S0-BPI-363

CHANGING
ORGANIZATIONAL
CULTURE

CHANGING
ORGANIZATIONAL
CULTURE

•

Strategy, Structure, and
Professionalism
in the
U.S. General Accounting Office

WALLACE EARL WALKER

Hd
9802
. W34
1986
WEST

The University of Tennessee Press
Knoxville

ASU WEST LIBRARY

Copyright © 1986 by The University of Tennessee Press / Knoxville.
Manufactured in the United States of America.
All rights reserved. First edition.

The United States Government is entitled to a royalty-free license
to duplicate and use all or parts of this work.

The paper used in this book meets the minimum requirements of the American
National Standard for Permanence of Paper for Printed Library Materials,
Z39.48-1984. Binding materials have been chosen for durability.

Library of Congress Cataloging-in-Publication Data

Walker, Wallace Earl, 1944–
    Changing organizational culture.

    Bibliography: p.
    Includes index.
    1. United States. General Accounting Office.
I. Title.
    HJ9802.W34   1986   353.0072′32   85-
29446
    ISBN 0-87049-502-X (alk. paper)

For Susan, Allen & Kathryn

Contents

Figures and Tables

Preface

This study seeks to understand professional change in a legislative organization. It is at once the study of professionals in an agency that evaluates other agencies and at the same time an effort to suggest how one might study public professionals and the organizations they inhabit. Furthermore, it is a story of cultural transformation, a tale of successful change in the General Accounting Office (GAO). In a little more than forty years—a modest period by the standards of government agencies—the role of GAO auditors was changed dramatically from clerk to evaluator.

Although change in the cumulative sense has been dramatic, year by year the GAO has shifted gradually as the organization has sought to satisfy its principal client, the Congress. Success, then, can best be understood as adaptation and alteration. As the Congress was transformed by such government developments as the New Deal, Great Society programs, and permanent military mobilization, by altered aspirations of its membership, and by organizational change, the GAO shifted accordingly and simultaneously managed to professionalize its staff and maintain control of its internal affairs. In the highly publicized, organizationally varied, and turbulent atmosphere that characterizes Congress,[1] the GAO's achievement is particularly significant.

This then is not a story of startling or rapid achievement. Such change is highly improbable among professionals in government organizations. Only cataclysmic performance failure seems capable of such immediate transformations. It is also not principally a story of GAO-congressional relations or of GAO-executive agency relations. Others have already reported on those facets of GAO behavior.[2] Instead this book seeks to understand why the behavior of GAO evaluators has changed over time and what the implications of these changes are for the GAO, the Congress, and the government at large.

The essence of this book is about professional behavior in government. I am interested in the role of professionals in government, in what motivates them to do what they do, and in how professional behavior is changed. My argument is that to change government organizations, one must first alter the behavior of government professionals, and to change professional behavior, one must transform organizational culture.

This book develops a cultural theory composed of a series of propositions which aspire to explain why GAO village life was as it was in the late 1970s. This theory reflects my conclusions about the truly central components of organizations and is garnered both from the literature on organizational behavior and my twenty years of work in various government bureaucracies. In essence I argue that to understand the professional behavior and ideology of GAO evaluators, one must first understand organizational history and design. Organizational design is composed of the strategies and structures fashioned to respond to external events and imposed by agency leadership.

To pursue this objective of understanding professional change, this book must tell several stories at once. The first story consists of a set of propositions about professionals in organizations, and about organizational culture and organizational design (Chapters 1 and 8). The second story is about the General Accounting Office and its auditors—how the Office looked and what the auditors did before 1940, with another snapshot during the period of the 1970s (Chapters 2, 6, and 7). The final story details the changes made by appointed and career leaders in the intervening thirty years (Chapters 3, 4, and 5).

Motivations.   As in any research endeavor that has stretched over a long period, my motivations and aspirations for this research have been altered by new interests. As a graduate student at the Massachusetts Institute of Technology in the early 1970s, I was fascinated by the intellectual fervor in American politics concerning the apparent unchecked powers of the American presidency. Like many others, I looked to Congress as the only viable counterweight to insure constitutional balance and the protection of American liberties. But the more I studied Congress, the more I found disarray and apparent helplessness in confronting the President and the executive branch. One bright hope seemed to be the General Accounting Office, which under Elmer Staats was shifting its orientation to better serve congressional needs.

Fostered by continued service as an active-duty Army officer and by a transforming experience as a White House Fellow, my interests and previous preoccupation have shifted to organizational change and professional behavior. Not organizations or professionals in the private sense but in the public sense. That is, I am interested here principally in public agencies, what many call bureaucracies. Thus the questions I keep asking myself are as follows: What is organizational change? What does it look like for government agencies? How should we study change and behavior in public organizations? What impact do environmental changes have on organizational arrangements? Are there seminal events and leaders which have so conditioned these agencies that succeeding developments are simply a gradual unfolding of previously established designs and commitments?

Out of these questions grew still others which were more specific to the General Accounting Office. Without doubt the GAO had changed over the forty-year period from 1940 to 1981. But how fundamental had this change been? What standards should we apply? Are the aspirations espoused by economists for organizational flexibility to meet altered market conditions appropriate for public organizations such as the GAO? Does the behavior of legislative bureaucracies differ from that of executive agencies? What impact did organizational change have on the activities of GAO professionals and the output of the Office? What differences did GAO change make in terms of Congress, the government at large, and American society? The answers to most of these questions almost invariably returned to focus on GAO professionals, that is on an informal group of people as opposed to a formal, inanimate organization. I found that studying the auditors themselves provided most of the answers.

Audiences. My answers to these questions will also, I hope, prove interesting to a broad array of audiences. Students of political science, public administration, and business administration will find here a scheme for studying and understanding organizational change as well as a longitudinal study of one particular organization from its founding in 1921 to 1981. Those most interested in my approach to organizational change should focus on the introductory chapter and the concluding one, which detail the roles that leaders, career elites, professional cadres, planning, reorganization, and personnel-management systems play in realigning professional behavior and which also examine criteria for assessing organizational success. Those students who are drawn to the historical study of organizations are invited to review Parts I and II, which suggest how the GAO changed over the forty-year period under study.

This book is also directed at four other communities: accountants and auditors in both the public and private sector, public-policy evaluators, senior public officials, and scholars interested in Congress. Accountants and auditors may wish to set their sights on chapters 2, 4, and 5, which detail the historical adaptation of their craft to government, the way the Office has gone about planning and structuring itself for the conduct of government audits, and the relationships between private and public accountants that emerged as the GAO established a personnel management system to instill the ideology and the myths of the profession into government. Members of the evaluation community should review chapter 6, which describes the audit ritual used to evaluate public programs and agency management.

Finally public servants and students of congressional oversight should steer to chapters 3 and 7. Chapter 3 discusses the preconditions for agency change, how leaders and senior managers went about transforming the GAO and how they coped with the inherent resistance of Congress to organizational change. Chapter 7 discusses the GAO as a congressional overseer and the impact that evaluations have on agencies and the Congress, a topic that all senior agency bureaucracies must ponder since no public organizations are exempt from GAO audit.

Research.   Although I wish I could provide a coherent design for describing the conduct of my research, alas I cannot. Since this project began in 1972, I have consulted such a broad array of sources that previous designs were continually being overwhelmed by opportunity and occasionally modified by shifting interests. My efforts have also been influenced by my duties in the Army, which have required that I lay aside my research and my manuscript for lengthy periods. The end product is almost certainly better as a result of these "sabbaticals."

The moorings of this study rest on field observation using an inductive approach. The foundation consists of research in primary, secondary and tertiary sources, as well as graduate study in accounting. In 1972, I was able to gain GAO sponsorship for this study. Over three summers and school holidays during the period 1972 to 1977, I interviewed 153 GAO employees at all levels of the organization. These employees included the senior leadership, nearly all of the GAO division and office directors, audit managers in all GAO audit divisions, and auditors in four of the GAO's regional offices.

Additionally, I discussed GAO activities with thirty-four executives and senior bureaucrats from six federal departments and agencies. These executives were selected based upon their knowledge of GAO activities or their association with a dozen audit reports which GAO executives had identified as among their best work. I also interviewed a total of seventeen congressmen and congressional staff members and eight newsmen, all of whom were familiar with GAO audit activities. Finally I was permitted to attend several GAO planning meetings chaired by the Comptroller General or the Deputy Comptroller General.

In all cases I promised interviewees anonymity—interviews are identified here by a number (as II 34, for example). This anonymity and my techniques of taking notes rather than recording interviews prompted a surprising candor. Interviewees were forthright about the GAO, their auditing experiences, and even intimate details of their personal lives.

In addition to these 212 interviews, numerous primary documents were studied. I reviewed all the Comptroller General's Annual Reports from 1921 to the present, studied dozens of GAO audit reports, and consulted scores of internal documents provided me by GAO employees. These documents detailed, among other things, organizational shifts in planning and administration, directives from the Comptroller General, and Office-wide announcements concerning changes in the GAO's personnel system. Secondary documents were also useful. I relied heavily on congressional appropriation hearings, GAO oversight hearings, committee reports on proposed legislation, and floor debates from the *Congressional Record.*

Furthermore, scores of tertiary sources consisting of books, dissertations, and journal articles that discussed the GAO or its audit activities were consulted. Finally, to better understand the accountant's discipline, I took a graduate level course in financial management and accounting taught in a business administration curriculum.

My efforts to describe the behavior of GAO evaluators and the changes in that organization began with my masters thesis, written in 1972. That was followed by a doctoral dissertation, completed in 1980. Some of my preliminary conclusions about organizational change and GAO behavior are contained in a paper I presented to the American Political Science Association in 1983. The *Journal of Evaluation and Program Planning* published extracts from my dissertation in 1985 and 1986. I am indebted to coeditor Jon Morrell for his assistance and to Pergamon Press for the authority to reproduce from these articles.

Acknowledgments. As in any writing endeavor, this study has benefited immeasurably from the kindness of others. I owe much to Professor Harvey Sapolsky of the Massachusetts Institute of Technology, who served as my dissertation adviser, trusted friend, and enthusiastic supporter not only on this study but in numerous other endeavors. Professor Walter Dean Burnham of MIT guided me through my graduate study and my masters thesis, and has continued to provide valued guidance and assistance ever since. The third member of my doctoral committee was Professor Frederick Mosher of the University of Virginia, who offered inspiration and encouragement. The late Jack Saloma suggested the GAO as a subject of research. Robert W. Porter, Jr., made the necessary introductions and has continued to be a sustaining force.

I am also grateful to: the West Point Dean's Research Fund, the Military Education Foundation, and the National War College Association, which supplied financial support for my research; to my aunt and late uncle Eddie and John Starkey and my sister-in-law and brother-in-law Celia and Lew Dollarhide, who furnished me room and board and so much more during my many stays in Washington; and to Colonel Lee Donne Olvey, my Department Chairman, who has been a source of strength and encouragement for a decade. My parents Evelyn and Dale Walker have provided unwavering support in more ways than they can understand or than I can ever repay.

This study could never have been done without the assistance of the 153 GAO evaluators who so generously gave of their valuable time and whose patience, interest, and trust in my guarantees of anonymity are tributes to their professional commitment to building better government. Many others have reviewed parts of this manuscript or discussed with me the ideas contained herein. Many have also ventured to West Point to discuss similar issues with my students. Their counsel has invariably been wise and judicious. Among the many contained in this group I should mention Harold Seidman, George Edwards, Tom Cronin, Louis Fisher, Michael Nelson, Dick Neustadt, Frank Rourke, Landis Jones, Edgar F. "Beau" Puryear, Jim Doig, Erwin Hargrove, Don Price, Don Haider, Arthur Maass, Roger Porter, Deborah Stone, Aaron Wildavsky, the late Jeffrey Pressman, Fernando Torres-Gil, James Gavin, Austin Ranney, Dorothy James, Sam Sarkesian, Bradley Patterson, and Richard Holwell.

Equally helpful have been a number of colleagues in the Military Academy's Department of Social Sciences: Jim Golden, George Osborn, Bill Wix, Fred Black, Dan Kaufman, Jim Bowden, Sherwood "Woody" Goldberg, Bob Kimmitt, and Richard Saunders. Ms. Vicky Lilos cheerfully typed many variants and rewrites of this and previous manuscripts, and Mrs. Barbara Thomas kept me out of administrative difficulties. The USMA Librarian Egon Weiss and his very able staff have been most helpful by providing research space and support. A number of editors and publishers have also been supportive: Cynthia Maude-Gembler, Mavis Bryant, Lee Weiskopf, Michael Ames, David Kellogg, James Sabin, and Arnold Zohn. The White House Fellows Program did a great deal to educate me about the pathways and mores of the federal government.

My biggest debt, however, is to my wife Susan, my son Allen, and my daughter Kathryn, whose love and forebearance sustained me through the research, writing, and seemingly endless rewriting of this manuscript. To them this book is dedicated.

This book exists because of the efforts of these many sources of inspiration and support. It would have been a better book still had I been more attentive to their wise counsel. To them belongs much of the credit. By right of authorship, I must claim the blame for what follows. I also should absolve my service. The material contained herein does not necessarily represent the views of the United States Army or the United States Military Academy, and indeed these views are mine alone.

Wallace Earl Walker
West Point, New York
September 1, 1985

CHANGING
ORGANIZATIONAL
CULTURE

CHAPTER 1

Introduction

Organizational change is a dominant concern of our age. Corporate executives seek to make their organizations more efficient and responsive. Newly elected Presidents use their staffs and political executives to bend existing organizational structures to fit the administration's philosophy and vision for governance. Like Presidents, members of Congress seek to fulfill electoral promises to reform government. Such promises invariably call for reshaping government agencies in some fashion.

The antecedent concern is not so much organizational change as an interest in altering the output or products of government. That output is viewed in different ways by different elected officials. Presidents consider such products in aggregate terms initially and concern themselves with expanding or limiting the presence of government in societal affairs. Presidential staffs and appointed officials flesh out their leader's philosophical disposition and apply it to achieve specific forms of governmental output. Given their opportunities as proscribed by subcommittee assignments and resources for gathering political information, members of Congress are preoccupied with demands for new or improved services from executive agencies to fit constituent needs.

Governmental products are as diverse as the smorgasbord of public agencies and their reporting bureaus.[1] What all government output has in common is behavior by public professionals representing the interests of their agency. That is, professionals recommend or make policy, generate estimates, consolidate data, manage loan programs, regulate commerce, and settle claims.

Organizational behavior is not random, nor is it easily changed. Organizational behavior is dominated by public professionals who are recruited and socialized by the government for service within the government. As all governmental actors come to realize sooner—and the rest of us usually later—altering the government's products requires organizational change. What few realize, however, is that change requires modifying organizational culture and thereby the behavior of highly professionalized bureaucrats who dominate public agencies and whose skills and training rival those of any profession found in the private sector. Equally imposing are the political resources and expertise these professionals possess about agency activities.

STUDYING THE GENERAL ACCOUNTING OFFICE

There are not many studies which detail the change within an organization over extended periods. Most often organizational studies focus on shifts which occur over the period of a decade or on short-term changes in the relationship between an organization and its environment. For instance Daniel Mazmanian and Jeanne Nienaber consider changes prompted by the environmental movement in the Army Corps of Engineers during the 1970s.[2] John Tierney considers the reorganization of the Post Office into the Postal Service in the 1970s, after passage of the Postal Reorganization Act.[3] Frederick Mosher's very fine study of the General Accounting Office does review the shift that the GAO has undergone in response to public demands for accountability.[4] His focus thus differs from this study's in that here I will provide a theory for studying organizational change, will emphasize the preconditions which affect behavior of the public professionals within the GAO, and will seek to assess the effectiveness of GAO auditors as agents of the Congress.[5] In many ways this study may be considered a companion piece to Mosher's. His looks from the outside in and the top down, mine from the inside out and the bottom up.

The General Accounting Office is a nonpartisan, independent agency in the legislative branch and is headed by a Comptroller General, appointed for a single, fifteen-year term and removable only by joint resolution. In 1981, the Comptroller noted that the GAO's major functions were to:

> assist the Congress in its legislative and oversight activities; audit and evaluate programs, activities and financial operations of Federal departments and agencies; and carry out financial control and related

functions with respect to most Federal Government programs and operations. . . .[6]

The GAO and its public professionals have experienced considerable change over the last forty years. In 1940, just after the first Comptroller General left office, the GAO's structural arrangements were not much different from those of the old Auditors of the Treasury whose functions, which date back to the early 1800s, the GAO inherited in the 1921 Budget and Accounting Act. The staff in 1940 was predominantly a clerical one whose principal function was to assess compliance of executive agency expenditures against rigid codes of performance. In essence the GAO and its clerks sought to control executive expenditures from the legislative branch.

In 1981, with the departure of the fourth Comptroller, Elmer Staats, the GAO was organized functionally to respond to the needs of a fractured Congress. The staff was a professional one that sought to evaluate the effectiveness of government programs, the efficiency of agency management, and the economy attained in government management and accounting systems.[7] Thus the GAO now seeks to oversee or review public policy and administration and not to control it.

Given this dramatic change in organizational output, how might one then seek to understand it? One could study the behavior of old and new institutional leaders, the alterations new leaders made in administrative systems, and their pronouncements about these changes. But such an approach ignores the actual behavior of what James Q. Wilson calls the "operators" in agencies, those that perform the central tasks of an organization.[8] The behavior of the operators, or what I call public professionals, is the essence of organizational output.

If the behavior of public professionals is so crucial, then perhaps one should focus on them. In the case of the GAO, we would then look at how the evaluators actually did their work, using a participant-observation approach. Such an approach would seek to study the conduct of several evaluation reports and the contact evaluators had with various components of Congress. Yet this approach is neither practicable nor likely to yield much in the way of understanding why the evaluators evaluate as they do. The relationships between GAO evaluators and elements in Congress are so extensive over such a wide array of subjects that generalization from any manageable sample would prove difficult if not impossible. Furthermore, the range of GAO reports is so diverse that to intensively study the conduct of three or four evaluations would not permit much in the way of generalization either. Even if these studies did provide some generalizations, we are not likely to find out why a particular format was used in one report and not in another or why the procedures the evaluators used were considered appropriate.

One way out of these dilemmas is both to focus on the development of organizational systems in the GAO and to seek from the auditors themselves and close observers specific details about how the auditors usually conduct their evaluations. With such information in hand, we can not only describe what the evaluators do, but also seek to understand why they do it. Clearly the place to search for explanation is the organization's administrative and group structures. The propositions developed in the next section argue that to understand "operator" behavior, one must study an organization's professional groups and its administrative arrangements—that is its hierarchical form and its planning and personnel systems. In the administrative arrangements and the professional struggles that occur within agencies, one will find the incentives which guide public professionals to do what they do. In Herbert Kaufman's words, administrative arrangements "preform decisions," "detect and discourage deviation," and insure the "will and capacity to conform."[9]

I should also make clear what I mean by the terms "professional" and "public professional." Like Mosher, I define both terms liberally and use them here interchangeably. As he has suggested, there are two classes of professionals in government. The "general professions" contain lawyers, doctors, and engineers, whose specialized skills fulfill certain government needs. There are also "public service professions."[10] In my view, here again there are two classes. In one class are recruits with more generalist backgrounds who are trained and socialized into a particular profession, such as military and foreign service officers.

The second class of public professionals labor in shops similar to those of the private sector. However, their pregovernment training and socialization do not properly suit the needs of the public agency. For the GAO this has meant that accountants, and more recently social scientists, must be retrained and resocialized to fit the Office's variant of auditing. Such "retailoring" creates considerable tension, as new evaluators find inconsistencies between their previous training and experience and the demands of public service. In the more general sense, all these classes of professionals serve public needs. Given their diverse backgrounds and perspectives, conflict among them is endemic.

My theory takes a cultural approach to the study of professional and organizational development and change. "Culture" is an elusive concept. As one observer recently suggested, seeking to understand the term is "like putting your hand in a cloud—seemingly all air and no substance."[11] Yet social scientists have found that the concept provides considerable insight into human behavior. For instance Mary Douglas and Aaron Wildavsky use it to explain why, in our technological age, we are so preoccupied with risk and pollution.[12] Terrence Deal and Allan Kennedy find the concept helpful in explaining corporate success.[13] Here I use the term in a historical and derivative sense. I argue that all organizations have a particular culture that is composed of an ideology, rituals, myths, and knowledge—that is knowledge of the organization, its environment, and its past.[14] The culture prescribes what work is to be done and how it can be changed over time. To discover an organization's culture, one must intensively study what institutional leaders, career managers, and "operators" say about themselves and their organization and what they do.

THE FRAMEWORK

My argument posits that professional change occurs only when an agency's culture is transformed. Cultural transformation means that the output of the organization will be dramatically altered. Incremental modifications are not changes in the fundamental sense which I discuss here. Rather such modifications are simply accommodations to new circumstances. Thus a new policy pronouncement by institutional leaders or a new law modifying agency responsibilities are usually only modifications to existing professional behavior. Where these policies or laws are accompanied by fundamental structural alterations which rearrange professional incentives, and thereby professional behavior, then organizational change can be said to have occurred.

Out of this argument grow a number of propositions. Over time, simple accommodations fail to keep pace with environmental shifts. As these environmental shifts accumulate and the gap between environmental demands and agency accommodations becomes more profound, elected officials or the task environment perceives organizational failure or catastrophe, and change is required. The failure to close this gap between the environment and public organizations—that is, the failure to change—will spell doom for the organization. It will ultimately be swallowed whole or in part by another organization, discarded, or condemned to a tidepool existence with many of its constituencies fleeing to other, more lucrative waters.

The environment of public organizations is complex. That environment includes not only the Congress (and all it encompasses, such as committees, subcommittees, parties, caucuses, staffers, and individual members) and the President, but also other government organizations, diverse constituencies and contributing technologies. Since public policy-making cuts across numerous interests, no government organization is an island. Its relationships with other agencies may range from friendly to hostile. The constituencies represented by public organizations can be both obvious and subtle. Subtle constituencies include professionals in the private sector who see themselves allied with public sector professionals who practice similar crafts. Technological advances also affect public organizations, because elected officials invariably find political capital in promoting new or altered technologies for use by government agencies.

Thus, true organizational change of the sort I am suggesting here is manifested in altered behavior patterns by public professionals. To alter that behavior, an organization's culture must be transformed. To do that, organizational design must be changed. An organizational design is composed of current and past arrangements which agency elites have fashioned to contend with conditions imposed by their environment (see Figure 1).

An individual culture evolves during a distinct epoch in the institution's history. Each epoch may last for only five to ten years or up to a century.[15] Within a cultural epoch are various eras in which one leader or a group of leaders may dominate. In each epoch a new series of institutional arrangements, which may be broadly grouped under strategy and structure, is generated.[16] These arrangements are seldom developed immediately, but rather unfold slowly as appointed leaders and career elites contend with environmental shifts. The resultant culture from each organizational design is manifested as rituals and an ideology that direct the behavior of professionals. Remnants of previous organizational strategies, structures, and cultures are carried along by the institution throughout its history.

Strategy.   A strategy is an institutional course of action that develops over time. It includes the key values the institution is to embody, the goals and objectives for the institution, and a partially explicit, partially implicit plan. This plan entails both various schemes to meet contingencies and programs for allocating resources.[17]

An institutional strategy is a product of historical experience, in-

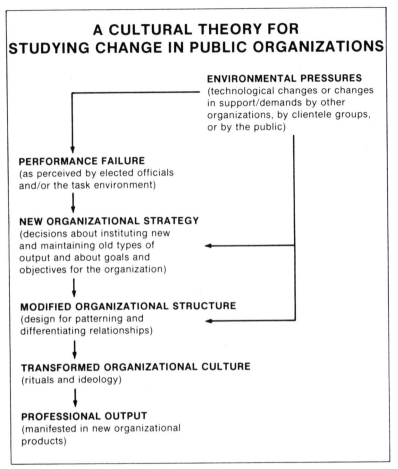

A CULTURAL THEORY FOR STUDYING CHANGE IN PUBLIC ORGANIZATIONS

ENVIRONMENTAL PRESSURES
(technological changes or changes in support/demands by other organizations, by clientele groups, or by the public)

PERFORMANCE FAILURE
(as perceived by elected officials and/or the task environment)

NEW ORGANIZATIONAL STRATEGY
(decisions about instituting new and maintaining old types of output and about goals and objectives for the organization)

MODIFIED ORGANIZATIONAL STRUCTURE
(design for patterning and differentiating relationships)

TRANSFORMED ORGANIZATIONAL CULTURE
(rituals and ideology)

PROFESSIONAL OUTPUT
(manifested in new organizational products)

Figure 1

cluding the traditional demands of the task environment, the character and latitude of the leaders appointed in the past, and the predispositions of the former career elite (see Figure 2). No bureaucratic institution can step out of its heritage. What it chooses to do today and in the future is contingent upon what it has learned from the past, the options provided by previous organizational designs, and what demands are placed upon it.

Institutional leadership plays a central role in generating a strategy. As Phillip Selznick has taught us, leaders are crucial for institutional regeneration.[18] Their character and latitude are worthy of study. Char-

---

ORGANIZATIONAL STRATEGY

STATEGY IS A PRODUCT OF:

—ORGANIZATIONAL EXPERIENCE AND ENVIRONMENTAL DEMANDS

—CHARACTER AND LATITUDE OF APPOINTED LEADERSHIP

—PREDISPOSITIONS OF THE AGENCY'S CAREER ELITE

—STATUTORY MANDATES AND PRESIDENTIAL ORDERS

Figure 2

acter includes the leader's style and belief system. The latitude of political executives is influenced by the length of their tenure, by their expertise, by the rigidity of institutional overseers, and by environmental circumstances.[19]

Another factor influencing institutional strategy is the predisposition of career elites. Mosher has suggested that professional groups array themselves in vertical bands within organizations. Generally one professional group becomes the elite corps of the organization, what I call here the elite profession. Those who occupy the highest career postions in the elite corps are called the career elite. This elite has considerable influence over not only the management of all professionals, but also the direction of the institution itself.

Therefore, although political executives are the prime movers in generating an institutional strategy, they must also hitch up career elites, as well as load considerable cultural baggage on the new wagon. Without the support of career elites, redirection of professionals within the institution is impossible. Furthermore, all institutional strategies must consider existing relationships with outside organizations, as well as the demands and expectations of the institution's constituencies.

Strategy and structure are frequently enshrined in law. Statutes protect institutional strategy from assault by other agencies or power centers and from pressures for alternative forms of output by forces within the institution's task environment. Laws also legitimate structure by specifying organizational relationships and arrangements for personnel management.

Structure. Out of an organization's strategy grows a structure. Structure provides the design for patterning and differentiating relationships within the institution.[20] Like strategies, structures are products of consultation, experimentation, and adaptation. There are three salient structural factors, each of which must be altered for public organizations to change: hierarchical arrangements, planning mechanisms, and the personnel system (see Figure 3).

Harold Seidman has pointed out that hierarchical arrangements have political implications.[21] They also have behavioral implications. That is, they are important determinants for the manner in which professionals carry out organizational functions. Where hierarchy is centralized in order to permit institutional reorganization, professionals must seek approval for non-routine actions through several decision-making levels. In a flatter arrangement, with numerous career elites reporting to a single political executive, the domain of professional disgression is expanded.[22] Thus, the organization's hierarchical arrangement sets outer limits on professional behavior and thereby affects the institution's culture.

A second critical aspect of institutional structure is the presence and use of planning mechanisms. Such mechanisms are dedicated to longer-term institutional issues, to questions of hierarchical design, or to more immediate coordination of output. Where technological or environ-

---

ORGANIZATIONAL STRUCTURE

THE ESSENTIAL COMPONENTS ARE:

—HIERARCHICAL ARRANGEMENTS

—PLANNING MECHANISMS

—PERSONNEL SYSTEM

- Composition of the career elite

- Types of professional cadres

- Personnel management (techniques for recruiting, socializing, training, and promoting)

Figure 3

mental shifts are seen as likely by farsighted political executives, a planning group is often created to explore alternative strategies for the institution. New strategies require structural decisions, such as redesign of the hierarchy. Also where output must satisfy diverse audiences or is dependent upon a multitude of internal units, a planning mechanism is necessary to coordinate bureaucratic behavior.[23]

The personnel system encompasses the composition of the career elite, types of professional cadres, and techniques for personnel management. The composition of the career elite is an important issue for the institution. Where a new organizational design has been devised, the elite may need to be partially reconstituted with new leaders; other career leaders less able to tolerate the new direction are moved to honorific positions or retired. Altering the career elite is a delicate matter that has great symbolic significance to professionals within the institution.

The type and number of professional cadres also influence institutional culture. Agencies with one professional group are heavily swayed by the ideals and procedures of that profession. Where several types of professionals exist in a single institution, considerable conflict is likely, and political executives have more room to maneuver in strategy-making and structural redesign.[24]

Within the institution's personnel system are factors which foster particular forms of professional behavior. The techniques for recruiting, socializing, training, and promoting professionals invariably condition what they do. The origins and educational experiences of recruits provide them with certain attitudes. Socializing new recruits into the ideals and work habits of the bureaucracy is crucial in adapting them to expected behavior.[25] Once recruited and socialized into a particular bureaucratic profession, the employee will receive various forms of training to prepare him or her for new job assignments or higher-level staff or supervisory responsibilities.[26] Finally, the standards required for promotion also influence the expectations and behavior of public professionals.

Thus the argument here is that organizational change can take place only when a chain of circumstances occurs. That is, environmental pressure for change must build to a crescendo, leaders bent on change must be in place within the organization, and these leaders must win acceptance for change from career elites. Leaders and elites formulate a new strategy for the institution and a structure to insure its implementation. Such a structure requires new planning mechanisms, hierarchical rearrangement, and a transformed personnel system. Only with such shifts in organizational design, that is in strategy and structure, will the culture and thus the behavior of public professionals be transformed. Such a transformation means that the output of the organization is thereby changed.

A PREVIEW

I find that the GAO's development follows these propositions. The GAO over the forty-year period from 1940 to 1981 transformed its culture from one of control to one of oversight. This transformation in culture changed the behavior of the GAO "operators," the auditors, recently retitled "evaluators." This transformation was prompted by significant environmental changes in the demands of the GAO's principal taskmaster—the Congress—and by alterations in the executive branch and the accounting profession.

With the advent of the New Deal, a permanently mobilized military, and the institutionalization of a Welfare State in the Great Society programs, executive branch agencies took on a complexity and a sophistication that defied traditional methods of congressional control. Furthermore a more assertive and media-conscious string of presidents, beginning with Franklin Roosevelt, threatened traditional congressional responsibilities and techniques for representation. In response to these developments, congressional power began to fragment such that subcommittees and individual members—"issue entrepreneurs" as Michael Malbin has labeled them[27]—have become the salient forces in executive-legislative relations.

Simultaneously, significant changes occurred in the professions. The accounting profession broadened to review not only financial systems, but management systems as well. Graduates of business administration schools sought to apply sophisticated new management techniques first to private corporations and then to public agencies. With the advent of the national security state and expansion of social programs, public policy specialists began to assess the effectiveness of government programs.

All of these developments impinged on the GAO's traditional methods of auditing. Old routines were no longer viable. A new repertoire was clearly needed. Comptrollers Lindsay Warren, Joseph Campbell, and Elmer Staats selected a new career elite for the GAO, composed initially of certified public accountants and then later intermixed with social science analysts. This career elite and the GAO leadership developed a new strategy that entailed responsiveness to congressional needs, close observation of executive branch operations, evaluation of agency management and programs, and professionalization of the Office's employees. The structure to implement this strategy was composed of new planning mechanisms to coordinate evaluations and to insure the GAO stayed in tune with congressional needs. Extensive reorganization flattened the GAO's hierarchy to better respond to a more fragmented Congress and also established new subunits to provide congressional liaison and an internal management review system. Finally the personnel system was totally redesigned with college-recruited accountants serving as the purveyors of the new management and program evaluations.

The incentives contained within this new strategy and structure insured a careful and dogged form of auditing that sought to find faults to report to Congress. The evaluation repertoire itself, then, reflects the strategic and structural choices not only of the culture of oversight but the culture of control as well.

The impact of these reports on Congress and the government vary from report to report. In the aggregate, it is clear that GAO evaluation reports serve the programmatic needs of members of Congress and enhance their reelection efforts. Thus GAO evaluations permit them to pursue politics through yet another medium. The reports also serve to enhance the size and scope of government by continually calling for more resources to be applied to management, more precise regulations to guide public managers, and more specific laws to suggest criteria for measuring public programs. Such calls are unlikely to be answered, for the evaluators' values are inconsistent with those of a democratic state. The GAO evaluators were born out of the accounting profession and out of a legislative mandate which prescribes the Office play a dominant role in making the government more businesslike. Businesslike government would require rationality, that is, economy and efficiency. The American system, however, celebrates liberty and freedom gained through consensus. The two value systems are inherently irreconcilable.

Yet the GAO has been successful in adapting itself to a transient and demanding environment. It has emerged with its responsibilities intact, its mandate for oversight extended, and its discretion protected. In effect it continues to serve as a comforting symbol to Congress that continuous oversight of executive agencies and programs is being effected. The task of assessing organizational success in government must, then, take account of unalterable conditions as well as achievements.

The sequence for this book is as follows: Part I is devoted to strategy, Part II to structure, and Part III to professional behavior. Each part consists of two chapters. Chapter 2 reviews the culture of control which dominated the government's auditors from 1776 to 1940. Chapter 3 explains why that culture disintegrated and describes the agendas which the GAO's new leadership pursued, the triumph of the certified public accountants, and the specific new strategy which was selected.

In Part II, the structural arrangements to institutionalize this new strategy are outlined. Chapter 4 describes the new planning mechanisms and hierarchical arrangements. Chapter 5 is devoted to the personnel system. Part III depicts the evaluation ritual and portrays the evaluator's ideology and myths in Chapter 6 and the impact this ritual has on the Congress and the government at large in Chapter 7. Finally Chapter 8, the concluding chapter, assesses organizational success in the GAO, applies the theory to another organization and then critiques the theory.

PART I

·

Strategy

CHAPTER 2

The Culture of Control

·

Auditing is an ancient craft. It has been historically associated with legislative efforts to control[1] funds as disbursed first by sovereigns and then by political leaders. The struggle is essentially over power and is endemic to the relationships among political executives, legislatures, and bureaucratic organizations.

Although the modern GAO has been influenced by all these struggles, which date back as far as Babylonian times, the most influential eras have been the American experiences with auditing during colonial times, the period from 1789 to 1921 in which the executive dominated the audit, and the GAO's culture of control from 1921 to 1940.

THE LEGACY OF AUDITING

One of the first records of legislative audit is provided by Polybius, who notes that public money was controlled by the Roman Senate before 216 B.C.[2] The Anglo-Saxon traditions of audit began some eighteen centuries later when the British Parliament sought to restrain James I through the Subsidy Act of 1624, which provided for treasurers to maintain accounts for public funds.[3] The American approach to auditing was influenced by the struggle between the British Parliament and the Crown over the control of expenditures. The American colonial and Revolutionary War periods were marked both by a multitude of audit forms and a clear commitment to legislative authority over expenditures. By the time the First Continental Congress met in 1774, it was a common colonial practice that taxes could not be levied, nor could public funds be disbursed, without a statute which had originated in the lower house of the assembly. Most of these assemblies had some mechanism to review the accounts of receipts or expenditures.[4] Borrowing titles from the British and specific duties from the colonial governments, the Continental and Confederation Congresses fashioned a form of auditing which was responsible to the legislature. Numerous mechanisms were used during this period. The most significant was the Office of Auditor General, which was created in 1776 to manage the Treasury Office of Accounts; this office was the first direct predecessor to the General Accounting Office.[5]

Executive responsibility for government auditing had its seeds in the Constitution, but did not grow to full flower until after the passage of the Treasury Department Act of 1789. The Constitution legitimated the function of auditing. Article I, Section 9 prescribed that "No money shall be drawn from the Treasury, but in consequence of Appropriation made by law; and a regular Statement and Account of the Receipts and Expenditures of all public money shall be published from time to time."

The Treasury Act of 1789 placed the accounting and auditing officers firmly in the executive orbit. Although nominated by the President and confirmed by the Senate, these officers became, in effect, bureau officials in the Department of the Treasury. They could be and were removed by presidents. They were seldom called upon by Congress to submit oral or written reports. The relationships of these officers with the executive departments were conditioned by their relationships with the President. Since the Congress never challenged their appointment and dismissal by the President, the Auditors and Comptrollers were hardly willing to seriously question the acts of department heads. And yet their relationships with the Congress were important, because their functions were based on validating the consistency of executive spending with congressional appropriations.[6]

Essentially these anomalies continued until the 1921 Budget and Accounting Act, in spite of the chaos in accounting caused by the Civil War[7] and the Progressive calls for reform in the period of 1890-1920.[8] The 1894 Dockery Act did rationalize the system somewhat by creating a Comptroller and Assistant Comptroller. In 1918, all auditing was placed under the administrative supervision of the Comptroller to meet the exigencies of World War I.

In spite of the changes made by the Dockery Act, the federal accounting and auditing system in 1921 looked much as it had in 1789. The basic arrangement laid down by the Congress in the Treasury Department Act of 1789 remained in force. It was widely agreed that the system was not effective, but Congress continued to bandage it rather than perform radical surgery.

CONTROLLING EXPENDITURES FROM THE LEGISLATIVE BRANCH

The 1921 Budget and Accounting Act reestablished legislative control over accounting and auditing, authority the Congress had not had since the ratification of the Constitution. However, in this reincarnation, the auditing officers had to contend with a fully established executive branch and a President of considerable power. Also unlike the legislative audit that had existed from 1776 to 1789, this new form of audit had a cultural heritage developed within the executive branch. These precedents and the new arrangements produced a congressional audit which sought to control administrative behavior from the legislative branch.

The Search for Businesslike Government

The motivations for the 1921 Act may be found in several developments peculiar to turn-of-the-century America. At this time, faith in business, science, and the scientific method was high. This faith was manifested in the rush to establish government corporations and in the proposals for government reform espoused by President Taft's Commission on Economy and Efficiency, known as the Cleveland Commission. The Cleveland Commission subscribed to the views, held by many in the public administration field, that scientific management techniques could cure the government's ailments. For the conduct of audit, it proposed that the Auditor's Office be consolidated under one supervisor and that modern business methods be used, thereby achieving greater efficiency and economy.[9]

Another development which spurred reform was a growing conviction in Congress that the auditing officers were constrained by their location in the Treasury Department from reporting questionable practices to the legislature. Although there is some disagreement on whether this conviction was accurate,[10] this perception became the congressional reality and dictated reform.[11]

The spark which ignited reform was World War I. Not only did the war overload the auditing system, it also so enhanced the influence of President Woodrow Wilson that Congress sought ways to protect its own powers.[12] Although Congress agreed that budgets should be formulated in the executive branch, it was not willing to add further to the President's powers by permitting that branch to then audit and settle accounts in the Office of the Comptroller of the Treasury. Thus it was considered prudent to create a General Accounting Office for audit in the legislative branch and a Budget Bureau in the executive branch.[13]

Although Wilson did veto the first version of the Act over the provisions for removal of the Comptroller General, there was no other strong resistance to this arrangement.[14] The Act was reintroduced with new provisions for removal of the Comptroller, then passed and signed on June 10, 1921. These provisions called for the GAO to assume the functions of the Auditors of the Treasury and for a Comptroller General to replace the Comptroller of the Treasury and to head the GAO. He and his Assistant would be appointed by the President, confirmed by the Senate, and serve fifteen-year terms, removable only for cause by a joint resolution, which must be passed by both houses and signed by the President. The Comptroller could not succeed himself. His Assistant was expected to ultimately "grow into" the position of Comptroller when the latter retired.[15]

Congressional expectations for the GAO and the Comptroller are ably reflected in the words of the Act's principal sponsor, Representative James Good. As he noted, "By creating this department (the GAO), Congress will have applied *practical business policy* to the administration of the Government's fiscal affairs. . . . This *independent* department will necessarily serve as a check against extravagance in the preparation of the budget."[16] Furthermore the General Accounting Office was mandated to perform all accounting and auditing for the federal government; to settle and adjust public claims; to establish accounting systems, procedures, and forms; and to provide advance decisions on fiscal matters.[17]

The Comptroller General was, again in Good's words, to "become the real guardian of the Treasury," to be "one of the most powerful and useful Government officials," and to promote "real economy and efficiency" in government. The Comptroller was "to discover the very facts that Congress ought to be in possession of and . . . fearlessly and without fear of removal present these facts to Congress and its committees." Good foresaw three results from the Act: to inform Congress of the expenditure of public funds, to "serve as a check on the President," and to force cabinet officers to realize their responsibility for prudent use of public funds.[18] Thus a powerful Comptroller General was created to perform two functions: (1) to guard the treasury and check the President and (2) to inform the Congress.

Therefore environmental pressures and the performance failure of government auditing forced not simply organizational change, but in fact a wholly new organization to conduct the audit. As the gap between environmental shifts—as reflected in the new technologies for management spawned by the industrial revolution and by such groups as the public administration profession—and the performance of the Auditors and Comptroller of the Treasury widened, simple accommodation was no longer possible. Elected officials and public reformers were convinced that the existing arrangements had failed to provide economic and efficient, that is to say businesslike, government. The new Comptroller General then fashioned an organizational strategy and imposed an organizational structure which created a distinct culture for the GAO.

The Stategy for Control

The organizational experience that the GAO and its first Comptroller General John Raymond McCarl had to rely on was that of the old Auditors and Comptrollers of the Treasury. Those officers, however, were subservient to the executive branch hierarchy. Now Comptroller McCarl and his Assistant Comptroller General Lurtin Ginn were subordinate to the Congress, which was neither organized nor inclined to give the GAO such direction. That is, neither chamber was disposed to form committees on public accounts to receive GAO reports, nor to designate committees to oversee GAO operations.[19]

With no advocates in the Congress for either the Office or for reporting to the legislature, McCarl chose the other function assigned to the GAO by the 1921 Act, that is, to guard the treasury and check the President. His conclusion, which is certainly a legitimate reading of the history of governmental auditing in general and of the legislative history of the 1921 Act in particular, was that Congress wanted him to settle problems and not to raise them.[20]

The character of John R. McCarl was particularly important in the formation of the GAO's strategy during this period. Since few of the senior leaders in the old Auditors offices became part of the new GAO, McCarl did not have to contend with an established career elite. Thus his style and belief system played a salient role in this new organization.

Before his appointment, McCarl had been a lawyer, party activist, and presidential confidant. A graduate of the University of Nebraska law school, he practiced law in McCook, Nebraska, from 1903 to 1914. Later he became a private secretary to Senator George W. Norris and then the executive secretary of the national Republican Congressional Campaign Committee. After advising President Harding against appointing several candidates for the Comptroller Generalship and failing to persuade several congressmen to take the position, he accepted it himself.[21]

These experiences conditioned his beliefs about government. As Harvey Mansfield's somewhat critical description suggests, his midwestern roots were important.

> Comptroller General McCarl was a man of crusading zeal who espoused the simple faith of pre-war midwestern progressivism—a creed that found equally abhorrent the privileged corruption of the Harding administration and the social welfare programs of the Roosevelt administration. He brought to his office abundant energy but little training in administration, [federal] law, or accounting that would equip him for his tasks.[22]

And yet as a lawyer and a strict constructionist of congressional appropriations, McCarl saw the law as the final arbiter of expenditures. As he pointed out in 1930,

> the problem of accounting for public money is not an accounting matter as that term is usually understood in commercial practice. The problem of appropriation control is *primarily a legal problem* . . . it is the duty and the responsibility of the General Accounting Office to carefully scrutinize all expenditures to see whether the restrictions, limitations, and directions in the law have been observed in connection therewith. The yardstick of control is that *stated by the Congress in the law.*[23]

Therefore McCarl found all forms of bureaucratic discretion repugnant. His annual reports and statements consistently voice concern about the lack of uniformity in the behavior of public officials and the tendency to give them wider latitude in spending government funds.

Finally the law gave direction to McCarl's choice of a strategy. The consolidation of authority under the 1921 Act made the Comptroller, in Mansfield's words, both "the arbiter of the law and the practice of financial administration."[24] That is, the Comptroller General was responsible not only for government accounting and auditing, the old role of the Auditors, but also for passing upon the validity of his auditors' determinations and interpreting the statutes governing federal expenditures, the old role of the Comptroller of the Treasury. Furthermore, the Comptroller General and his GAO were responsible for settling all government claims and dictating accounting forms and systems for all agencies.[25]

More specifically, three responsibilities made the Comptroller a force in financial administration: the authority to settle accounts, to prescribe accounting procedures, and to countersign warrants and requisitions. Inherent in the authority to settle accounts were the options to disallow disbursements, make advance decisions, and pre-audit. If disbursements did not conform with the GAO's interpretation of congressional appropriations, they could be voided. To preclude such embarrassments, department and agency heads sought advanced decisions by the GAO before their financial officers disbursed various categories of expenditures. Or executive leaders would seek a pre-audit of vouchers before actual payments were made.[26]

The Comptroller's other two responsibilities also gave him leverage over the executive branch. The prescription of accounting systems provided GAO access to all accounts and permitted the Office to influence agency policy. The Comptroller's countersignature and requisition-approval authority provided him the power to appropriate funds, since he could refuse his signature in instances where he felt an agency's use of funds was illegal.

Given the circumstances of his office and his own philosophical inclinations, McCarl's strategy for the new institution was to continue the work carried on in the old Treasury Auditors and Comptrollers' Offices, to build new GAO offices and divisions to accommodate the responsibilities added by the 1921 Act, and to exert maximum control over government expenditures to insure that the value of economy was properly celebrated. He reserved virtually all organizational decisions to himself. Finally, his strategy also included correct, but distant relations with Congress and a pugnacious and somewhat overbearing attitude toward executive agencies.

The Structure for Control

The GAO's structure reflected the strategy of Comptroller McCarl. Unwilling to delegate responsibility, McCarl was not interested in a planning mechanism to consider goals and objectives for the GAO or to design courses of action to achieve them. The organizational hierarchy was designed to reflect McCarl's disposition for centralized control and the ideals of a businesslike government.

With the en masse transfer of career employees to the GAO in 1921 and the lack of a single building to house them, the initial scheme was simply to transform the Auditor's offices into GAO divisions. These divisions were subsequently reorganized on a functional basis to increase, in McCarl's words, the "efficiency and economy of the work of auditing accounts"[27] and to deal with the many responsibilities contained in the 1921 Act. Thus the Office of the General Counsel was responsible for appeals, the Investigations Division prescribed and investigated accounting systems, the Bookkeeping Division controlled the disbursement of appropriated funds, and the Audit Division audited and settled accounts of all federal agencies.

Very few of these activities took place beyond the GAO's walls. The meager use of field investigations and field pre-audits was more a bone thrown to satisfy his statutory responsibilities and the explosion of government in the New Deal than a concentrated effort to decentralize operations. The Office of the Comptroller General was a bottleneck which constrained internal operations and external relationships. Controversy among his division directors was often not resolved. Informal arrangements made by his directors with executive agencies were occasionally repudiated.[28] Described by many as a "red-tape despot," he was concerned with all the affairs of the GAO, including the elimination of red tape itself. As he observed in 1923:

Among the other things being furnished the divisions where it was thought a saving could be made, were *large quantities of red tape* being used to tie papers and documents for filing. On investigation, cheaper soft twine was substituted, resulting in a considerable saving.[29]

The staff the GAO inherited from the Treasury was beset by routine and poor salaries. No effort was made to change the personnel profile of this staff. Neither a career elite nor a headquarters staff was groomed to embody or defend the values of the new legislative audit. Furthermore the GAO did not seek skilled accountants or any other professional group to fill its ranks.

Since McCarl felt that the GAO's function was to determine the compliance of government expenditures with law, the only professionals were thirty or so lawyers. All other employees were clerks whose salaries were meager. The titles of these clerks reflect their skills: audit clerk, clerk-checker, special computer, computer-checker, audit clerk-typist, reconciliation clerk, tabulating machine operator, bookkeeping machine operator, comptometer operator, and bookkeeper. Even those titled auditor were to simply review vouchers.[30]

The Culture for Control

Out of this organizational design, a culture for auditing was spawned. The ideology revolved around the value of economy in government. During McCarl's time this value meant, to use Dwight Waldo's words, "penny-pinching."[31] The principal norm for operationalizing this value was strict compliance with a rigid and narrow interpretation of the intent of Congress as divined from committee reports and hearings and from the *Congressional Record*. The dominant myth in this culture was that all Congress wanted, or ever would want, was for the GAO to check presidential digression by controlling executive expenditures from the legislative branch.

The principal ritual in the culture of control was the compliance audit, a repertoire similar to that practiced by the Treasury Auditors. Thus the GAO auditors compared expenditures with appropriation authority granted by Congress to insure mathematical correctness. Seated at desks and organized into small work teams, the auditors would daily confront huge stacks of paper. Armed with colored pencils and rubber stamps and reinforced by the "coffee grinder" adding machines, they would check, stamp, tick, and turn over each voucher.[32]

The differences between this ritual and that practiced in the Treasury were that now the auditors were free of the executive branch and that the Comptroller had great authority in his own right. Where the "tick-and-turn-over" audit revealed noncompliance, the Comptroller would disallow expenditures or lecture cabinet members for their inattention to financial matters. To cite several examples, a payment to General Pershing was disallowed, because he could not find his ticket receipts. Lacking appropriate legislative authority, the Bureau of Engraving was not permitted to buy wooden shoes for its employees who were required to work on floors covered with acid. Finally, when the Navy accepted a bid that was $250 higher than the lowest bid on the grounds that only that bid fit its requirements, McCarl proceeded to criticize Navy Secretary Swanson for his inattention to the authority of the GAO to make determinations on government contracts.[33]

Each agency's response to these imperious tactics reflected its relative status in the overall government pecking order. The Treasury and War Departments often ignored the GAO. The Navy Department would fight back. In the case noted above, Secretary Swanson sharply responded to McCarl's claim of authority by noting that his action was reviewable only by the President and the federal courts. Some complied willingly. When McCarl objected that the GAO had not audited all vouchers prepared by the Civil Works Administration, Harry Hopkins loaded fifteen barrels with government checks, deposited them at the GAO and told McCarl, "Let me know if you find anything wrong."[34] Still other agencies sought relief in the pre-audit or in congressional action to relieve the disbursing officers of responsibility. A final agency strategy was to seek legislative action to exempt expenditure from GAO control. Government corporations such as the Tennessee Valley Authority were successful in avoiding GAO control and centralized audit—though not a field audit—until the Government Corporation Control Act of 1945.[35]

THE INTERREGNUM: 1936–40

The late 1930s was a period of rebuke for the General Accounting Office. Comptroller John McCarl retired on June 20, 1936, at the end of his fifteen-year term. Although another Comptroller was appointed in 1939, he almost immediately developed a serious illness and resigned. Therefore Assistant Comptroller Richard Elliott acted as the Comptroller for most of the period 1936 to 1940; he was careful not to disturb the Office.[36]

The Roosevelt Administration, smarting under the disallowances of the GAO, did seek to change the GAO's charter during this period. In early 1936, the Brownlow Committee was appointed to examine management in the executive branch. Suspicious of any system which divided authority and responsibility, the President's Committee found, not surprisingly, that the auditing system deprived the President of the power to discharge his responsibilities. The Committee was particularly concerned that the Comptroller controlled by issuing rules and regulations governing administrative procedures and by pre-auditing vouchers, and then audited the actions that executive officials performed under his own rules and regulations.[37]

The Committee's philosophical predispositions about the proper control and auditing arrangements for the federal government led it and President Roosevelt to recommend the abolishment of the General Accounting Office. They proposed that a General Auditing Office be created in the legislative branch to conduct field audits at the site of agency operations and report its conclusions to the Congress. Control functions were to be shifted to the Treasury Department, along with the responsibility to settle claims.[38]

The bills growing out of this proposal were defeated in 1938. Having insisted upon a measure of control in the 1921 Act and having observed the active presidency of Franklin Roosevelt, Congress, as an institution, was not disposed to relinquish its influence in budgetary affairs. Thus congressmen were not willing to dispense with their equivalent of the Bureau of the Budget, because the GAO had the authority to countervail presidential and bureaucratic power.[39]

Denied the option of eliminating the GAO, President Roosevelt chose to influence its performance by careful selection of the next Comptroller General. After much prodding from Roosevelt, Representative Lindsay Carter Warren, a highly respected Democrat from North Carolina accepted in 1940.[40] Roosevelt's persistence was to pay off. Warren and his successors thoroughly revolutionized auditing to the point that the Comptroller General and the GAO were ultimately to become comparable in practice to what the President had proposed in 1937—an Auditor General and a General Auditing Office.

CHAPTER 3

Strategy and Agendas
in the Culture of Oversight

.

Organizational strategies are not born fully grown. Rather they must be nurtured and matured slowly as organizations review the new conditions which have forced them to change. New circumstances require organizations to study the task environment, emerging technologies, and alternative plans. Once such studies have been completed, institutional leaders must then test their new courses of action against the expectations of the organization's constituencies.

Successful organizational strategies are composed of simple themes or principles. These principles highlight what an organization is to do and how it is to relate to its environment. Complicated formulations can be misunderstood by the many executives and career elites who will be responsible for translating the goals and objectives of a strategy into specific organizational reforms and professional routines. Thus the old Army maxim for field commanders about to design a plan for sending troops into battle dictates "KISS," that is "Keep It Simple (Stupid)." If it isn't simple, commanders are convinced the plan will not be understood and implemented effectively.

The same dictum applies to organizational strategies, not only because of the many hierarchical layers required to respond to them, but also because individual leaders seldom survive long enough or have sufficient latitude to see their strategies fully implemented. With an average tenure of twenty-two months, most leaders in the executive branch have insufficient longevity to influence bureaucratic behavior.[1] Even where their tenure is longer, they are often constrained by the policy preferences of overseeing congressional committee chairmen and committee staff members and by the executive branch hierarchy, which includes cabinet secretaries, White House assistants, Office of Management and Budget analysts, and the President himself.[2]

As new leaders are appointed, they must build on the work of their predecessors. While the strategy remains constant, a new leader's agenda for implementing that strategy and its principles will differ from that of the last incumbent. Strategies cannot be easily modified, because they are almost invariably legitimized by statutes. Thus the ultimate achievement for the leader of any public organization is to see his strategy or his specific agenda to implement that strategy enshrined in laws or presidential orders. Therefore, organizational strategies are usually designed within the organization and then accepted by the actions of elected representatives. To cite an example, Secretary of War Elihu Root took particular care to see that the new strategy of "preparedness," which he designed after the Army's cataclysmic performance failure during the Spanish-American War, was endorsed by the General Staff and Militia Acts of 1903.[3]

The character of institutional leaders also influences strategy. Character includes an individual's style and belief system. A leader's style results from his experiences and his habits of work, of interpersonal relationship, and of communication. The first years of professional experience are usually formative, and when subsequent experience reinforces early professional learning, leaders carry techniques, practices, and expectations along to subsequent positions. For instance, Dwight D. Eisenhower's experiences and work habits as a military officer conditioned his leadership style as President.[4]

The interpersonal behavior patterns of leaders are also important, because they influence the relative compatibility between leaders and subordinates. Where resonance does not exist between political executives and bureaucratic professionals, disharmony and organizational tension ensue. Finally, the techniques a leader uses to communicate can also affect his plans. The most success is enjoyed by political executives who use a variety of communication channels to sell the dominant strategy and their particular agenda. Such channels include conferences, meetings, memoranda, awards, ceremonies, visits to bureaus and regional offices, and organizational newsletters.[5]

The character of institutional leaders is also influenced by their belief system—that is, their values and attitudes. Out of this belief system grows a style or pattern of leadership and management. An executive who values order and correct relationships tends to believe in strict hierarchy. This attitude, in turn, influences him to form habits of interpersonal relationships which reinforce regularity within the organization but reduce attention to details not channeled strictly through the hierarchy. Ultimately the concern for regularity and hierarchy may become in itself an agenda for the institution.

The final factor influencing institutional strategy is the predisposition of the career elite. This elite has considerable influence over not only the management of professionals, but also the direction of the institution itself. Thus without an overriding strategy refreshed by new agendas, environmental ambiguity will confuse and derail the rituals of public professionals.[6] With these propositions, let us now turn to the efforts of GAO leaders.

PERFORMANCE FAILURE

The events of the era 1940 to 1981 and the efforts of three Comptrollers General realigned the GAO's culture. The New Deal, World War II, and the Cold War provided the impetus for realigning the GAO into the culture of oversight. The evolution of American business corporations, the Brownlow and Hoover Commissions, and a reassertive Congress provided the broad scheme for the culture. Lindsay Carter Warren designed the new strategy. Joseph Campbell and Elmer Baker Staats filled in the details with their own agendas.

The New Deal created numerous agencies, much larger budgets, and broad discretionary powers for public servants. This explosion of government strained the existing accounting and auditing systems. As E.L. Normanton has observed, compliance auditing or the "control of regularity is not merely insufficient but terribly inadequate in this epoch of heavy spending."[7]

Although the New Deal strained the auditing arrangements, World War II and the Cold War shattered the culture of control. As in all previous wars, mobilization of men and material overwhelmed the audit. Millions of vouchers piled up in government warehouses, while at the same time most of the experienced audit clerks were drafted or enlisted in the armed services. At war's end, Comptroller General Warren estimated that in the area of transportation vouchers alone, it would require ten years to audit vouchers generated between 1942 and 1945.[8]

The Cold War called for the deployment of American armed forces in Europe and Asia. This deployment and the shift to a permanently mobilized defense establishment made centralized audits impractical.

By 1948 the defense budget alone was larger than the entire federal government budget for any fiscal year from 1921 to 1940, during the GAO's culture of control.[9]

These events created a crisis for government auditing. The resolution of this situation was suggested by new technologies developed outside government. As large industrial enterprises began to restructure in the 1920s and 1930s to drive down unit costs and to reduce the impact of market fluctuations, they began to turn more and more to professional accountants who emphasized efficient and effective uses for resources.[10] Given American preoccupation with businesslike government, this emphasis came to be celebrated as the panacea for the ills generated by the national security state.

The celebrants for these values of efficient and effective government were the Brownlow and Hoover Commissions. Staffed by students of public administration and scientific management, these Commissions found the government in general and government auditing specifically to be a maze of divided responsibility and accountability, which engendered wasteful conflict and duplication. These reformers thought that by straightening lines of responsibility and authority, government auditing would be more responsive to both the President and Congress, and the government itself would be more accountable. The scheme of the first Hoover Commission was similar to that of the Brownlow Committee. It called for splitting up the GAO, thereby giving the authority for accounting methods and procedures to an Accountant General residing in the Treasury Department. The Comptroller General was to perform legislative audits on a decentralized and spot-sampling basis.[11]

This redesign was hardly acceptable to the Congress. Both the House and Senate Committees on Expenditures noted that the Comptroller General's authority to prescribe accounting requirements "is an essential legislative control over public financial transactions, and must be held inviolate."[12] However, Congress was much more receptive to the recommendations for decentralized and professionalized auditing. Beginning with acts in 1945, Congress encouraged the GAO to restructure the legislative audit.

Another element in the congressional calculus was the disturbing growth of presidential influence in the 1930s and early 1940s. The Depression and the war had drained the Congress of considerable authority and invested it in the executive branch. "Crises in policies with politics as usual"[13] called for new techniques of congressional control over the functioning of a more powerful executive.

DETERMINANTS FOR THE NEW STRATEGY

L indsay Warren personified the new values of efficient and effective government espoused by the reformers. His background, personality, and philosophy were infused with an abhorrence of waste, overlap, and duplication. Born into a patrician family in Washington, North Carolina, Warren followed his ancestors into law and then politics. In 1924 he was elected to the House of Representatives at the age of thirty five. For the next sixteen years he faced no opposition in North Carolina's First District.

As a classic Southern Democrat, Warren supported New Deal legislation and government reorganization. He chaired the House Accounts Committee from 1932 to 1940 and was known for his interest in matters relating to more efficient government. He was widely known and respected in the House, and many congressmen believed that he was slated to become the Majority Leader.[14]

As Comptroller General, Warren's appearances before Congress were always colorful and forthright. For instance, he observed in 1949:

> Any bureau can put up a case, at least to suit itself, why it should be retained. Congress can set up a bureau for the edification of the Three Blind Mice or for the Rehabilitation of Humpty Dumpty, and within a year those who head them can come in with glowing accounts of their work.[15]

Warren's testimony frequently combined facts with, what one observer called, a "spectacular sense of outrage." He was so effective that congressmen seldom took issue with him. In a debate with former President Herbert Hoover over Hoover's recommendations before the Senate Expenditures Committee in March 1950, the Comptroller won hands down.[16]

Like his predecessor John Raymond McCarl, Lindsay Warren was indignant with the discretion Congress had granted to the executive agencies. Unlike McCarl, however, Warren was also concerned about the effect of bureaucratic latitude on congressional powers and public confidence. Warren found the waste in big government particularly appalling. He labeled the cost-plus method of contracting used extensively during the Second World War as the "greatest device ever invented for pumping money out of the Treasury." He characterized many bureau heads as "empire builders." Long before the Hoover Commission report, Warren described the government as a "hodge-podge and crazy-quilt of duplications, overlapping inefficiencies and inconsistencies," full of "tax-eaters and those who wish to keep themselves perpetually attached to the payroll."[17]

To respond to the external pressures and to Warren's philosophy, a new executive and a new career elite had to be established. The new executives were GAO veterans with progressive ideas, while the career elite was composed of newcomers with credentials as certified public accountants. With the retirement of Judge Elliott as Assistant Comptroller General, Warren persuaded the President to appoint Frank Yates, who had been with the GAO since its inception and had served as a legal advisor to the Comptroller General. Another GAO veteran, Frank Weitzel, was pulled into the Comptroller's Office and served as one of Warren's assistants from 1945 to 1953. Upon Yates's death, Warren convinced President Dwight Eisenhower to nominate Weitzel as Assistant Comptroller. Both of these men were entrusted with considerable responsibility.[18]

However the principal forces for change were the newcomers with their commercial auditing expertise. Displaced by the war, these certified public accountants were interested in government work and disposed to an audit reliant upon generally accepted principles of auditing. Furthermore they sought to hire young accountants, to eliminate the clerks and investigators responsible for the old compliance audit, and to model the GAO after a large public accounting firm.[19]

Warren, his executive elite, and the new career elite designed a new strategy which sought to fulfill the second function Congress had prescribed for the GAO in the formative 1921 Budget and Accounting Act. Thus they recognized that the GAO could not successfully control executive behavior, but could only oversee it. That is the GAO could not guard the treasury and check the President; what it could do was to study government operations, gather information, and report faults in management and programs to Congress. The Congress would therefore be responsible for seeing to it that the deficiencies discovered by the auditors were corrected.[20]

Building on this core, Warren and his elite redesigned the Office under the guidance of five principles: responsiveness, cognizance, professionalization, precision, and evaluation. The origins of these principles lie in the experiences of government auditors and the GAO, in the philosophy of Lindsay Warren, and in the philosophy of the accounting profession itself. Although never articulated as such, these principles, I argue, were manifested in the behavior of Warren and his successors Campbell and Staats, as well as in the behavior of the GAO executive and career elites during the culture of oversight.

The principle of *responsiveness* refers to the GAO's responsibility to respond to congressional demands and needs. That is, the GAO should provide reports to Congress, lend auditors to congressional committees and subcommittees to conduct investigations, provide the Comptroller and members of his elite to testify before Congress and to review executive branch proposals as requested by Congress. However these reports should not be primarily initiated by congressional requests; that is, the GAO auditors themselves should be responsible for initiating reports in areas which they think Congress will be, is, or should be interested.[21]

Cognizance meant that GAO auditors would maintain an audit presence within federal agencies both in Washington, D.C., and in the field. The centralized form of voucher review was discarded, and the auditors were sent out to agency sites to investigate financial systems, management, and programs. In practice, cognizance meant that GAO auditors would maintain small field offices colocated with agency headquarters in Washington and regional offices around the country and overseas. Auditors located in these offices were then able to interview executive bureaucrats in their own headquarters, request and review files on site, inspect government warehouses and contractor plants, and view the operation of federal programs as well as state and local programs that used federal funds.

The principle of cognizance brought several advantages. It provided more information on government operations than did the rather sterile "vouching" of the old centralized audit. It also permitted the GAO to go beyond investigating the simple compliance of federal financial systems into analyzing the programmatic and managerial affairs of government agencies. Finally, it was also more lively, more interesting than the review of tax forms and vouchers which had been the fare for most CPAs in the private sector. As Lindsay Warren observed in his 1951 report to Congress, the advantages to site auditing were "continually being demonstrated."[22]

Warren and his elites decided that the GAO could no longer rely on technicians to do the audit. Only college-educated, professionally-trained analysts were adequate to the task. The only acceptable analysts were experienced accountants or younger, college-educated accounting majors who could be properly reared in GAO training programs. As one observer commented the GAO placed itself "in the hands of the accounting profession."[23]

The principle of *precision* meant that the GAO was to be totally accurate and fair in its reporting. This was a response to the McCarl era, in which the GAO was not known for its fair play with executive agencies, and also a response to the realization that inaccurate reporting of even the most minute detail would damage the GAO's reputation with Congress. As Lindsay Warren observed in 1952, "we have three rules in making our audits and investigations—first, to be right; second, to be fair; and third, to go down the middle of the road."[24]

Finally the GAO was to *evaluate* agency financial systems, management, and programs. Reporting details was not enough. As a critic, the GAO was to compare agency performance with the standards promulgated in the laws, orders, and regulations of the government and to find faults. Again using Warren's own words, the GAO was "not an office of programs and policies." Rather it was to "criticize wasteful and extravagant practices observed in audits and investigations" and to suggest "successful means of getting the job done with fewer employees and at lower cost."[25]

These principles composed the strategy Warren emplaced during his tenure as Comptroller General from 1940 to 1954. They continued to influence the Office throughout the culture of oversight. Although succeeding Comptrollers sought to modify them, the principles endured, because they were legitimized by legislation and institutionalized by the structure constructed by Warren and his elites.

LEGITIMIZING THE NEW CULTURE

The origins of enabling legislation for government organizations are as complex as laws of a more programmatic nature. In the case of the GAO, the burst of legislation which legitimized the new strategy of evaluation during Warren's tenure reflected many sources and interests. As discussed above, presidential dissatisfaction with the GAO, congressional needs, as well as the interests of the accounting profession, the government reformers, and executive agencies all influenced the outcome. However, a review of the legislative history for these laws suggests that Lindsay Warren had a strong hand in all of them. In the aggregate, these laws directed the GAO into the culture of oversight by emphasizing the five principles that constituted the new strategy.

Each principle was emphasized in the landmark Budget and Accounting Improvement Act of 1950, and most were amplified by other laws passed from 1945 to 1951. The precursor to the 1950 Budget Act was an informal arrangement called the Joint Accounting Improvement Program. Worked out in 1949 by Warren, the Secretary of the Treasury, and the Director of the Bureau of the Budget, the Program was essentially a rapprochement between the executive and legislative branches. It resolved many of the disputes over the responsibility for accounting which had plagued the government since the 1921 Budget and Accounting Act. The Program shifted the responsibility for maintenance of accounting systems and production of financial reports to the Treasury Department and made the GAO responsible for specifying accounting principles and standards.[26]

The 1950 Budget and Accounting Act enshrined these arrangements and further specified that the GAO's responsibilities were to audit and report to Congress, thereby emphasizing Warren's strategic principle of responsiveness. The 1950 Act also approved the use of site audits and invested the Comptroller with the discretion to decide when audits and accounting system reviews were necessary—the components of the two principles of cognizance and precision. Finally, the Act emphasized the principles of professionalization and evaluation by approving the use of commercial audit techniques for all government agencies.[27]

These principles were amplified by other laws during this period. The George and Government Corporation Control Acts of 1945 required the GAO to conduct professional evaluations of all wholly-owned and mixed-ownership corporations at corporate sites.[28] The 1945 Reorganization Act and 1946 Legislative Reorganization Acts emphasized the GAO's responsiveness to Congress by declaring the Office to be part of the legislative branch and designating a committee in each chamber to receive GAO reports.[29] Cognizance and precision were promoted by laws in 1946, 1947, and 1951 that gave the GAO access to the records of all federal contractors.[30]

Two other laws were also important. The 1949 Federal Property and Administrative Services Act specified GAO site audits, the use of generally accepted principles of professional auditing, and evaluations of agency effectiveness to oversee an "efficient, businesslike system of property management" in the federal government.[31] Finally, a 1950 Act transferred GAO responsibilities for postal accounting to the Post Office Department and called for GAO site audits, to be conducted as the Comptroller saw fit.[32]

Warren's health began to fade in 1952. Two operations and a rigid diet were not enough to restore his vigor. On the advice of his doctors, he retired in April, 1954.[33]

Lindsay Warren proved to be the embodiment of congressional imperatives in the post-War area. His concern for economy and efficiency in government and his sense of outrage over government waste were consistent with congressional concerns for reasserting legislative power and redesigning the government's financial mechanisms. His artful leadership blunted the managerial, executive-oriented proposals for accounting reform proposed by the Hoover Commission, and yet created a compromise which was satisfactory to the agencies, the Congress, and the GAO. In the end, Warren and his elites had not only fended off calls for reform without sacrificing organizational integrity, they had also fashioned a new strategy which expanded the GAO's mandate and responsibilities.

REFINING WARREN'S STRATEGY DURING AN ERA OF CONGRESSIONAL RESURGENCE

Although Warren's strategy and its supporting principles have dominated the GAO to the present, they were strained by subsequent shifts in Congress, the government, and society. First we will discuss these broader shifts, then suggest what their impact was on the eras of Campbell and Staats. Then, as each of these eras is discussed, the more specific guidance which Congress gave the GAO in that period will be detailed.

The period from 1954 to 1981 was a high risk one for the GAO. The Cold War, Great Society programs, rapid economic growth, followed by stagnation in the 1970s, cultural upheaval in the 1960s and an ill-fated war in Southeast Asia all imposed considerable strains on government, the Congress, and therefore on the Office. Although the New Deal continued to dominate government during this era, it was variously interpreted by conservative President Dwight Eisenhower, moderates such as Richard Nixon and Jimmy Carter, and the more liberal Lyndon Johnson.

While the number of executive branch employees did not grow substantially during this period, federal budgets and responsibilities expanded dramatically. Inflation could account only partly for the growth in budget outlays from $60.3 billion in fiscal year 1955 to $657.2 billion in 1981.[34] The principal components of this growth were the Great

Society programs committed to achieving racial equality, social justice, and economic opportunity.

Among the primary proponents for these commitments were activists in both the House and the Senate.[35] Many of these activists were in the vanguard not only for programs seeking to achieve these social goals, but also for congressional control and oversight mechanisms to ensure that executive agencies carried them out. That is, chastened by the presidential penchant for worldwide military incursions and by Richard Nixon's defiance of congressional demands, many in Congress felt that stronger controls over public policy and administration were necessary to achieve political accountability.[36]

Members of Congress also found their traditional relationships with constituents undergoing unexpected changes. Post-Korean War presidents discovered that television and polling permitted them to proselytize and test constituencies nationwide. Interest groups recognized that grassroots campaigning through targeted mail techniques and lobbying Congress through large coalitions were effective devices for achieving their legislative purposes.

The Congressional response to the many pressures from within and without was to disaggregate. Where committee structures had dominated congressional policy making since the beginning of the twentieth century, subcommittees and individual legislators themselves came to play a dominant role.[37] Such a shift required more staff to provide subcommittee chairmen and members themselves sufficient resources to influence legislative details. The number of personal and committee staff members grew from 4,489 in 1957 to 13,969 in 1979.[38] New support staffs to provide analytical assistance were created in the Office of Technology Assessment in 1972 and the Congressional Budget Office in 1974. The Legislative References Service became the Congressional Research Service in 1970 with new responsibility to provide policy analysis. By the late 1970s, these changes had transformed congresssional offices into what Robert Salisbury and Kenneth Shepsle have called "member-centered enterprises."[39]

Congress also redefined its terms and promoted new control mechanisms for influencing public policy. In a 1970 Act and subsequent rules adapted by the House, legislators distinguished between "oversight" and "control" of public policy. Oversight is an information-gathering function that includes the responsibility of each standing committee to review and study the behavior of federal agencies to insure it conforms to the intent of Congress.[40] Control, on the other hand, entails actions growing out of oversight which seek to modify or reform agency behavior.

The most favored devices for control of executive behavior during the period 1954 to 1981 were nonstatutory controls and the legislative veto. Nonstatutory controls were used in appropriations hearings and reports to coax, cajole, and badger executive agencies into compliance with congressional desires.[41] When federal agencies found ways to evade these controls, Congress shifted to the legislative veto. The legislative veto reserved to a committee, to one or to both chambers the opportunity to disapprove contemplated action by the executive branch.[42] During the 1970s, it was used with increasing regularity and was contained in key provisions of two landmark pieces of legislation: the 1973 War Powers Resolution and the 1974 Budget and Impoundment Control Act.

The Campbell Era

These political developments were accompanied by both broad and specific guidance for the GAO from Congress. Broad guidance came from the Government Operations Committees, which had been charged by the 1946 Legislative Reorganization Act to oversee the GAO and receive its reports. During this period the House Committee considered federal supply management in general and individual aspects of agency operations more specifically, with a view to "bringing out fresh opportunities to achieve increased efficiency and economy."[43]

More specific guidance was contained in the Lispcomb Report and the "Zink Stink." In 1956 Congressman Glenard Lipscomb (R, Calif.) authored a report criticizing the GAO for its audit practices. The report stated that audit findings were too often repeated from report to report and that auditors were unwilling or unable to state unqualified opinions on the financial management of agencies. It also found little or no coverage of the Defense Department. Finally, the audits were too late in reaching the Congress to be of much use.[44]

The Zink Stink involved the congressional response to a GAO report critical of zinc mining executives who constituted a Defense Department advisory committee on stockpiling critical materials. In spite of considerable efforts to obtain documents and interview the zinc company employees, GAO investigators failed to nail down every detail. Consequently their report was loudly disputed by several zinc company presidents. The Comptroller General was forced to concede publicly that his investigators had issued a report which contained errors. Further the GAO found itself rebuked by several senators.

Senator BRICKER (R, Ohio). GAO in making a charge of this kind is supposed to be absolutely accurate, when reporting to the Congress as to the facts. I would not [accept] a statement like that in a letter unless I checked it and we do not expect you to. . . .

My criticism of you is for submitting a report that was erroneous when you could have found out the truth and submitted it factually to this committee.

.   .   .   .

Senator CAPEHART (R, Indiana). You do not think if you came up here and misrepresent to the Congress that that amounts to anything? . . . Why haven't you already withdrawn your allegations and admitted you made a mistake? [45]

These events played a significant role in generating Campbell's agenda for the GAO.

Campbell's Style.   An equally important component in Joseph Campbell's agenda was his personality, specifically his style and philosophy. Campbell was a self-made man who financed his education at Columbia University through scholarships. loans, and private employment. As a certified public accountant in New York City from 1924 until 1941, he was a partner in an accounting firm and comptroller of Valspar Corporation. Columbia University then selected him assistant treasurer and later treasurer and vice president. There he served under recently retired General Dwight Eisenhower who became Columbia's president in 1948.

After his election to the U.S. presidency, Eisenhower first appointed Campbell to the Atomic Energy Commission and then nominated him as the Comptroller General.[46] His nomination did not please many Democrats in Congress, who supported one of their own. But in the end, Campbell's unquestionable qualifications as an accountant and the solid support of the accounting profession won out, and he was confirmed in March, 1955.[47]

The GAO auditors found him to be a tough, autocratic, and rather distant leader. He worked primarily through his division directors and expected them and their immediate subordinates to attend to the technical details of managing the audit. His supervisors were expected to have the details of individual audits immediately available at his every call, a technique which promoted elaborate systems of minute-by-minute accountability and information recall.

He was impatient with bureaucracy. He showed no interest whatsoever in learning the civil service grade structure. Yet, men were expected to get the job done quickly and without mistakes. It was widely believed that Campbell might tolerate one, but certainly not two mistakes from his auditors.[48]

His managerial style was succinctly articulated in testimony before the House Post Office and Civil Service Committee.

> [Good leadership] requires strong supervision, intelligent direction, independent internal review, and evaluation of the performance of both workers and supervisors.
>
> Costly and wasteful deficiencies usually result from the failure of one or a number of individuals to properly carry out their duties. When this occurs, the error made by one person is compounded or leads to others, because each individual is concerned only with his own activity.
>
> All personnel must be made fully aware of their responsibilities and of the nature and consequences of their actions and that inefficiency will be a first consideration in evaluating personal work performance for promotion, demotion and reassignment.[49]

Campbell's philosophy was that of a disciplined pragmatist who believed in the value of audit. He felt auditors should be aloof. He shunned the social festivities of Capitol Hill and Washington out of the conviction that auditors ought not to mingle with their clients. He also felt that auditors should find deficiencies.

> In planning and conducting our audits, we place primary emphasis on agency, contractor, or subcontractor operations and activities in which opportunities for improvement appear to exist. . . . Application of this policy results in placing particular emphasis on known or suspected weaknesses, such as ineffectiveness, inefficiency, waste and extravagance, improper expenditures, failure to comply with laws or congressional intent, or other problem areas.[50]

As one committee staff member fondly remembered him, "Campbell had a classic sense of the jugular vein."

Campbell's Agenda.   The body of legislation enacted by Lindsay Warren and his elites prescribed the strategy for the Campbell era. Furthermore, since an auditing elite had been installed by Warren, and since Campbell shared with those CPA's the perspectives of the accounting profession, he maintained them in their positions. Thus the strategy of reporting to Congress and its attendant principles dominated Campbell's tenure as Comptroller General.

Campbell's agenda, however, tended to accentuate professionalism and precision over the other principles laid down by Warren. Chapter 5 will describe in detail the professional system which Campbell and his career elite instituted. Suffice it to say here that the values and norms of the certified public accounting profession were consciously adopted by Campbell and his elite. Professional behavior meant loyalty to the GAO and high ethical standards. If auditors left to pursue an assignment in another agency or the private sector, they were not permitted to return.[51] Ethical standards were codified in a Comptroller General's order which was distributed to each GAO auditor and were carefully policed.

Those who are familiar with the personnel system developed during Joseph Campbell's tenure agree that it was very successful. Given the disparity between the government salary structure and the marketplace for accountants, the GAO was able to obtain and develop capable accountants.

Campbell also emphasized precision. To GAO auditors, chastened by the Zink Stink, precision meant complete accuracy in reporting. No fact or conclusion could be included in GAO reports without a careful checking process called *referencing* (see chapter 6). As one senior GAO official recalled, the auditors of that era would "prove it over and over before writing about it—they would leave nothing to chance."

Precision also meant emphasizing deficiencies and actually citing names of government officials and contractors thought to be responsible for mismanagement. Audit reports of this period would also recommend that contractors voluntarily refund extraordinary profits derived from negotiated contracts.[52] As another GAO veteran observed, "We became a wholly independent bunch of auditors. Campbell made tigers out of us."

Of less importance were the principles of responsiveness, cognizance, and evaluation. Reponsiveness to Congress and agency cognizance appeared to be splendid ideals, but they should not erode the independent viewpoint necessary for objective reporting, according to Campbell. The GAO should be responsive to congressional requests, but generally follow its own audit program to root out waste and inefficiency. Campbell did extend site auditing, but insisted that his auditors maintain an aloof relationship with "clients."[53]

The principle of evaluation was not given much attention either, because it was thought to be synonymous with commercial auditing practices. These practices had already been accepted by the GAO career elite, which was composed of experienced CPAs. Auditors needed only to apply their training learned in accounting curriculums and GAO training courses to the affairs of government. Thus GAO auditing practices came to parallel those of the large public accounting firms.[54]

In the end, the auditors became too aggressive in the eyes of some within Congress, particularly those dependent upon political support from defense contractors. These congressmen pressured Representative Chester Holifield (D, Calif.), the Chairman of the Government Operations Committee, to investigate and modify GAO audit procedures. The Holifield Hearings were conducted in 1965 and a report released in 1966. They were unhappy with the style, format, and content of GAO reports; the frequency and scope of reporting; the distribution and release of reports; the handling of confidential business data; the naming of officials in audit reports; the practice of seeking voluntary refunds from contractors; and the referral of reports to the Justice Department.[55] In essence, Holifield's subcommittee was dissatisfied with the Campbell audit. The report refocused GAO auditing.

These events also prompted Campbell's departure. By 1965, his health was failing and the strain of the hearings proved to be too much. He was forced to seek a disability retirement.

THE STAATS ERA

With Campbell's retirement, his deputy, Frank Weitzel, assumed responsibility for the GAO as the Acting Comptroller General until the confirmation of Elmer Boyd Staats in March, 1966. The period of Staats's Comptrollership (1966 to 1981) was turbulent.

Paralleling the social and institutional shifts discussed above were changes in the accounting profession itself. Faced with the widespread expectation that the auditor's opinion was definitive and that the auditors were responsible for discovering corporate fraud, large public accounting firms created the Financial Accounting Standards Board (FASB) in 1973 as an independent entity to provide standards for the profession. This effort was not enough to stave off the criticism of the Senate Committee on Government Affairs. That Committee published a staff study in 1976 asserting that the large firms were so thoroughly intertwined with the management of American corporations that CPA independence was nonexistent and that accounting standards should be promulgated by the federal government. These assaults did nothing to enhance the reputation of the accountant in either the government or the GAO.[56]

The assaults did not, however, impede the growth of the evaluative audit in the private sector. Recognizing public demands for greater accountability of government at all levels, some auditors began to conduct evaluative audits for regulatory commissions and agencies at the state and local levels. These audits generally used standards derived from, or similar to, those promulgated by the GAO. Others began to apply these techniques to business as well.[57]

Also affecting the accounting profession were other new technologies developed in the nation's leading business administration schools and then applied to government. Operations research and systems analysis, cost-benefit analysis, zero-based budgeting, and the planning, programming, and budgeting system were used to enhance management of public agencies and their programs. As these techniques appeared in executive branch agencies, congressmen also begin to call for their use by GAO auditors.[58]

Staats's Style.   The background and philosophy of Elmer Staats was suited to satisfy this clamoring for a broader audit repertorie. He had strong ties with the academic community, the executive branch, and Congress. A Phi Beta Kappa graduate of McPherson College, he earned a doctoral degree from the University of Minnesota in public administration in 1939. He was active in the American Society for Public Administration, serving as President of the Washington, D.C., chapter from 1948 to 1949 and as National President from 1960 to 1961.

His service in the executive branch was principally to the President. From 1939 to 1966, he worked his way up from a management analyst to become the Deputy Director of the Bureau of the Budget (BOB) under Presidents Truman, Eisenhower, Kennedy, and Johnson, and Executive Officer of the Operations Coordinating Board of the National Security Council (NSC) under President Eisenhower. These experiences gave him an unusually broad overview of the operations of the federal government and a keen sense of legislative affairs.[59] As one old BOB hand observed, "I at first thought Elmer was rather slow, but I soon learned that he was terribly sensitive to the Hill—he knew what Congressmen wanted."

Thus Staats was a consummate public servant who possessed a keen sense of congressional and bureaucratic politics. It was widely believed that "Elmer always sat on a three-cornered cushion—one side was for the Democrats, one for the Republicans and one for vague situations."[60] This flexibility won him many supporters. As President Lyndon Johnson remarked during Staats's swearing-in ceremony on March 8, 1966, he was appointed for his faithful service and wise counsel to four administrations; "Elmer Staats has always been a builder, a believer— not a doubter."[61]

This background clearly influenced Staats's style and philosophy as Comptroller General. To survive the political shoals in the Exective Office, one had to be circumspect and had to work to a consensus. To deal with public professionals and with the Congress, one developed a collegial, participative style of leadership. Hugh Heclo has described this style as "due-process" leadership, in which the views of all are given a fair hearing prior to the announcement of a decision.[62]

Due-process leadership, incremental change, and looking out for the GAO's interests characterized Staats's approach to the Comptrollership. In line with his experience in the BOB and NSC, Staats would hold lengthy conferences to consider legislative strategy or internal matters. Division and office directors would present their budgets and their plans for future audit work in forums similar to the agency budget hearings held by the BOB.

Staats favored both incremental change and daily management delegated to his directors. According to him, change had to

> start modestly and expand slowly. There must be gradual development built on experience gained—the auditor must walk before attempting to run. . . . It behooves the auditor who is expanding his efforts beyond financial and accounting matters to develop his competence gradually, but surely.[63]

Content to leave most of the day-to-day management to his direct subordinates, Staats was primarily interested in the broad directions of the Office. Where he felt it necessary to intervene in such matters as organizational policies or new audit directions, his technique was that of "leaning into matters. He never gets mad, and he never gets tired."

Much of his workday was spent "looking out" for GAO interests. As several senior auditors observed, Staats "listens and watches for the undercurrents . . . he knows and meets lots of people." He was "personally involved in a wide range of issues with congressmen and people outside of government." For instance, in fiscal years 1968 and 1969 he spoke before forty-eight business and professional organizations.[64] During the first ten years of his Comptrollership, the testified before Congress a total of 187 times[65] and was always ready to meet with congressmen or to discuss matters on the telephone.[66] His speeches were published widely.[67]

Staats's philosophy and values were derived from the field of public administration. He believed in better government. This concern was not just limited to decreasing waste and mismanagement—the traditional preoccupation of previous comptrollers general—but also included an interest in improving personnel management, internal auditing and budgeting, and program performance. These interests were reflected in his focus on the concept of accountability. To enhance public confidence in government, "the need is for accountability."[68]

The work of his auditors was to enhance accountability,[69] which he felt could be achieved by publicizing the faults of government and its programs. Staats was convinced that such publicity would pressure agencies and the Congress to improve management and program effectiveness and so enhance the reputation of government. Thus finding fault with all aspects of agency peformance became virtuous, because it enhanced accountability.

New Enabling Legislation.   Just as Lindsay Warren had worked with the Congress to legitimize his strategy for the GAO, so too did Elmer Staats seek legislative support for his agenda. Yet given the turbulence of this era, Staats as often found himself responding to congressional demands for an altered GAO repertoire as influencing and shaping these demands.

The Staats era rivaled that of Warren in producing GAO-related legislation. Seven principal pieces of legislation were enacted during the period 1966 to 1981, as well as over eighty others which expanded or reasserted GAO audit authority in virtually every endeavor of the federal government. At the end of this period, the following previously sacrosanct agencies were subjected to the legislative audit: Federal Bureau of Investigation, Internal Revenue Service, Federal Reserve System, Comptroller of the Currency, and Bureau of Alcohol, Tobacco and Firearms. For a brief period, Congress even required the GAO to monitor presidential campaign contributions.[70]

Of the seven principal pieces of legislation, three influenced the audit directly, while the other four were intended to free the GAO from the last vestiges of executive branch control. The first to directly affect the audit was a 1967 Amendment to the Economic Opportunity Act, introduced by Senator Winston Prouty of Vermont, which called on the GAO to provide "an impartial and businesslike investigation of the poverty program."[71] By calling on the auditors to review the efficiency and effectiveness of a program, to hire consultants, and to contract out much of the work, the Prouty Amendment suggested a new routine in the evaluative repertoire of GAO auditors.

Of more significance were the 1970 Legislative Reorganization Act and the 1974 Budget and Impoundment Control Act. The 1970 Act required the GAO to "review and analyze the results of government programs and activities" and conduct cost-benefit studies. To carry out this mandate, the Comptroller was specifically authorized to reorganize the GAO. Office reviews were to be given wider availability, and executive agencies were required to respond to all auditor recommendations to the House and Senate Government Operations Committee within sixty days of report issuance.[72]

The 1974 Budget Act further expanded the GAO's mandate to perform program audits and the Comptroller's role as an agent of Congress. The Act sought to "clarify and strengthen the role of the Comptroller General in program evaluation" by requiring him to cultivate criteria for evaluating government programs and to assist committees in inserting such criteria into legislation. The Act also reinforced the status of the Comptroller by making him the principal agent of Congress in coordinating with the executive branch on budgetary matters.[73]

The remaining four laws firmly established GAO independence of the executive branch. The GAO was exempted from all personnel controls of the Office of Personnel Management and permitted to establish its own career system. Where agencies would not produce documents, the Comptroller General was empowered to seek redress in the federal courts. For organizations outside the federal government, the GAO was allowed to issue subpoenas. These laws also required congressional leaders to advise the President on their preferences for filling vacancies in the offices of the Comptroller and Deputy Comptroller General.[74]

The New Agenda.   In spite of all this legislation, Lindsay Warren's strategy of reporting to Congress was not altered, nor were his strategic principles abandoned. Rather these principles were refined, that is, brought forward and modified to meet the new circumstances facing the GAO. Whereas Joseph Campbell emphasized the principles of precision and professionalism. Elmer Staats had a broader agenda, one which addressed all of Warren's principles.[75]

The principle of responsiveness was to consist of more than issuing reports and occasional testimony before Congress by the Comptroller and a few career elites. Rather responsiveness came to mean energetic oversight of established programs, frequent testimony and coordination with members of Congress and their staffs, and forecasting of the legislature's agenda. Energetic oversight was "getting our money's worth from old and established programs. From our vantage point, it appears that both the executive and legislative branches have been more concerned with starting new programs than with making certain that those we already have are working satisfactorily or could be improved."[76] Testifying before Congress increased from an average of two times a month in the mid 1960s to an average of fifteen times a month by the end of the 1970s.[77] Furthermore auditors had to establish congressional interest in an area before they began to audit (see Chapter 6). Finally, the Comptroller sought to lead Congress into new areas of oversight, rather than follow. Staats said in 1977,

> We try to focus on issues which we think are coming up or that we think Congress should get interested in. There are many issues we identify where there doesn't seem to be much interest in the Congress. We try to get their attention to get something done about it [*sic*].[78]

Staats also broadened the principle of cognizance to encompass areas beyond site auditing. The chill which Campbell had imposed on relations with executive agencies was lifted, with Staats and his auditors candidly discussing audits with agency appointees and senior bureaucrats. Staats also opened up new relationships with a broad array of federal and nonfederal agencies by campaigning for an inspector general to be installed in all federal departments and by publishing pamphlets detailing GAO auditing standards and procedures to assist nonfederal audit agencies. His auditors were encouraged to join professional associations other than those of accounting and auditing. Finally the GAO became an active force in the International Organization of Supreme Audit Institutions, with one of Staats's Assistant Comptrollers serving as editor of the organization's journal.[79]

Precision was to be achieved by new mechanisms to oversee the auditors and the audit process. That is, a large headquarters staff was designed which consolidated the functions of personnel management, budgeting, and program planning. An information system was imposed to calculate the resources assigned to various lines of audit, and a program planning system emplaced to design and coordinate the audit effort (see Chapter 4). Evaluation came to mean more than review of agency financial systems and management. The new star was program auditing, which was to assess the effectiveness of federal programs in achieving the objectives contained within the law (see Chapter 6).

Elite Redesign.   To broaden the principle of professionalization, Staats sought out professions other than accounting to add to the GAO's ranks, and redesigned both the executive and career elites. Social scientists, engineers, graduates of business administration curriculums, and even a few doctors were hired.

Upon his arrival at the GAO, Staats found no executive elite and the career elite of CPAs in shambles. Confused and feeling betrayed by the Holifield Hearings, the career elite had no sense of direction, was badly split internally, and was slowly disintegrating.

To rectify this situation, Staats gradually eliminated the old career elite from operational control by promoting them out of their line positions to serve as his assistants; as expected, they soon retired. In their place, he created three new classes: an executive elite, a novitiate career elite, and a counter-elite.

The executive elite initially was composed of the Deputy Comptroller General and the General Counsel, both of whom Staats selected himself. That is, Staats persuaded President Johnson to appoint Robert Keller as the Deputy Comptroller General when Frank Weitzel retired after fifteen years of service. Keller had served the GAO for thirty-one years, working his way up to be General Counsel.[80] To replace Keller as General Counsel, Staats chose Paul Dembling, who had served in that position at the National Aeronautics and Space Administration.

To further expand this group, Staats persuaded Congress to provide five Assistant Comptroller General positions and the authority to appoint them as he saw fit. For these Executive Level IV positions, Staats chose outsiders such as Tom Morris and Sam Hughes, both of whom had extensive management experience in the executive branch. Later he turned to bright and energetic GAO auditors such as John Heller, who shared his interest in changing the Office.[81]

The novitiate career elite was expanded dramatically as Staats created new divisions and staff offices. Chosen to fill these positions were positive and enthusiastic auditors who had risen quickly in the GAO.

All CPAs, they embraced the values traditionally linked to the accounting profession. When I queried them about the values they associated with the GAO, they named accounting virtues: independence, objectivity, impartiality, integrity, authoritativeness, and accuracy. Although finding the novitiate initially inclined to avoid audits of top-level policy issues, Staats worked hard to broaden their horizons. Frequent conferences were held to discuss new audit directions and to include the auditors in projected organizational changes. They were called upon to chair GAO-wide committees on issues facing the GAO and to prepare memoranda for division director meetings. Training programs were begun to expose them to new analytical tools as well as to the broader issues facing all of government.[82]

Finally, a counter-elite was installed to set the pattern for the new form of evaluation and to force existing auditors to follow it. Two outside policy analysts, comfortable with social science evaluative techniques, were brought in at the highest civil service grade, quickly elevated to the august position of division director, and provided line auditing divisions. As an insider from one of these divisions observed, "our reason for being is institutional change."

Other émigrés were chosen to fill newly created staff positions in areas which Staats thought needed particular attention. A journalist was brought in to be an Information Officer, a systems analyst was employed to create an internal management-information system, and personnel management experts were hired to manage the GAO's equal employment opportunity program.

The counter-elite was further bolstered by a staff which consisted of auditing heretics who were to implement the program planning and personnel management systems suggested by Assistant Comptroller Tom Morris. These accountant auditors served to erode the dominance of the career elite by implementing systems for resource allocation and personnel management which provided the executive elite access to the auditors' professional sanctuaries. Their heresy was to work against the brethren by advocating the new administrative ideology. Thus the counter-elite consisted of several division directors, nonaccounting professionals recruited for specific tasks, and staff accountants dedicated to the new audit agenda.

SUMMARY, PART I

Organizational history is as important as organizational culture in influencing the behavior of public professionals. An organization's lineage influences present behavior. Thus the GAO auditor-evaluators can point to distant ancestors who were tasked by the Roman Senate and the British Parliament to review expenditures made by executive officers. These ancestors influenced the American colonial auditors, who in turn set the stage for the constitutional provisions that regular statements and accounts of public receipts and expenditures would be published. To implement these provisions, the Treasury Act of 1789 lodged the Comptroller and Auditors in the executive branch.

Not until 1921 were these provisions modified. The Progressive Era and World War I were instrumental in promoting the Budget and Accounting Act which moved the government auditors to the legislative branch. That Act called on the General Accounting Office to promote businesslike government and perform two functions: to check the President and inform the Congress.

Given congressional disinterest in assisting the GAO in these tasks, the first Comptroller General John McCarl pursued the first function of checking the President as his strategy. The structure for the culture of control was a centralized hierarchy and a personnel system almost entirely composed of clerical and technical employees. The output during this cultural epoch was the compliance audit, a ritual of arduous comparison of expenditures with appropriation authority.

McCarl's strategy and structure failed to keep the GAO abreast of congressional and governmental changes. The Brownlow Committee, appointed by President Roosevelt, demanded reform as New Deal programs were threatened by the slow-moving compliance audit. Finally World War II and the Cold War forced change. Out of the ruins of the culture of control grew a new culture of oversight.

The next Comptroller was Lindsay Warren; he realized the GAO could not realistically check the President, so he pursued the second function of reporting to Congress as the principal plank in his strategy. To develop this strategy, certified public accountants were hired as the Office's new career elite. Warren and this elite formulated five principles during his tenure which were to dominate the GAO for the next forty years: responsiveness to Congress, cognizance of agency operations through site auditing, professionalization of the audit ranks, precision in reporting, and evaluation of agency performance. The strategy of reporting was legitimized by seven statutes which also served to institutionalize these principles.

Warren's successors were Joseph Campbell and Elmer Staats. Campbell faced a Congress increasingly more dissatisfied with executive branch behavior and presidential intransigence. By Staats's term, the Congress was in open revolt and sought to reassert itself through such statutes as the War Powers Resolution and the Budget and Impoundment Control Act. Simultaneously, it also tripled its staff, created new support agencies, and accelerated its decentralization such that subcommittees and individual members came to dominate legislative proceedings.

Not disposed to mix with his client, the Congress, Campbell was not aware of these stirrings. His efforts were focused internally on professionalizing the Office. This agenda was not satisfactory to some congressmen, and the GAO found itself severely criticized for its aggressive reporting.

Responding to these criticisms, Elmer Staats created a new set of elites and a new agenda. These elites were composed of an executive group, a counter-elite of experienced policy analysts and other outsiders, and a novitiate career elite of younger, more aggressive auditors promoted from the ranks. These elites and Staats then refined Warren's principles to fit the new congressional circumstances.

Sometimes in frustration and sometimes at Staats's intitiative, Congress passed a number of new laws which served in the end to promote his program. Few executive agencies were any longer exempted from the audit, and the GAO was completely divorced from administrative restrictions previously exercised by executive branch agencies.

Thus by 1981 the GAO had survived intact a period of profound congressional change. The Staats era ended just as the Warren one had: with the GAO possessing even more formal authority to oversee the executive branch.

The viability of government organizations is not realized without a structure which institutionalizes a strategy and its attendant principles. Part II will discuss the hierarchical designs and personnel systems instituted by Campbell and Staats.

PART II

·

Structure

CHAPTER 4

Hierarchy and Planning
in the Culture of Oversight

.

Structure has three functions. It polices strategy. It also imposes predictability and maintains values. The essential components of an organizational structure are hierarchical arrangements, planning mechanisms, and the personnel system (see Figure 3). Each of these components must contribute to the three functions of structure if organizations are to change.

Cultural shifts in public organizations must overcome many resisting factors. Among those which tend to damp change are the inherent opposition of professionals to the uncertainty which always accompanies structural alterations, the interdependence of the organization and its environment, internal obstacles such as resource limitations and sunk costs, as well as the collective benefits that stability brings to every member of the organization.[1] Most of these inhibiting elements derive from conflict among contending groups over values. That is, the factors which damp change in public organizations are inherently political. Because villagers in public organizations often have no mechanism for resolving these political issues, they seek to turn problems of politics into problems of administration.[2] The argument then is seldom over ends, but rather over means.

Therefore leaders cannot simply announce a new strategy and its attendant principles or proclaim an agenda. Such proclamations are not enough. New strategies must be policed by new or redesigned structural components. Thus members of organizations are "enmeshed in intricate procedures and restrictions, watched and reviewed and inspected and investigated and called to account every step of the way."[3]

Structure also seeks to impose some measure of predictability on the organization's environment and internal processes. Herbert Kaufman has argued that the most prominent driving force for organizational leaders is an aversion to unpredictability.[4] This aversion drives them to create organizational units both to smooth or at least predict environmental fluctuations and to dominate their subordinates.

The third and final function of structure is to maintain organizational values.[5] These values are protected by both institutional leaders and the career elite and are frequently codified in the preambles to enabling statutes that created and have subsequently altered public organizations. A universal value for the leaders of all organizations, be they public or private, is the achievement of their goals as well as the goals decreed for the organization by its environment. Thus structure expresses commitment, influences program direction, and orders priorities.[6]

These functions of structure are achieved by the hierarchical arrangements, planning mechanisms, and personnel systems created by organizational leaders and career elites. The hierarchical arrangements are composed of suborganizations, which come in many shapes and sizes: bureaus, divisions, offices, departments, elements, groups, and committees. In the armed forces other terms are used: corps, wings, task forces, brigades, regiments, battalions, companies, batteries, platoons, and sections. In most instances these suborganizations may be labeled either as staff units dedicated to serving institutional or suborganizational leaders or as line units preoccupied with carrying out institutional repertoires.

The choices available for hierarchical arrangements involve the degrees of centralization, staff power, and layering.[7] Organizational leaders must decide whether centralization of power in agency headquarters is preferable to decentralization in the field, whether they should rely more on staffs or provide line career elites with the guidance and resources to achieve institutional goals, and whether to flatten their organizations, thereby giving career elites direct access to senior agency executives. Choices are seldom clear cut or enduring. Frequently leaders must choose the least undesirable option, which is often somewhere between the extremes of each of these three continuums. Furthermore, choices are frequently modified as leaders seek to fine-tune arrangements to fit their purposes.

Organizational leaders must also insure that hierarchical arrangements achieve the functions of structure discussed above. That is, arrangements must contribute to the policing function by insuring that an organizational unit serves as a custodian for the principles emphasized by a new strategy or agenda. Hierarchy must also promote predictability and value maintenance by entrusting still other units with the responsibility for surveillance of key environmental elements, for ongoing administration, and for performing central organizational repertoires.

Planning mechanisms are also used to attain the functions of structure. These mechanisms vary in the ends they seek to serve. That is, planning may try to coordinate output among diverse units within the organization. It may seek to watch for environmental shifts, to assess their impact on the organization, and to provide alternative responses to these shifts. Or it may seek to formulate and phase hierarchical changes to respond to the goals of organizational leaders. Regardless of its end, planning centralizes authority within the organization. it does this through intervention, monitoring, and assesssment.[8]

Finally the organization's personnel system is central to policing strategy, imposing predictability, and maintaining values. How the executive or career elite is structured, what professional cadres are selected, and how new personnel are recruited, socialized, trained, and promoted are central structural issues which leaders must oversee.

ARRANGEMENTS IN THE WARREN AND CAMPBELL ERAS

Driven by the principles embodied in Lindsay Warren's new strategy for the GAO and the agendas adapted by Joseph Campbell and Elmer Staats, GAO leaders created a new structure for the Office. In this chapter we will use the propositions developed above as guideposts to direct our discussion of GAO hierarchical arrangements and planning mechanisms. In the next chapter we will turn to the personnel system.

The prime contractor for the structural components of hierarchy and planning was Elmer Staats. Lindsay Warren was preoccupied with designing a new strategy, a task which exhausted him. Joseph Campbell focused on the personnel system, in line with his emphasis on the principles of professionalization and precision. During the eras of both these Comptrollers, the career elite of certified public accountants was pretty much left alone to erect the GAO's hierarchical arrangements and planning mechanism. Staats entered the Office at a time when the career elite had been assailed by Congress. In turmoil Staats found opportunity. This chapter will first address the hierarchy and planning mechanisms erected during the Warren and Campbell eras and then turn to the reconstruction of these structural elements by Staats.

Planning.   Warren and Campbell differed on the need for planning mechanisms. Soon after assuming the Comptrollership, Warren established a Committee on Organization and Planning and a Planning and Budget Office to redesign the GAO. Initially composed of established GAO officials, it ultimately came to be dominated by accountants.[9]

The reports of the accountant planners during this period demonstrate the attitude of the newly emergent professional elite. They speak of how divisions, offices, or sections could use resources more economically and efficiently. For instance, their reports observed that the centralized voucher audit in the Washington headquarters served no worthwhile purpose, because collections did not equal salary costs and because centralized auditors had "no knowledge of agency activities or operations."[10] The Investigations Division was particularly inefficient. It was found to have "an unusually high percentage of incompetent personnel" who had responsibilities inferior to "the level of their positions."[11]

Most other suborganizations were equally culpable. The most explosive conflict, however, involved the GAO's attorneys. Two major deficiencies were "apparent" in the review of the operations of the Office of the General Counsel:

> First, the number of cases, a great many of which deal with *insignificant issues*, does not warrant the number of employees presently constituting the Office. Secondly, in considering material issues the Counsel's Office consistently shows a strong tendency to side with the agency's position.[12]

The General Counsel's response emphasizes the existent tension between the two professional cadres. He noted that since 1945 more attention was given to supporting the Congress and executive agencies, matters which he felt were far from insignificant. As to the charge of bias, he observed that "we have to be guided by legal principles in our determinations and not by . . . our concept of what the law ought to be." Perhaps "we would have been more enlightened to have consulted the Audit Division but that would not necessarily have changed the conclusion."[13]

Campbell saw no further need for Warren's planning office or for a mechanism to coordinate GAO output. He left all program planning and coordination to his line division directors. They in turn decentralized planning to field offices and audit sites such that audit directions were decided from the bottom up. He was responsible for establishing a legislative liaison office to monitor relations with the Congress. However, it was installed in the Office of the General Counsel and did not seek to coordinate relations with the Congress.

Hierarchy. The two Comptrollers did seem to agree on hierarchical arrangements. The choices made by Warren and Campbell were to initially reorganize the Office in keeping with their strategic principles and then to decentralize activity to field units and line career elites at GAO headquarters. As each Comptroller decentralized, he also tended to deepen the hierarchy by creating fewer line divisions and offices reporting directly to the Comptroller General.

During the Warren era, decentralization to field units and restructuring of headquarters divisions were the principal hierarchical changes. Modest decentralization had already been initiated in the middle 1930s to contend with such New Deal activities as agricultural adjustment and soil conservation programs. Given their experiences with auditing financial transactions at agency sites, the established GAO elites applied the same technique to resolve the difficulties engendered by World War II. By June, 1944, almost forty percent of all GAO employees were located outside of Washington.[14]

The results of these decentralized or site audits were so satisfactory that this technique was expanded after the war. Site audits permitted the auditors access to all agency documents and familiarity with agency operations. In 1948, Warren observed, "It is my purpose to extend such audits to other areas." By 1952, site audits were conducted at 944 department, independent agency, or contractor locations and overseas in a European Branch.

The restructuring of headquarters divisions responded to the observations and proposals of the accountant planners in Warren's Planning and Budget Office. They were successful in rearranging the Audit Division under a Director of Audits, who of course was to be a certified public accountant. The Office of Investigations was overhauled to emphasize greater responsiveness to Congress.

Campbell and his career elite of CPAs did not overhaul the GAO's organization as Warren had. They did not need to. As Philip Selznick has observed, a unified outlook resulting from common experiences precludes the need for centralization in administration.[15] Thus, given the internalization of the CPA norms, decision making on audit and administrative matters was decentralized to the division directors, regional managers, and their immediate subordinates.

Using some of the recommendations of Warren's planning staff and responding to the Zink Stink and the Lipscomb Report discussed in the last chapter, Campbell did rearrange the accounting and auditing divisions. Citing the need for consistent application of auditing policy and for more emphasis on defense activities, the Defense and Civil Divisions were created in 1956.[16] The operations of all the regional auditing and investigative offices were subject to the direction of the new audit divisions. Administrative supervision of these offices was placed under the Field Operations Division located at GAO headquarters in Washington. This separation of control further decentralized GAO operations. Campbell designated his regional managers as his personal representatives outside Washington and gave them great latitude in hiring and promotion. Most of these offices soon became powerful fiefdoms and exercised a surprising degree of autonomy from central headquarters.[17]

The creation of two separate audit divisions within the headquarters was significant. The Civil and Defense Divisions came to be quite different and rival organizations. The Civil Division emphasized personnel management; it carefully recruited and trained its own accountants and rotated them through agency sites in Washington. It was known as a people-oriented Division, and many of its graduates later were promoted to the career elite during the Comptrollership of Elmer Staats. The Defense Division was more product-oriented and paid less attention to personnel management. Many of its auditors had been hired from the ranks of retired armed services personnel; what entry-level accountants it did employ were usually recruited and trained by the Civil Division. The focus of the Division was producing reports on the deficiencies found in Defense Department and contractor operations.[18]

The hierarchical arrangements and planning mechanisms used by Warren and Campbell were used to enforce their strategic principles. Thus responsiveness to Congress was to be achieved through a planning office emplaced by Warren and an office of congressional liaison established by Campbell. Cognizance over agency activities was pursued by decentralization of audit activities to various audit sites colocated with agency offices in Washington and in the field. Professionalization and precision were sought through a personnel system emplaced by Campbell (to be discussed in the next chapter). Evaluation was to be achieved through heavily layered divisions in GAO headquarters that were supposed to insure that audit reports were truly analytical in character.

Warren's and Campbell's structural arrangements also sought to promote predictability and value maintenance. Predictability, like the principle of responsiveness, was to be superintended by the planning office, which provided intelligence about organizational affairs to the career elite, the congressional liaison office, and a layered GAO headquarters that would insure compliance with the principles of the Comptroller Generals. Value maintenance was the task of the career elites and the personnel system.

Unfortunately for the GAO, these structural arrangements failed to properly perform two functions: to police the strategic principles of responsiveness and evaluation and to insure predictability. The structure established during the Warren era and refined during Campbell's tenure did not keep abreast of changes in Congress and the society at large. The government changed so rapidly in the 1950s and 1960s that Congress no longer felt the Office was responsive to its needs for information or evaluation. Furthermore, the hierarchical arrangements did not provide early warning of these changes. Without a planning mechanism and with the congressional liaison office buried in the General Counsel's Office, Campbell and his career elite were not aware of the significance of these environmental shifts. The ensuring turmoil provided the next Comptroller, Elmer Staats, an opportunity to restructure the Office.

STAATS REARRANGES THE FURNITURE

Elmer Staats and his executive elite found the GAO to be an archaic organization that more resembled a confederation than a coherent government agency. To address this problem, Staats chose to centralize planning into the hands of the executive and career elite, to balance the power of the career elite with a new staff, and to flatten the organization to provide greater access to the senior executives.

Planning Mechanisms. In his first year as Comptroller General, Staats created a program planning staff in his immediate office to consider new audit and organizational initiatives. After seven years of experimentation with alternative designs, the staff proposed, and Staats accepted, a system which embodied lead divisions, issue areas, and lines of effort. Later this staff became the Office of Program Planning, entrusted with the custodianship of this new mechanism to coordinate organizational output. Each line division was to lead in developing plans and coordinating resources committed to predesignated fields of congressional and national interest. These fields were designated as "issue areas" and included such national concerns as food, consumer and worker protection, transportation, national productivity, military preparedness, law enforcement, procurement, tax policy, and national resources.

Within each issue area were "lines of effort" which provided more specific guidance for individual audits and which were given varying priorities as congressional interests shifted. Lines of effort supporting an issue area were scattered across several divisions.[19] For instance, the issue area of food included the following lines of effort: "effectiveness of food information systems," "policy options involving a system of national food reserves," and "domestic food assistance programs designed to promote social welfare."

Also proposed by the Program Planning Staff was a financial management information system. This system was designed to provide data on program costs, proposed and actual allocation of audit time to specific audits, payroll costs, and productivity.[20] The program planning and financial information systems permitted another initiative to oversee division audit efforts. Since the Office of Program Planning received data from the information system on all proposed audits, to include the number of actual audit days to be expended on each, the planners began to question the necessity of certain audits that appeared to be narrow in scope or a repetition of previous reviews. Consequently, in 1976 an Assignment Review Group was created to review the need for specific audits.

By instituting a program-planning system, Staats was able to intervene and gain some control over GAO priorities. The system also permitted Staats to monitor and assess the operation of each division by comparing plans with actual auditing efforts, to judge younger auditors who were frequently called upon to brief Staats at planning meetings, and to learn about new developments in each issue area.

Coordination of output thus became the province of the Office of Program Planning and the executive and career elites. These elites were also charged with formulating and phasing hierarchical changes. Staats frequently convened elite committees led by staff, office or audit division directors to consider structural or environmental issues identified by the leadership. Once the committee had issued its report, Staats and his executive elite would decide upon a course of action to address the issue. Thus Staats and both elite groups sought to identify and monitor environmental and organizational developments that needed attention.

Hierarchical Arrangements.   The creation of a staff was perhaps Staats's biggest structural contribution. As planning and administration functions became centralized, the career elite, which dominated the audit divisions, became more subject to review and intervention by the senior leadership. The career elite initially resisted this development, but resistance crumbled when it became clear that the staff directors spoke for Staats.

In addition to the Office of Program Planning, Staats established an Information Office to provide a low-key, press liaison program. He also created Offices of Personnel Management and later Staff Development to centralize the recruiting, socializing, training, and promotion of auditors. He moved the congressional liaison office away from the General Counsel and subject to his direct review. Subsequently, Offices of Policy, Budget, and Internal Review were installed to establish Office-wide policies for auditing, to review audit reports, to centralize Office budgeting, and to conduct evaluations of GAO suborganizations. Finally an Equal Opportunity Office was established to insure that minorities and women were hired and treated equitably.[21] Thus the new GAO staff served several functions. The Offices of Planning, Policy, and Internal Review enforced the principles of evaluation and precision. The Information Office and newly resurrected congressional liaison office promoted responsiveness to Congress. Furthermore the entire staff served the function of imposing predictability.

The second principal change in the hierarchical arrangements was the functionalization of the audit divisions. That is, nine new audit divisions were created out of the Civil and Defense Divisions and given responsibility for cognizance over various agencies. Later, as the program planning system was implemented, these nine divisions were also given the lead in various issue areas.[22] For example, the Community and Economic Development Division was the "lead Division" for the environment and economic development areas and such agencies as the Department of Agriculture, the Department of Housing and Urban Development, the Atomic Energy Commission, and the Environmental Protection Agency.

Staats advised all employees that his reorganization was to accelerate program and functional expertise among the senior auditors, to provide new opportunities for auditor growth, and to facilitate more timely completion of audits. [23] In other words, he wanted to shift career elite attention from administration and personnel management to overseeing the audit itself. As one confidant noted, Staats wanted to open the organization up to see what the audit actually entailed. A second purpose was to flatten the organization to correspond with a fragmented Congress, many separate parts of which were increasingly requesting more evaluative audits. Thus functionalizing the headquarters audit divisions served to insure that the principles of cognizance of agency activities, responsiveness to Congress, and evaluative audits were attained.

The final initiative was to further enhance agency cognizance and to insure predictability. By the late 1960s, the regional offices, which contained about one-half of the professional audit staff, were dominated by older, line auditors who were not always responsive to the headquarters' demands for programmatic information to support the audit repertoire. To redirect these offices, the executive elite began to rotate regional and assistant regional managers and to send out promising middle-grade auditors with headquarters experience as regional managers. Staats also installed a new director of the Field Operations Division who was more inclined to rationalize the structure of the regional offices and to demand more consistent administrative policies. [24]

CHAPTER 5

Building Professionals: The GAO Personnel System

.

Although Elmer Staats was the prime contractor for creating the hierarchical arrangements and the planning mechanisms for the culture of oversight, he shared the responsibility with Joseph Campbell for the personnel system. Campbell's system paralleled those used in the large private accounting firms, systems with which he and his career elite of certified public accountants were very familiar. During the Staats era, the system was centralized and refined, and the ranks were expanded to include some professionals with schooling beyond accounting.

Statistics from the period 1940 to 1981 reflect the professionalization of the GAO, as Lindsay Warren, Campbell and Staats all sought to eliminate the centralized compliance audit practiced by technicians and to install more advanced techniques borrowed from the accounting and public administration fields. By 1956, just after Warren's departure, 24 percent of all GAO employees were professional accountants. Just before Campbell's departure in 1965, 48 percent were professional accountants.[1] When Elmer Staats departed in 1981, 72 percent were either professional evaluators who actually conducted GAO audits or other professionals who directly assisted in GAO audit procedures such as program analysts, engineers, economists, actuaries, and mathematicians.[2]

A personnel system is conceptualized here as having three components: composition of the career elite, types of professional cadres, and personnel management (see Figure 3). The GAO's career elite consisted almost entirely of CPAs, with a few exceptions who were later hired by Elmer Staats (see Chapter Three). The dominant professional cadre, or the elite profession, had been accountants ever since Lindsay Warren transformed the GAO. There was a small complement of attorneys to deal with the GAO's ancillary functions of handling claims, providing legal analysis to the Congress and the Comptroller General, and writing the Comptroller's legal opinions.

This chapter will concentrate principally on personnel management during the Campbell and Staats eras. We will address four facets: recruitment, socialization, training, and promotion of GAO auditors. Each of these facets has contributed to the dominant strategic principles contained in the GAO culture of oversight.

CAMPBELL'S SYSTEM TO PROFESSIONALIZE THE GAO

J oseph Campbell believed in accountants. As he observed, "A smaller number of more efficient, more professional men can do a better job than a larger number of voucher clerks without professional training."[3] In Campell's mind professional and efficient (read precise) people were accountants. Thus his goals of professionalization and precision were reinforced by his personnel system.

During Campbell's term, the standards for personnel management were established by the Civil Division. In fact for a period, the Civil Division recruited and socialized recruits for the entire headquarters. Later, when the Defense Division moved to its own recruiting and training, it copied the procedures of its sister division. In the regional offices, these same standards were used. Since there was very little geographical rotation, those that were hired by a regional office remained there throughout their career. Finally, Civil Division personnel procedures were also adopted by the GAO Office of Personnel Management when Elmer Staats centralized procedures in the late 1960s.

Recruiting.   GAO recruiting depended on the creation of a favorable climate in schools of accounting and business administration and on well-socialized, intermediate-grade auditors who served part time as recruiters. A climate conducive to GAO recruiting was created by hiring consultants and providing faculty orientation programs. Educators from schools of business administration were hired to advise the Comptroller General on the recruitment and development of the auditing staff. Orientation programs were given to faculty members of accounting and business administration schools in order to acquaint them with GAO work.[4]

Those selected as recruiters were considered among the best middle-grade auditors in the GAO. They were expected to recruit college-educated accountants with backgrounds much like their own. That is, entry-level accountants were expected to become senior journeymen auditors in seven or eight years. Since only the most favored were selected, recruiting duty became an important milestone in one's career.[5]

The recruiting standards themselves were a mix of objective and subjective criteria. Entry-level auditors were expected to stand in the upper quarter of their graduating class and to have demonstrated a capacity for leadership. The recruiters were looking for quick learners who could easily adapt to new surroundings. Entry-level auditors were to have a sense of urgency and a hunger to succeed. As one experienced staff developer noted, the people the GAO was after had a sparkle in their eyes and a brightness to their personality that came out very quickly. Appearance was also an important indicator of a good candidate.[6]

The assessment of these characteristics was dependent upon the recruiter's conversation with university faculty members and interviews with candidates. Generally speaking, those that satisfied the recruiters were white males of second or third generation ethnic stock. They had come out of working-class homes and were among the first in their families to have received a college education.

Their education was often financed through considerable family deprivation. Consequently these young candidates had secured a practical education which would provide them a secure future. Many of those selected had found accounting to be an uninspiring experience and were, therefore, quite susceptible to the recruiter's pitch that GAO auditing was not limited simply to debits and credits. Candidates were also told that successful GAO auditors were promoted rapidly and had diverse, challenging assignments that called for considerable travel.[7]

Females and blacks were not favored. Some limited experience with both had convinced the recruiters that neither would remain long enough to justify a GAO investment. The staff developers generally believed that it took three to four years to develop an auditor, at a cost of $50,000 or so in salary and training. Females were prone to leave the rolls for marriage or pregnancy, and blacks found themselves isolated on the professional staff.

Where the GAO recruited was as important as the criteria used for recruiting. The headquarters and each region recruited from its own area. Generally speaking, the recruiters learned that small schools located in economically depressed areas yielded hungry candidates.[8]

The myths that were developed during this period when college-level recruiting was initiated have continued to influence the auditors. The recruiters and the candidates they hired were convinced that the GAO was getting the cream of accounting school graduates. The Comptroller General's reports for 1961 through 1969 note the acquisition of "high quality students, with accounting as their major field of study." This self-image enhanced the auditors' sense of worth and also convinced the more ambitious ones that they needed to work hard. "We've always been told that the GAO hires above average people. So within the Office above average is average. Thus to be above average [and get ahead], one must be superior."[9]

Preliminary Socialization. The socialization process for the young accountant-turned-government-auditor began immediately. His first year was designed so as to acquaint him with the rudiments of auditing and also to assess his fitness for further GAO service.

The basic premise behind all GAO training was that the GAO needed creative accountants with broad interests. Although such men were termed "generalists" in the GAO, an accounting background was considered essential. This premise was based both on GAO's experience with frequent, short-notice congressional assignments and with the GAO-imposed rotation sequence for auditors. Such assignments required auditors to move in quickly to an agency site or contractor plant, assess the organization's financial and managerial condition, and then issue a report to Congress on the deficiencies.[10]

Regardless of whether the recruit's first assignment was in the GAO headquarters or at a regional office, he was sent to the headquarters for a three-week orientation course designed to acquaint him with the policies and procedures of the Office. The course included lectures and practical exercises in collecting evidence, interviewing, maintaining work papers, and writing audit papers.[11]

Recruits were expected to assimilate norms of appearance and behavior that paralleled those found in the large public accounting firms. That is, auditors were expected to maintain a professional image and attitude. One's image was dependent upon a dress code that was provided to all new auditors during their first three weeks with the GAO. Auditors were expected to wear blue, grey or brown suits and a white shirt. Ties were to be conservative in color. Hair was to be short and well groomed. In their preliminary training sessions, the young auditors were told "sport coats are for the race track." In agency offices or contractor plants, auditors were told to keep their suit coat on at all times. Wearing the coat maintained a professional, management-like image. Compliance with the dress code became one of the first tests for a new auditor.

Other norms were an enthusiastic approach to auditing, tolerance for frequent rotation among assignments, an ability to quickly discover the managerial deficiencies in an agency, and a willingness to work extra hours. All of these GAO norms have also been articulated by CPAs as the "unwritten rules" of their profession.[12] Given Joseph Campbell's background and managerial style, it is not surprising that he emphasized them.

The personnel managers also used this critical period to survey and assess the new recruits. Not only were they watched during classroom sessions, the recruits were also interviewed individually. Thus the orientation course was an important period for the new auditor. The impressions he made on GAO supervisors and personnel managers influenced his subsequent assignments and his promotions. As one division director told the GAO's training coordinator, "I can tell within three days whether a man will be a good auditor."

In the first six months, the new auditor was rotated through three different assignments, each lasting two months. These assignments were intended to reinforce the fundamentals of auditing that he had received in his orientation course. Of equal importance, his supervisors and the personnel managers would assess his potential for the legislative audit. The personnel managers conducted interviews and seminars in which such open-ended questions as "What have you learned?" and "How do you evaluate your performance and your progress?" were asked. The answers to these questions yielded valuable feedback not only on the recruits, but also on the performance of their supervisors.

At the end of the first six months, the recruit's performance and potential were reviewed. Those who had made a good impression and who had received positive reports on their performance at job sites were sent out for a six-month assignment. Those who had not fared so well were advised that they were not "working out" in their first-year probationary period and were assisted in finding a position in another federal agency.

The final evaluation during the recruit's probationary period was conducted near the end of his six-month assignment. Those who were considered in the top of their peer group were promoted immediately at the end of twelve months.[13] The rest were promoted six months later. Thus the GAO's preliminary socialization process was much like that of the large public accounting firms. They too had an initial, intensive training period which lasted from one to four weeks. This training was followed by frequent rotation through rather dull assignments that required "detail work" such as "vouching" (verifying statements by referring to the source documents), recomputing calculations, and conducting inventories. Careful evaluation of performance and aptitude also characterized the first year of a young accountant employed by these firms, just as they did for the GAO auditor-recruit.[14]

Rotation and Subsequent Training.   The remainder of the socialization process for legislative auditors was monitored by the personnel managers within the audit divisions. Preferring to leave a man in one place to gain and then use his expertise, the Defense Division infrequently rotated its auditors among assignments. The International Division felt rotation from an overseas assignment was imperative to maintain currency with the audit. The Civil Division rotated auditors frequently and according to a predetermined sequence. Although field auditors were almost never rotated out of their region, they were moved from site to site as the workload dictated. Both the headquarters and the regional offices used training courses to prepare auditors for the CPA examination and subsequent responsibility.[15]

Many in the GAO career elite felt that rotation was useful in maintaining a freshness of auditor viewpoint. Thus rotation among audit sites was structured. Entry-level auditors stayed at a site for one year, whereas the journeymen auditors usually remained at a site for two years. The senior journeymen auditors usually remained for three or four years. During these periods, auditors were assigned to the review of many different aspects of agency operations, but they worked out of the site office, which was either in the agency building or in an adjacent one.

Rotation of auditors among assignments is an established norm in large public accounting firms. Entry-grade "juniors" and journeymen "seniors" in these firms spend their time at offices of the firm's clients. Even some of the senior journeymen supervisors rotate to meet the needs of the firm's larger clients. Not until the public accountant reaches the level of manager does he consistently work out of one of the firm's offices.[16]

Once a date had been set for an auditor's rotation, personnel managers would gather to decide upon a new site. Those whose past performance was outstanding and who were considered to have excellent potential would generally be sent to the best audit sites. The best sites were agencies which had attracted the most public and congressional interest and had the most imaginative supervisors. In some instances where an agency would suddenly generate considerable attention, the managers would have to infuse the site with their best talent to satisfy congressional demands. In discussing one outstanding auditor, a personnel manager noted, "Wherever we put him, the site would get hot."

The younger auditors were also interested in audit sites where the senior career leaders had established their reputations. During the early 1960s, Civil Division auditors all yearned to work at the Department of Health, Education and Welfare, the National Aeronautics and Space Administration, or the Atomic Energy Commission. Agencies with established, routinized programs were not sought after. Some of these sites were the Post Office Department, the Veterans Administration, The Civil Service Commission, and the District of Columbia government.

Training was also an important part of the socialization process, particularly when it led to the CPA certificate. Auditors were encouraged to obtain the certificate, and it was clearly a prerequisite for promotion to the upper grades. Young auditors were frequently queried about their plans for obtaining it. Those actively pursuing it were given classes and free time to prepare for the examination. Since certification required both the successful completion of the written test and a certain period of experience in public accounting, the GAO campaigned to convince state CPA Boards to accept GAO experience.[17]

Other training was also employed. An intermediate training course was given to staff members in grades GS-9 and GS-11. The Advanced Audit Management Course was provided to GS-12s, GS-13s and GS-14s. A few, more senior managers were sent to graduate schools for periods ranging from four to sixteen weeks.[18]

A final aspect of the auditor socialization process was emphasis on ethical standards. All auditors were provided a copy of the Comptroller General's order on auditor conduct.[19] Unwritten rules were equally important. Fraternization with executive agency personnel was forbidden. Even in some instances where established friendships had developed among senior GAO officials and high ranking executive officers prior to Campbell's term, the auditors became reluctant to join old friends for lunch.

Promotion.   The GAO promotion system was designed to enhance recruiting and to retain the best auditors. Since the Office could not alter salaries to compete with the public accounting firms and the business community in the tight accountant market, it chose to promote its auditors very rapidly. By expanding the number of career elite positions and by use of a rapid promotion plan, the GAO was able to lower its Office-wide attrition rate from an average of 22 percent in the late 1950s to 12 to 13 percent in the mid-1960s, a figure below the government average of 15 percent.[20]

Auditors were promoted based on their performance and potential ratings and on the assessment of the Division managers. The best record was attained by a CPA with a law degree who was promoted on an average of every 13 months to a senior career elite position in only ten years.

Those selected for rapid promotion had fulfilled the prophecy decreed for them while they were still in their probationary first year. Identified during the recruiting season or the three-week orientation at GAO headquarters, they were given the best audit sites and the most attention by the personnel managers. Such exposure quickly socialized them to the ethic of the GAO auditor. Those whose personal qualifications and inclinations were sympathetic to the values and norms which constituted the auditor's ideology were recognized and promoted rapidly.[21] One such "fair-haired boy" noted:

> My philosophy was ingrained in me by two of the men I worked for. These men were ethical and professional, and their standards were high. They drummed this into me . . . All I had to do was just listen—I learned the ropes by osmosis.[22]

Yet, one promotion criterion was universal for all. Auditors were expected to produce audit reports. In considering the promotion of one auditor, a personnel manager told division leadership, "He has produced only five reports in five and one-half years—he is not an operator." The auditors were well aware of this criterion. Auditors noted that "the overwhelming motivation was would what we were looking at result in a report to Congress?" and that "the number of reports was what was rewarded."[23]

The Defense Division was particularly energetic in producing reports. Reports with a single finding were encouraged by the division leadership. One defense auditor who was promoted to direct a division during Elmer Staats's Comptrollership was remembered for his ability to get six reports from a pair of pants. He would report on the lack of commonality among buckles, zippers, snaps, buttons, cuffs, and belt loops in the various trousers required for wear in the armed services.[24]

The Congress fully approved of the GAO promotion policy but was to rebuke the auditors for their emphasis on multiple reporting. The House Appropriations Subcommittee responsible for GAO funding routinely expressed concern in the annual hearings on the adequacy of Office staffing and career elite positions.[25] However, the Holifield committee was not as sanguine about the frequency of GAO reporting. It criticized the "sheer mass of GAO reports" that dealt with "minor events or problems of no great interest to the Congress."[26]

Thus Campbell and the GAO career elite sought to instill the values and norms of the large New York City accounting firms. Their personnel policies were similar to those of the U.S. Forest Service. Both agencies hired young recruits with educational backgrounds consistent with the underlying philosophy of the dominant professional elites. Furthermore, both agencies emphasized rotation, counseling, and continued education to enhance conformance with the dominant ethic. Finally those who could not conform were encouraged to "select themselves out."[27] Such procedures are routinely used in the milling of public professionals.

STAATS CENTRALIZES AND BROADENS THE SYSTEM

Congressional demands for broader audit together with a shortage of college-trained accountants forced Staats to modify the GAO's personnel system. To meet the need for auditors, to satisfy congressional requests, and to perform broader audits, the GAO leadership turned to college graduates with degrees in management, engineering, social sciences, and the liberal arts. To provide the necessary infusion of developed talent, the executive group insisted on hiring people with programmatic expertise and installing them in the intermediate audit grades. By 1978, over one-third of all GAO auditors had college concentrations in fields other than accounting. Still, in spite of official rhetoric, some training in accountancy was still required, and accountants remained dominant.

Staats and his elites also sought to inculcate all of Warren's principles into personnel management, principles which Staats embraced with equal enthusiasm. The principles of professionalization and precision were already institutionalized into the GAO personnel procedures. Cognizance was to be achieved by reducing the amount of auditor rotation among audit sites. Responsiveness and evaluation were emphasized by recruiting procedures and training techniques which promoted skills other than those of accounting.

Looking for People Like Themselves. The mechanics of recruiting were not substantially changed. Enthusiastic, middle-grade auditors were still dispatched to small schools to search for students who stood in the upper quarter of their graduating class, had demonstrated potential for leadership, and possessed the zeal and the ambition thought to be needed for the legislative audit.[28]

Most of the college graduates recruited by the GAO were accounting majors. Predominantly, those who were recruited out of the graduate schools held degrees other than accounting. Since each group constituted about one-half of the new recruits, the 50 percent accountant–50 percent nonaccountant goal was realized.

Yet these official statistics are misleading. Many recruiters sought candidates with undergraduate degrees in accounting and a graduate degree in some other field. Also, although many college graduates were hired with degrees in business administration or management, they had to have six hours of accounting to be placed on the register and hired. Thus the career elite could proclaim that the auditor career system was being broadened to include specialties other than accounting, while at the same time insuring that most of those recruited had received the "proper" educational background.

The auditors had confidence only in their own recruiting techniques. Before legislation in 1980 removed its personnel system from control by the Civil Service Commission, the GAO could maintain its own Service-approved registers and recruit to fill those registers. The career auditors were reluctant to consider people on other registers. Such people were not thought to be of sufficiently high quality to do the legislative audit. As one close observer noted, "GAO says it can't get good people off the Commission's [general] register, but then again it hasn't really tried."

The career elite was equally reluctant to recruit at the larger, more prestigious schools. Suspicious of all GAO upper-level hires, the career elite was unwilling to send out anyone but accountants, who were almost all educated in small state schools. As one upper-level hire with a graduate degree from the Massachusetts Institute of Technology observed,

> Some of the young auditors coming in are sharp, but it is remarkable how many slow ones there are. The GAO could get people from MIT in planning and Harvard's JFK School. Yet no one has ever asked me to interview anyone up there. They are wrong when they say they cannot get such people.

Graduates of prestigious schools were perceived to be too intellectual and thus unwilling to do the vouching required of all entry-level auditors.

Although 231 upper-level hires were brought into the GAO during the period September, 1970, to February, 1976, this procedure was clearly antithetical to established recruiting policies. Most of these were males who had worked for the federal government in Washington and had become aware of an opening through a GAO auditor. As might be expected given the dichotomy between the old Defense Division's orientation to expertise and the Civil Division's emphasis on rotation, 90 percent of these hires worked in the new divisions fathered by the Defense Division. Yet this small concession to expertise was considered atypical even by the Comptroller General. As he pointed out, "Our basic policy is to hire at the entry level and promote from within.[29]

Upper-level hires were no more welcome in the field offices than they were in the headquarters divisions spawned by the Civil Division. In 1976, only 10 percent of those in the regional offices were hired in grades other than those prescribed for entry level auditors. As one experienced field auditor observed, "upper-level hires are acceptable at headquarters, but not in the field. Here you want an auditor—an accountant to do the menial jobs."

Thus, although compelled to hire recruits with backgrounds other than accounting, the auditors were still able to insure that most new auditors had some acquaintance with accounting. As one GAO consultant noted, "The GAO's recruiting system has duplicated itself over time. The auditors are looking for people like themselves."

Bringing People Up Right.   Like the recruiting procedures, the socialization process for new recruits developed by the old Civil Division during the Campbell era was refined and applied Office-wide during the Staats years. This process differed somewhat between the headquarters and the regional offices, but in all locations the emphasis was on extended conditioning by senior line auditors. All headquarters training was consolidated under the Director of Personnel, while regional training was supervised by regional coordinators who usually worked directly for the regional manager. As an Assistant Comptroller General pointed out to the House Appropriations Committee, "People are brought up right in the GAO."[30]

On-the-job training programs emphasized the proper accumulation of factual data. Recruits were given small tasks to locate certain facts and then queried on what they had found out and how. As one regional manager noted, "auditors are trained to be technically correct." Another auditor noted, "We ask our young auditors, 'Did you get the facts?,' 'What did you do to get the facts?,' and 'How do you know that?' "

To reconcile the GAO audit managers and the elites to the new educational profile of the young auditors, internal associations were formed to provide feedback. A Youth Advisory Committee was created and consulted regularly on new management proposals. The Committee was also encouraged to report its views on existing organizational policies.[31]

Intermediate-level training opportunities were legion. Staats believed very strongly in training courses and significantly expanded the GAO's program. When he arrived, internally administered GAO training had reached only 1,200 professionals. In 1972 alone, under Staats, 2,200 auditors received such training. The emphasis in these courses was on developing auditor capacity for the broader evaluation audit and for supervising junior auditors.[32] Externally administered training was enlarged even more dramatically. Whereas in 1966 only 136 professional staff members received outside training, by 1972 such training was provided to 1,775 auditors.

Another tool used to acquaint auditors with the techniques of the broader audit was the *GAO Review*. This quarterly magazine was expanded, and the executive group gave it considerable attention. Speeches by the Comptroller General were frequently used as lead articles, and Assistant Comptroller General Ellsworth Morse devoted much of his time to editing the *Review*. Essentially it provided a forum for auditors to discuss their experiences and was generally geared toward articles that focused on broader auditing techniques or on better procedures to serve the Congress.[33]

Managing Well-Brought-Up Auditors. Staats and the GAO elites also sought to design a management system that could be applied Office-wide. During the Campbell years, the career elite had managed promotions and auditor assignments, coming to the Comptroller General only to receive his blessing for promotions to the senior audit levels. The perception of the executive group and the staff during Staats's early years was that sponsorship by a supergrade auditor was a clear prerequisite for promotion and that the career system was a haphazard affair. Early in his tenure, Staats expressed skepticism that the auditors whose names were given to him for promotion were the best qualified.[34]

Organizational changes and rapid promotions in these early years put strains on the rather primitive personnel system. The 1972 reorganization and the expansion of the professional staff called for numerous promotions to fill supervisory levels and established promotion expectations for more junior auditors. The shift in all professional grades during this period foreclosed later promotion prospects for auditors located both in the headquarters and in the regional offices (see Table 1). Essentially by the late 1970s, the GAO was running out of room at the top.

Staats's response to these issues was one of methodical experimentation. The creation of the GAO's Office of Personnel Management centralized personnel decisions in a staff working for the executive group. Convinced that mandatory rotation among headquarters divisions was contrary to providing sophisticated analysis to Congress, he eliminated this policy. Rather than having personnel managers shift auditors from place to place, the individual auditor was made responsible for seeking a change in position. Simultaneously with this decision to dispense with rotation, he created the Office of Staff Development to provide a separate organ for managing auditor growth.[35]

To contend with the auditor-dominated promotion system, a competitive selection process was installed. This process required auditors to compete for promotions before a board which would review their files, conduct interviews with applicants, and then select the five best-qualified candidates for each opening. The final selection was left to the division director or regional manager. Of course this system did not entirely preclude what has been labeled "job tailoring,"[36] for new

TABLE 1. Number of Auditors by Grade, 1966 and 1979

Grade	As of 30 Jun 1966	As of 10 Feb 1979[1]
GS-18	4	9
GS-17	7	35
GS-16	25	43
GS-15	25	331
GS-14	282	651
GS-13	387	940
GS-12	569	1195
GS-11	583	454
GS-09	564	245
GS-07	465	299
TOTAL	2960[2]	4202[2]
MEDIAN GRADE	GS-11	GS-12

1. U.S. Comptroller General, *Comptroller General's Annual Report, 1966* (Washington: U.S. Government Printing Office, 1966) p. 276; and U.S. Congress, House, Appropriations Committee, *Legislative Branch Appropriations for 1980, Hearings,* 96th Cong., 1st Sess., 1979.
   2. Not all in the lower grades were considered professional staff; many were technical staff members in supervisory positions.

openings could still be described with a particular auditor in mind. Yet it did open the process up considerably to greater internal review, by providing the career elite alternatives for each selection and the executive group opportunities for overseeing promotions.

Other management tools were also developed by Staats to enhance auditor performance. Upon his arrival, he revised the incentive awards program by adding new awards and by establishing an Honor Awards Ceremony. The ceremony was an evening function held in the historic old Pension Building, complete with a keynote address and music by the Marine Corps Band.[37] Another tool was the *GAO Management News* published by the Information Office. A mouthpiece of the Comptroller General and the executive group, the *News* was distributed weekly to all professional staff members. Designed to enhance intra-Office communication, it contained details on organizational, personnel, and auditing developments.

Equal Opportunity in the GAO. The preoccupation of the white, male accountants with their own career system and with auditing precluded recognition of racial and gender issues in the GAO. Minority and female auditors were not sought after in the recruiting process. For instance, in 1966 only forty-five non-whites were interviewed for professional positions, and only nine were actually hired nationwide out of a total of four hundred new recruits who joined GAO in that year. Thus minorities and females were hired to fill support and technical positions and then were generally ignored.[38]

Increasingly more disgruntled by the conditions under which they worked, black employees formed a Black Caucus and finally staged a protest march around GAO headquarters during their lunch hour on March 18, 1971. After the march, considerable outside pressure was put on the GAO, first by the Citizen's Advocate Center, a civil rights group, then by black and other minority congressmen, and finally by a 1972 law which required the GAO to adhere to the provisions of the 1964 Civil Rights Act.[39]

The response to this internal and external pressure was at first perfunctory and then more determined, as the Comptroller General found himself questioned on a yearly basis before both the House and Senate Appropriations Committees on the GAO's equal opportunity plan.[40] Having established an Equal Employment Opportunity (EEO) Advisory Council in 1971 and a full-time deputy director for EEO in 1972, the Comptroller began to exert more effort to hire minorities as professionals. By the end of 1976 there were 74 black auditors and 42 other minorities as auditors; in late December 1978 these figures had grown to 359 blacks and 146 other minorities for a total of 12 percent minority employment in the professional grades.[41]

Simultaneous with these employment efforts, the GAO dispensed with the transportation rate function in 1975. Since many of the most dissatisfied blacks were employed in technical positions by the GAO Transportation Division, much of the open racial dissatisfaction with GAO policies was thereby eliminated.[42] The GAO also moved to adapt the established, white auditors to the new equal opportunity programs through classes on functional racism.[43]

The ethnocentrism in the GAO was hardly unique to federal agencies, but the efforts to combat it were significant to the culture of oversight. As one black GAO professional observed,

> There is a racial problem in GAO, but these problems also exist outside GAO. It is just as bad at the Veterans Administration or the Civil Service Commission. But you drop your bucket where you are, rather than go

elsewhere where the conditions are as bad. It's better to stay and fight until your ends are achieved.

By 1979 the profile of minority employment in the professional grades was better than that of the rest of the government.[44]

All these personnel management alterations were essentially designed to adapt the accountants to a broader definition of purpose and to legitimate their role in a broader audit. Shifting the accountants was not an easy task. The essentially conservative, apolitical world view of the accountant was averse to this sort of auditing. Since, like most public professionals, the auditors owed their primary allegiance to the rather ad hoc career system which had promoted them so rapidly, the most effective way to shift their orientation was to retrain them and to build in new reward mechanisms which would emphasize acceptance of the broader audit.

FRICTION

To anyone who has never experienced extensive organizational change, the process appears simple; but the reality is quite different. As Clausewitz says of war:

> The simplest thing is difficult. The difficulties accumulate and end by producing a kind of friction that is inconceivable unless one has experienced [such change] . . . . Countless minor incidents—the kind you never really foresee—combine to lower the general level of performance, so that one always falls far short of the intended goal.[45]

Just as rough materials passing over each other are impeded by the many irregularities on their surfaces, so too does friction hinder profesional and organizational change.

Thus all the changes in strategy and structure made by Warren, Campbell, Staats, and their allies in the career elite met considerable internal resistance. Changing the world view and behavior of professionals is not an easy or bloodless task. Some professional groups and their senior spokesmen are invaribly pushed aside, old procedures are modified at the expense of promotion prospects for some professional subgroups or individuals, and dominant behavioral patterns of the elite profession as well as cooperative arrangements among offices within the larger organization must be shifted.[46] Organizational change creates great uncertainty and anxiety as professionals are forced to alter their perspectives, their daily routines, and their longer-term expectations. Flexibility does not come easily to public professionals socialized to think and act in established ways.[47] To demonstrate how traumatic these shifts were for GAO professionals, a number of specific examples can be provided from the eras of all three Comptroller Generals. During the Warren era, the newly hired accountants warred with the lawyers, the established audit clerks, and the investigators. As described in this chapter, the accountants were critical of the voucher audit clerks for their ignorance of agency operations, of the investigators for their alleged incompetence, and of the lawyers for their preoccupation with "insignificant issues."

Each of these groups rebelled in one fashion or another. The voucher auditors sparked congressional hearings after World War II by alleging that new acountants would not insure that wartime transportation vouchers would be properly audited. As a result of these hearings, the investigating House committee criticized the new spot-sampling techniques instituted by the accountants as "basically defective and grossly mismanaged."[48] The investigators were able to hang on in the face of the accountant onslaught until the Zink Stink permitted Joseph Campbell to destroy their division, disburse them among the audit divisions, and allow them to be eliminated by attrition. The lawyers endured because the accountants were not able to fill their role of producing the Comptrollers' legal opinions, which were required by law.

The running battle between the accountants on one side and the lawyers and the clerks on the other continued through the Staats era. During Campbell's time as Comptroller, the accountants consciously avoided the lawyers, while simultaneously denying them access to outside professional meetings and in some cases promotions. These actions seemed to stem primarily from accountant suspicion that the lawyers would somehow claim their audit approach or methods were inappropriate or even illegal.[49]

This mutual accountant-lawyer suspicion forced the Comptroller General to issue a formal order specifying how the two groups would communicate. Thus, according to the Comprehensive Audit Manual, "the preparation of formal submissions is the responsibility of the audit group . . . this submission process should be followed so that *an authoritative legal interpretation* is available in support of the report comments."[50] The form and content of these submissions was carefully prescribed. Essentially the auditor was required to do all the legal research and then submit the matter to the lawyers for an authoritative interpretation. As one lawyer later noted:

The memo would come back six months to one year later written in "legalese." It was a hopeless and amusing relationship. So if a legal question came up the auditors would avoid it—get around it. If they needed a legal opinion, they would go to the legal shop of the agency they were working with.

The accountants also had difficulty in dominating the clerks, primarily because legal loopholes not closed by Warren or Campbell still required the GAO to perform essentially technical and clerical tasks. For example, both the Transportation and Claims Divisions were responsible for receiving vouchers and ruling on their compliance with existing government regulations. As described above, these Divisions were dominated by minorities. The tension manifested by the march of the Black Caucus on March 18, 1971, and widely perceived by outsiders as racism, was at least equally attributable to professional-clerical tension. Clearly the accountants did not feel these functions belonged in the GAO and continued to frown on the last vestiges of the old voucher audit.

With the addition of new management controls and professional groups during the Staats era, the accountants again found themselves defending their dominance over the Office. The career elite initially resisted the introduction of the program planning system, grumbled at the creation of an executive group, resisted the new staff composed of journalists and other outsiders, and were appalled when Staats installed a counter-elite of policy analysts. By Staats's departure in 1981, the accounting career elite was still preeminent, because they conceded to many of his management initiatives, quietly ignored outsiders installed in the staff, and waited patiently for the departure of the counter-elite, confident that with a new Comptroller, this heresy would be eliminated.

The professional corps of accountants also resisted the new professional groups introduced as policy experts. As we shall see in the next chapter, the accountants had continual differences with these outsiders—described there as auditor advocates—over the approach to and procedures for evaluating government programs. As noted earlier, field auditors also resisted these outsiders, hired for upper level positions, because they saw the outsiders as unfit for their line of work.

All the structured changes instituted by Staats, when combined with the GAO's effort to combat racial and sexual prejudice, imposed considerable strain on the accountants. A number of indicators confirm their level of tension. In my interviews with the auditors, they were quite open in discussing their confusion and their anxieties with the alterations in the institutional fabric. One interview resembled a psychotherapeutic session, complete with a senior auditor almost fully reclined in his executive chair, background music as a relaxant, and an extended outpouring of frustration.

Letters and leaks were also employed to vent frustration. An anonymous letter from several GAO professionals was sent to the Deputy Comptroller General in December, 1978, complaining of the changes instituted by the new planning process and the new personnel management system. A copy of this letter was also supplied to the House Appropriations Committee and to columnist Jack Anderson. Derogatory information on the GAO's competitive selection process, the new career management system, and on racial matters was regularly made available to the *Federal Times*.[51]

Thus organizational change is frought with friction. For the GAO, Staats and his allies among the career elite were able to prevail because of environmental pressure. Congressional transformation meant the GAO too had to alter its repertoire. Staats and his allies realized that without change, the Office faced slow disintegration as it became less and less useful to a Congress more intent on oversight.

SUMMARY, PART II

Thus personnel systems are one component of structure that programs public professionals and bends them to conform to organizational strategies. Personnel systems promote regularity and maintain organizational values. Such systems consist of executive elites, career elites, and personnel management procedures. Executive elites are needed to set the tone of policy discourse and broaden options.[52] Career elites play a crucial mediating role between organizational leadership and public professionals. Personnel management procedures promote organizational identification.

Organizational identification is the acceptance of the ideology and strategic principles of an organization such that an individual becomes emotionally committed to it.[53] Such identification is achieved through carefully constructed subsystems to recruit, socialize, train, and promote professionals. Recruiting must be done carefully to insure that professionals can adjust to the organization. Selecting recruits who had been schooled as accountants during the Campbell era meant that their outlook, style, and technical background would conform to the GAO's ideals and ideology. By hiring recruits with backgrounds other than accounting, Staats hoped to import skills which would broaden the audit to conform to congressional demands.

The GAO's socialization techniques of preliminary training and job rotation were designed to program new recruits.[54] Such programming sought to insure both that the auditors could conform to the demands of an evaluative audit responsive to Congress and that they would internalize the values central to the Office. Thus the ideal of organizational socialization is for strategy and structure to be "gradually accepted as one's own premise of thought and action, until compliance with them is no longer reluctant, or even indifferent, obedience, but an expression of personal preference and will."[55] As discussed above, such acceptance comes slowly and is accompanied by considerable grumbling in the face of organizational changes.

The GAO training programs instituted principally during the Staats era were another important facet of socialization. Continuing education was part of the indoctrination process, for it sought both to instruct evaluators on organizational values and to teach them new procedures and audit techniques.

Promotion was a reward for commitment to the GAO and for acceptance of its strategic principles. The decentralized promotion subsystem used during the Campbell era enhanced professionalization and precision. The centralized promotion procedures instituted by Staats and his elites sought to reward both expertise (or cognizance) of executive agency programs and performance of the broader audit format which was responsive to Congress.

Therefore, personnel management procedures seek to program professionals. The common values professionals acquire in schools, the socialization they receive through constant association with other professionals, the continuing education, and the internalization of norms which they must demonstrate for promotion—all these shape their rituals.

The two other structural components also shape professional rituals. The GAO's program planning mechanism directed the auditors into evaluations which aspired to assess managerial efficiency and program performance. The flat hierarchical arrangements of the Staats era promoted GAO responsiveness to Congress.

In the next part we will discuss the dominant professional ritual in the GAO—the evaluation repertoire—and the types of auditors who perform that ritual. We will also infer from the discussion of strategy and structure as well as from the description of this repertoire the GAO ideology. Then we will turn to the impact that GAO evaluations have on Congress and the government.

PART III

Professional Behavior

CHAPTER 6

The Evaluation Ritual and the Ideology of Oversight

.

Out of a transformed strategy and structure comes a different organizational culture. This culture is not completely new; rather it carries inheritances from the organization's history, including both predecessor organizations and previous cultural experiences and lessons. Contained within a culture are rituals and an ideology. Rituals in an organizational culture are manifested in rites of passage such as graduations and promotions, in ceremonies such as parades and awards convocations, in established procedures such as staff requirements, and in repertoires. Each repertoire consists of a collection of skills, techniques, methods and routines used to achieve some organizational output. Usually each organization has a number of repertoires, with one being dominant and influencing the remainder.

Thus in the United States Army, there are repertoires for defense, for movement to contact with the enemy, for resupply of combat troops on the front lines, and for gathering intelligence. But the dominant repertoire is the attack. All others are merely subsidiary to that overriding effort. The same is true in the General Accounting Office. The dominant repertoire there is conducting evaluations of government management and programs. Other repertoires, such as commenting on proposed legislation or reviewing government impoundments, are subsidiary. This dominant repertoire of evaluation produces the principal professional output of the Office: reports for Congress.

Crucial to each repertoire are the types of people needed to perform it. Such people may or may not have the same professional background. What is important is that a repertoire demands varied skills and roles. Again, to use the U.S. Army as an example, to attack the enemy requires three types of officers: line officers skilled in the use of infantry and tanks; combat support officers who provide support in communications and crossing obstacles; and combat service support officers who supervise the supply of ammunition, spare parts, and food.

A culture also contains an ideology composed of values, norms, and myths. Just as is true for organizational rituals, the organizational ideology also reflects history and design. The history of accounting and public audit, associated as it is with the struggle for power between the legislature and the executive, has influenced the ideals and principles of evaluators as well as their norms, that is their standards for behavior. This history also contributed to the GAO's culture of oversight. First I will describe the four types of evaluators, or auditors, who performed the evaluation repertoire in the last half of the 1970s. We will then turn to examine that repertoire by describing how the evaluators actually conduct their reviews for Congress. Finally, we will discuss the auditors' ideology. In the next chapter, we will discuss the GAO audit reports and their impact on government.

Both of these chapters then should provide us with several important insights. First, we will be able to appreciate the extent of change in the behavior of GAO auditors since the beginning of the culture of oversight in 1940. Furthermore, by exploring this ideology and the dominant repertoire—management and program evaluation—we can approach the central thesis of this book, which is that professionals dominate the output and behavior of government organizations. Finally, we should also be able to see the influence of strategic and structural changes on the professional evaluators in the GAO, another key concern of this book.

AUDITOR TYPES

Four types of auditors conduct the evaluation repertoire: line auditors, auditor managers, auditor advocates, and staff auditors.[1] Each contributes to the issuance of a GAO report.

The line auditors are normally found at audit sites located adjacent to agency operations or contractors' plants around the country. They are in the entry or lower-middle civil service grade. They collect information for evaluations by sifting agency data to discover deficiencies in agency operations and programs.

The auditor managers supervise the evaluation process. They are concerned with the three phases of evaluation: survey, review, and report. Auditor managers not only supervise line auditors, but are also responsible for guiding surveys and reports through the GAO's internal review process. Like the auditor advocates and staff auditors, they are in the middle and upper grades and are located in the regional headquarters or the GAO headquarters. They think of themselves as professional evaluators.

The auditor advocates plan and market GAO evaluations. Unlike the auditor managers, they see themselves as policy analysts. They reach across GAO division boundaries to plan and coordinate reviews to satisfy the demands of the new Office planning process. As advocates, they market GAO reports to congressmen, congressional staffers, agency bureaucrats, and the press. They maintain contacts outside the GAO with other policy analysts interested in their topical area.

The role of the staff auditors is to promote organizational change espoused by the Comptroller General and to insure that reports do not damage the GAO's reputation. They also provide administrative support to the other three types of auditors and carry out maintenance tasks for the institution.

On occasion, auditors will slip from one role to another out of necessity. That is, the requirements of a particular audit may require an auditor manager to assume the role of an auditor advocate. However, auditor managers quickly return to the fold. Their professional orientations, derived from their educational backgrounds and their experiences, inhibit them from straying into a new role.

The auditor managers and the auditor advocates are the most interesting types at the GAO because they are the movers behind each evaluation report. Yet they have very different perspectives, which occasions considerable conflict.

Auditor Managers. The auditor managers and the line auditors have the attitude of an external auditor who uses accounting tools and investigative skills. As external auditors they survey, review, and report on government programs to the management—in this case the Congress. In their eyes, "progress is reports [for Congress] that are on solid ground." Audits (and audit reports) are "ends in themselves rather than a means to the end." Their research strategy is strictly inductive. "Auditors feel that they can say something only if they gather all the information and verify it by adding it up twice." They would rather be "99 percent accurate and two months late than 90 percent accurate and on time."

As accountants, GAO auditors concentrate on figures and work papers, employ accounting logic, and insist that facts and figures be completely reliable. Auditors "go out and try to find something quantifiable; they prefer that to making judgments which cannot be quantified." They think in terms of "rules and regulations, dollars and cents." Auditors like to count and "are very detail oriented." Workpapers are very important. "Auditors are always happy with a piece of paper."

Accounting logic is also important to GAO audits. At the GAO, "the technique and logic of accounting are applied to a different set of circumstances." Auditing requires inquisitiveness. "Accountants fit into this pattern, [because they] can be trained" to "sort out facts from judgment" and to "avoid theoretical and normative assessments." "Accountants make good auditors because they think logically."

Auditors in the GAO are also investigators. They are perceived by executive agency officials as being sent by the Congress to discover flaws in their operations. Auditors feel that there "must be something wrong out there" with every program. That is part of their training—"if there is any smoke you will find fire." An agency deputy administrator commented that auditors are like "inspectors on an assembly line looking for reject parts"; they want lots of information from my agency and "select out only the things that are rejects." Another official who had studied all the GAO reports on his agency noted that a visit by the GAO is to be called on by an "investigative auditor who must find every memo [in the files] himself." This "investigative mode traps them in arduous audits of simple things."

Most of the auditors in the headquarters and the regional offices also identified themselves as investigators. They continually commented on the importance of gathering information and of consulting with many sources to insure they got "the true facts." "We are not programmatic people—we don't have enough experience in those areas. We don't need programmatic people. We are people who have an investigative knack."

Another characteristic of GAO auditors which is reminiscent of an investigator is their enormous command of facts. To interview auditors is to face a barrage of details about agency programs and management. In fact they are masters of detail—they can readily provide numbers, dates, and the names of agency officials. Around the coffee pot and at lunch tables, the tales they tell are of findings unearthed in executive agencies.

Auditor Advocates. The auditor advocates are, for the most part, social scientists educated in public administration or economics and trained as policy specialists. The successful advocate is intimately acquainted with the multitude of government programs which constitute his chosen field. In order to maintain relationships with and market GAO products to the Congress, the executive branch, the universities, and interests groups, the advocate must reach out and maintain contacts with like-minded policy specialists.

A principal way to reach out is through the use of consultants, who are now playing a large role in many GAO audits. Many of the audits most popular with Elmer Staats employed consultant panels. For instance, for the series of three reports on the service academies completed in 1975 and 1976, the GAO employed a panel of seventeen consultants, which consisted of former service academy superintendents and educators from the civilian community.[2] Another report, the "Liquid Metal Fast Breeder Reactor"(LMFBR) audit, also employed a panel of experts, in this case drawn from power companies and the academic community.[3] The use of consultants is an important technique in legitimating GAO audits, in forging alliances with policy specialists not formally affiliated with government agencies, and in gaining intelligence about agency operations.[4]

Consultants, however, are not universally loved. Auditor managers and line auditors are suspicious of them. To the auditors, many of the consultants either have insufficient business or government experience or are too willing to draw conclusions based on their professional judgment. Auditors are not comfortable with judgment; they prefer facts. As one auditor noted, "so often we don't take advice consultants give us." A consultant used by the auditors for his engineering skills observed that "people here have a problem working with professional expertise— they aren't comfortable with it."

The managers and advocates thus differ in terms not only of their backgrounds, but also their horizons. Conflict is exacerbated by the fact that accountants have traditionally been considered the "more elite" group.[5] One auditor manager noted the tensions between the accountants and the economists. "It is hard for these two groups to communicate. When I worked with an economist, I found that we thought on different wavelengths."

This tension is further enhanced by the fact that many auditor advocates originally joined the GAO as upper-level hires. That is, they did not work their way up from the entry level and consequently were not socialized as were the accountant auditors. Auditor advocates are not seen as part of the team by the managers; they "act on their own thinking" or "don't understand working papers and documentation." This tension complicates auditing. Both the advocates and managers perform roles that are important in the evaluation repertoire. Reconciling the roles of each group and their relative status was costly for Elmer Staats and the GAO leadership, who had to invest considerable time installing and legitimizing the interdisciplinary staff.

THE AUDIT REPERTOIRE

A GAO evaluation is designed to determine whether federal agencies are being run in an efficient manner (a management audit), or programs are achieving the benefits or results intended by the Congress and the administration (a program audit). The evaluators also conduct financial audits to assess whether an agency is using proper accounting methods and controls. The response of the line auditor or auditor manager upon entering these realms is predictable. As a generalist schooled in accounting techniques and trained as an investigator, he applies a standard repertoire to the evaluation at hand. His lack of policy acumen, his reluctance to generalize from disparate data—he will "only express opinions on hard facts"—and his unwillingness to "face the macro problems of government" preclude the use of policy analytic techniques used by social scientists. As one close observer noted, "Auditors use a standard procedure whether it is a management audit or a program audit. They sort of smell trouble and follow their noses."[6]

Line auditors and auditor managers conceptualize all auditing in terms of "cause, criteria, and effect." In interviews these three terms are used repeatedly. All three apply to findings, which, in their minds, are synonymous with deficiencies in agency operations. The "cause" of the deficiency is an attempt to explain why the financial system, the management, or the program failed to meet the standards required. The required standards for measuring performance are the "criteria" and may be found in audit standards established by CPAs, laws, agency regulations, or codes established by private professional groups.

Once the criteria are applied and the cause of a deficiency has been settled upon, the "effect" is sought. The "effect" is the impact a condition or deficiency has on the government, the agency, or the public. Generally speaking, the impacts of deficiencies must be adjudged serious or severe, or auditors will seek to close out the review and move on to more fertile ground.[7]

So all evaluations are alike. Auditors apply simple, easily remembered formulas to their work. Armed with the skills of an accountant and investigator, auditors use a host of unwritten rules, techniques, and procedures which constitute the evaluator's fault-finding repertoire. These shortcuts were developed over decades of auditing and passed on to new auditors as part of the socialization process.

The GAO evaluation repertoire is organized into three phases. The survey phase discovers deficiencies. The review phase fits facts to the faults found during the survey. Finally, the report phase records deficiencies for delivery to the Congress.

Discovering Deficiencies

Evaluations, or audits as the accountants still consider them, are initiated primarily to catch or sustain congressional interest. The GAO has distinguished between congressionally-requested evaluations and GAO-initiated evaluations. Congressional requests may be contained in laws which require the GAO to review certain areas on either a one-time or recurring basis. Or the requests may come from a committee chairman or any member of Congress. Elmer Staats decided that only 35 to 40 percent of all GAO evaluation resources would be dedicated to congressional requests. This ceiling was imposed to protect GAO independence—the classic value of any audit organization.[8]

The GAO-initiated evaluations are considered necessary because of GAO's government-wide horizons; further, since GAO auditors are close to agency operations both at sites in Washington and in the field, auditor managers are more aware of agency and program difficulties. In fact, the distinction between congressional and GAO-initiated evaluations is illusory.[9] Essentially the reason for GAO-initiated evaluations is self-protection. That is, the auditors prefer to protect themselves from reviews which are blatantly political in nature and to stockpile reviews against periods of low congressional activity.

Where congressional interest does not exist, auditors either have to stir it up or the evaluation will not be completed. Of the auditors queried, most indicated that such interest was imperative. As one put it, "If Congress is making a lot of noise about a program, we would be interested—we're here to serve Congress."

Soliciting evaluations usually involves negotiation between committee staff members and auditors. Each party notes its area of interest. Once an interesting topic is agreed upon, the auditors provide the committee staff a draft letter to be sent to GAO headquarters. The committee staff refines the letter, obtains the chairman's signature, and sends it off to the Comptroller General. As one committee counsel noted, "We help them set their priorities in our area of interest."

Forecasting and the Twitching Nose.   Auditor managers and advocates use a number of aids to calculate probable congressional interest. These aids tell them what agencies and programs are "ripe for audit." Within those areas, they follow their noses to find the deficiencies.

The most frequently used aids are congressional documents, such as hearings, committee reports, and *The Congressional Record.* Other indicators of likely congressional interest are the dollar amount or population coverage of federal programs and the degree of interest taken by the press. As one bureaucrat familiar with GAO routines commented, "Where a matter hits the press, you can bet the GAO will be knocking at the door."

Agency publications and previous audits also provide areas "ripe for audit." In some cases agencies will make certain claims about the success of some program or the efficiency of their management. If these seem particularly inflated, an audit will be initiated. For example, a Defense Department publication may indicate that a weapon system is in production or has been deployed to the field. Auditor managers find this an opportune time to compare the system's cost and performance with DOD claims, especially as those claims are contained in congressional documents. Another technique is to follow up on a particularly successful audit conducted several years before.

> Where the Department of Defense has said it has made changes [in any area we previously audited], we go back to see how many of our recommendations have been implemented, are being implemented, or are not being implemented.

Finally, audits which yielded notable deficiencies in one agency or department may be repeated in a similar agency. This is a favorite device to use on the Department of Defense, since one can apply the audit techniques learned in an audit of the Army to the Air Force and the Navy.

Thus these aids to calculation provide the general target for an audit. Based on these broad areas, the auditor managers located in the GAO headquarters will query other auditors located at agency sites in Washington and at the regional offices. Auditors at these locations have gained considerable experience with agency operations and are aware of interesting threads to pursue in others. More often, regional offices develop their own reviews and then sell them at headquarters. However, an auditor manager is still required at the GAO headquarters to sponsor the audit.

Once the area for evaluation or audit has been arbitrated between headquarters managers and regional or site auditors, a survey, or what the auditors call a "fishing expedition," is initiated. A survey is a broadbrush dip into the audit area to discover "conditions" (read deficiencies) which would warrant a full review. The "auditor's nose"[10] is most important during this stage; it "begins to twitch" when downwind from deficiencies. One auditor described the intuitional process as follows:

> If someone won't give me information, then something is there. Also if [agency] people resist, then something is there. You take a rapid look at regulations and statistics to see whether things are good or bad especially in terms of what [the agency] should be doing.

He described one example where he got the twitch. His group had decided to audit the Right to Read Program, which had been allocated 25 million dollars to teach 25 million people to read in five or six years. "Can the administration make 25 million people literate by 1980? That is one dollar a year. Right away you know—it's absurd."

Intuition strikes in various places. It may come in interviews, in observing or speaking with participants in social grant programs, while walking through a laboratory, or while conducting an inventory. One line auditor described his most memorable finding: a warehouse full of toilet paper at a military installation.

Auditors agree that the survey is critical. The survey blazes the trail that other auditors will follow in the audit itself. As one auditor noted, "The actual review should not yield much you don't know . . . . The review will prove the [survey's] hypothesis and/or expand the scope of the issue or will identify other possibilities."

Survey completion at a region or site initiates a round of GAO auditor manager bargaining. Regional and site auditor managers must now convince the headquarters manager and his reporting chain that the deficiencies discovered in the survey are worthy of a full-blown review.

Where a sponsor cannot be found, auditors will alter their product slightly for marketing purposes. Once an auditor manager agrees to the audit, he must face a peer review board which screens surveys for the division director. A successful peer review generally leads to approval of the audit by the division director. The proposal is then considered by the Office of Program Planning. If it appears to be repetitive of previous work or requires more than 1,500 staff days, the Assignment Review Group will consider it. Once this check is completed, the audit or evaluation is initiated.

Harvesting Facts

The review phase and the report phase are also group endeavors. Each auditor does but a small piece of the work, all of which is reviewed extensively, not only at the regional offices and audit sites, but also at headquarters. Furthermore, there is extensive layering in planning and organizing audit efforts. The emphasis is on obtaining the correct facts to fit the deficiencies discovered in the survey.

Obtaining facts is not an easy task. Political executives, career administrators, and program managers are not willing to reveal any more about their agency's operations and program administration than necessary. Not only must the auditors pierce the institutional veneers that executive agencies and bureaus maintain, they must also penetrate the professional groups that dominate each agency. These groups are unwilling to reveal their professional secrets to auditors, nor will they willingly permit auditors (or any other professional group) access to information that will damage the institution they have struggled so hard to create and maintain.

Because the audit is so dependent on agency employees, the line auditors have developed various techniques for gathering facts and tactics for dealing with particularly recalcitrant agencies. The techniques are employed to sort out fact from opinion and to manage the conflict and tension inherent in audit. The tactics are either confrontational or circumventional.

Sorting Out Fact from Fiction.   The auditor's basic tool is an agency document. It may be a memorandum, a report, or even scribbled notes. The document may be an official document such as a regulation, a policy statement, a mission description, or an organization chart and, therefore, contained in manuals or binders. All are copied for placement in the workpapers. Complete records are essential to sustain an audit through the GAO review process and to fortify it against its most demanding critics—auditor managers and auditor advocates.

Observation is another good device for finding facts. Observation involves a tour of a facility, installation, or plant. Quite often auditors back up tours with photographs, which are also placed in the workpapers.

The least reliable technique for finding facts is the interview. Though they can guide auditor-evaluators to the facts, interviews themselves are considered to be too full of opinions to be a direct source of fact. Where oral evidence must be taken, very strict rules are used. First, auditors must prepare an outline of what the interview will cover. Then two people must be present in the interview, both of whom are taking notes. At the conclusion of the interview, a written record must be immediately prepared, "preferably signed by [the] persons interviewed."[11]

Auditors recognize that in spite of all these caveats, interviews are very important. Interviews guide auditors to documents. "You don't ask [agency people], 'let me see your records.' If they are smart, they will give you all of them." It is believed that the best facts can be found several echelons below the organization's top leadership or in the regional or field office of federal agencies.

Managing Conflict: Don't Ruffle Their Feathers.   Auditing is essentially adversarial; the auditors recognize they have to scratch for every fact. To manage this tension, line auditors have developed techniques to smooth relationships. They subsume their efforts under the title "good working relationships." Agency managers describe these techniques as "doing the little things that business people do to get along with you."

Auditors know to initiate contact at the top of each organization under review. This initial visit is used to identify the subject of the audit, to request agency assistance, and to specify what work space and other support may be required. Another objective in starting at the top is to try to obtain willing cooperation from the organization. A favorite tactic is to argue that external auditors can provide top management with insight into their organization. Such insight, auditors argue, will permit managers to save resources and to gain better control over their operations. To some managers, convinced that the bureaucracy below them is neither disciplined nor responsive, this claim has appeal.

Auditors also know how to use the chain of command. The initial interview is followed by successive visits to each hierarchical level in the chain. This precludes "ruffled feathers" which can erect "impediments to audit." "Ruffled feathers" are also avoided by the auditor's being tactful and open. Tactful auditors use "diplomacy programs" and "cooperative, helpful, work-along-with type of approaches." In this way they are able to convince agency officials to help them and to contribute to the report. Thus, the auditors have found that a tactful demeanor and candor about findings "yields information in larger quantities" than if they act in an adversarial manner.

Tact and candor must be established over a period of time. Auditors learn to be patient and yet persistent. They try to avoid occupying busy agency officials for extended periods by planning their questions ahead of time and "doing their homework."

To the auditors, "good working relationships" are not cozy—the socialization process from the Joseph Campbell years still inhibits auditors from developing close associations. Rather "good working relationships" means that auditors will not be denied access to documents, will not be held up in their work, and will be given free access to all members of the organization. Such relationships do not mean that needed facts to support a deficiency will be readily provided. "All auditors know you have to dig for every piece of information."

Auditors contend that for the most part, these techniques are successful in leading them to the facts they are seeking. This low key, nonadversarial style is characteristic of more recent GAO audits. During the Joseph Campbell years, auditors were much more austere and generally withheld their findings from the organization under review.

Circumventional Tactics. Circumventional tactics attempt to envelop agency resistance and are preferred over confrontational tactics. Circumventional tactics include the use of informers, new leaders, and committee or congressional staff. Auditors complain that reliable informers in agencies are rare. Yet, on occasion, informers do surface and break up the logjams that their peers have constructed.

Another circumventional tactic is the use of new leaders or managers. New helmsmen want, of course, to make an impact, and to make an impact, change is necessary. Change is reform, and to legitimate reform, deficiencies must be found and pointed out to superiors and interested congressmen. There is no better way to find deficiencies than through the use of GAO auditors. Another added benefit clearly is that auditors report to Congress. As one political executive told Hugh Helco, "The

General Accounting Office is a good ally. We've got one of their men in working on a particular set of plans."[12] So auditors and new managers find it mutually advantageous to cooperate; auditors find the facts and expose deficiencies which new managers can rectify to enhance their prestige and reputation.

If agencies resist, auditors can also seek congressional support. Legislative and oversight committee staff members are interested in deficiencies in executive agencies. Staff members can supply a list of questions signed by the committee chairman in an audit area or will have the congressman request a report on the topic the auditors are reviewing. Such questions and requests usually persuade agencies to respond to GAO auditors. Of course, this tactic is used sparingly, since congressional staffers can change the direction of the GAO-intiated study. Auditors prefer to do their own studies.

Confrontational Tactics: "The Smoke 'Em Out." When "good working relationships" do not succeed and when circumventional tactics are exhausted, auditors use adversarial techniques to do evaluations. Where auditors cannot find documents that they know or suspect exist, they will confront an agency with a written summary of the facts they have found and ask for a formal comment. If this does not succeed, they will prepare their draft report and circulate it to the agency for comment. Often, the agency will complain that the auditors do not have all the facts which, of course, brings the rejoinder that the agency did not provide all the documents the auditors requested and that the GAO will alter the written summary or the draft report if the proper documents are provided. "So we try to smoke them out . . . our ultimate weapon is the draft report. Agencies want to comment on that."

In cases where agencies or contractors show a continual pattern of resistance to GAO auditors, the Comptroller General will lodge a formal complaint with the Congress. These complaints may be in the form of a letter, in testimony given by the Comptroller General before committees investigating agency activities, or in the *Comptroller General's Annual Report*.

Obtaining facts for audit entails considerable GAO-agency conflict. Each side employs numerous tactics to either avoid audit or delay it or, in the case of the auditor, to penetrate agencies in the pursuit of deficiencies. Auditors feel that they get what they are after. Agency managers and professionals are equally convinced that the auditors obtain only what is given to them. The point, of course, is that both sides see the conflict in different terms. The GAO auditors look for deficiencies to trumpet to the Congress and the press. The agencies want to protect their most closely held institutional values and professional independence. The outcome is such that both are usually satisfied.

Preparing the Report

Once the auditors have obtained sufficient facts to substantiate the deficiency discovered in the survey, the line auditors and auditor managers write the report. The managers and advocates then process the report. Finally the auditor advocates market the report to outsiders.

The report phase involves writing the draft, obtaining agency comments, and processing the final report. If, as some observers complain, GAO reports are mushy and timid, then the report phase is the culprit. As several auditors and outside observers have noted, GAO workpapers are better than their reports.

Writing the Draft.   The first draft of a GAO report is usually written at one of the regional offices or at one of the Washington site locations. The initial problem for each GAO evaluation is to find an auditor that can write. It has been widely acknowledged inside the GAO that most auditors are not skilled writers. Elmer Staats was also unhappy with GAO prose. One staff auditor noted that effective writing was always on the agenda for the Comptroller's meetings with division directors. The auditor writing style "drives [Staats] wild. What he always says he will do is go out and buy a *Wall Street Journal, New York Times,* or a *Washington Post* to find out what each report is about."

The reason that audit reports are full of turgid prose is best explained by the audience for which the auditors write and the report review process. Auditors write for other auditors.[13] As they put it, they "write for our next level of review." "Everyone below puts in something that someone higher up might ask."

Once a suitable writer has been found for the report, the massive collection of workpapers must be sorted to find the right facts to support the deficiency. About four or five large file drawers provide the necessary workpapers for a single GAO report. Once the report is written, the workpapers are assembled in sequence to substantiate "each figure, date, proper name and citation to legal and other reference material" used in the report. Further, each conclusion, deficiency, and recommendation must be adequately substantiated by the workpapers.

The report review process is arduous. The draft must be processed through multiple layers. Auditors talk of needing "patience and endurance" to push reports through the system. They describe the system as "picayunish and repetitive," and the final reports as "watered down." They find that "doing audit work is the easy part." and that internal conflict among accountants and other professionals is the norm.

At the regional and site offices, auditor managers review the report. The report is then sent to headquarters, where the responsible division assistant director reviews the report and has an independent auditor "reference" it. "Referencing" entails a careful examination of the draft report against the workpapers to assure complete accuracy. A red check mark is placed over each figure, name, or date and in the left margin next to each line. If the referencer is not satisfied, the unsubstantiated facts are removed or more documents are found.[14]

After referencing, the report is forwarded to an associate director for his review. If he is satisfied, a final draft report is prepared and sent to the agency or contractor for comment.

Agency Comments.   Auditors feel that a report is incomplete without obtaining agency comments.[15] Agency comments are sought because of the delicate position in which the GAO has found itself relative to the Congress and the agencies. Since agency executive appointees and career officials have built numerous bridges across the consitutional chasm between the executive and legislative branches, the GAO is constantly in danger of being challenged on its findings by coalitions established across the two branches. To defend itself, it can always argue that its report is based on the best information the agencies would release and that furthermore, the agency involved had a chance to correct the written record.

The tactics that bureaucrats use to protect their agencies run the gamut from apparent cooperation to armed confrontation. Armed with what they believe is the support of loyal congressmen, bureaucrats may stonewall or intimidate auditors. Other less confrontational techniques include obfuscation, unwillingness to provide comments, and retention of critical documents for use in presenting a case to Congress. Agency professionals have even been known to cooperate, particularly where their interests can be enhanced by a GAO report to Congress.

The auditors' tactics to deal with agency resistance are to limit agency comments or to extract from these comments the points the auditors feel are relevant. That is, auditors decide which comments are, to quote their *Report Manual,* "too voluminous" to use in the final report and which are "pertinent" to the findings in their audits. What auditors judge to be appropriate comments are not necessarily synonymous with the judgment of agency administrators and professionals.

Recently Congress has discouraged the GAO from seeking agency comments. It has recognized that there is little "play" left in GAO reports once a report is released. Almost certainly this initiative will make auditors more careful and more dependent on agency professionals during the survey and the fact-finding phases.

Processing the Final Report.   Once the report is declared by the associate director to be in final form, the second tier of processing begins. This tier is required to satisfy the division director that all is well with the report and the headquarters staff that the report is safe for the institution. Once the division director has reviewed it, the report advances to the staff for consideration. The gauntlet here involves not only the staff auditors, but also the lawyers and the journalists. Staff auditors in both the Office of Policy and the Office of Congressional Relations assess all reports to be signed by the Comptroller General. Staff auditors in the Office of Policy check to insure that all the standards and requirements listed in the GAO's *Comprehensive Audit Manuals* and *Report Manual* are satisfied. Staff auditors in the Office of Congressional Relations examine the congressional contact memoranda which accompany the report and try to assess the impact of the report on interested congressmen and committee staff members.

The senior lawyers in the Office of the General Counsel also review the report. They are interested not only in legal sufficiency but also in institutional protection. Journalists in the GAO Information Office are particularly concerned with the readability of the report, principally the digest.

The last hurdle is approval by the Deputy Comptroller General and the Comptroller General. With the Comptroller General's signature, the report is printed and distributed.

The review process is not unlike the choke points described by Jeffrey Pressman and Aaron Wildavsky in the implementation of an Economic Development Administration program in Berkeley, California. "The cards in this world are stacked against things happening, as so much effort is required to make them move. The remarkable thing is that new programs work at all."[16] It is equally surprising that any GAO reports are issued, given the numerous choke points which characterize the auditor's review process.

The GAO "audit trail" is now complete. From the survey, through the review, to the report phase a report may take eighteen months to three years. The cast has included not only four types of auditors within GAO, but also congressmen, congressional staff members, outside consultants, agency political appointees and career administrators, agency bureaucrats, and outside contractors. At one point or another each auditor—whether line auditor, manager, advocate, or staff—has found himself in contention with every other member of the cast. So auditing is adversarial. It is adversarial because public professionals inside and outside the GAO see their roles in different ways and value different things.

THE AUDITORS' IDEOLOGY

I n spite of their different horizons and training, all four types of GAO auditors think of themselves as something more than fact-finders. Their ideology provides them a host of justifications for their actions. The values they embrace reflect the GAO's history and design. Auditors value audit, involvement, and government that is economical, efficient, and effective. Their norms for proper behavior, developed during their socialization and training (and as discussed in Chapter 5), seek to insure these values are properly celebrated by government. Their myths include a feeling of superiority to the rest of those in government, as well as a belief that government can be made more businesslike.

Because they value audit, evaluators feel that they should enhance the reputation of and climate for audit. In their minds, the GAO should maintain a strong audit presence in federal organizations. Maintaining such a presence involves continuous audit of some aspect of agency operations. For example, between May, 1967, and June, 1977, the auditors completed some 56 evaluations on the Food and Drug Administration. Between the inception of the Postal Service in July, 1971, and March, 1976, auditors issued 126 reports on postal operations. As the first sentence in a recent report proudly announces, "Both before and after passage of the Postal Reorganization Act, GAO has maintained a strong audit presence in postal operations."[17]

Auditors are equally energetic about enhancing the climate for audit. They spend considerable time reviewing agency internal audit organizations. For instance the Army, Navy, and Air Force audit organizations were recently studied by GAO auditors and criticized for their failure to comply with GAO audit standards (See Chapter 7).[18]

The auditor value of involvement reflects their myth that they are an exceptional group within the government. As one member of the career elite told me:

> I guess we do tend to feel like the elite of the federal establishment. I share this attitude that we are above average. We do have higher quality people; we do conduct ourselves better. I guess you could say there is a crusading zeal here . . . . The origins of this attitude are the roles we play. We scrutinize federal agencies and find defects. Since we find defects—a job really for internal management—we tend to feel smarter and somewhat superior. The agencies also feed this feeling—they respect us.

Finally, auditors value good government. Good government is economical, efficient, and effective—as they come to view those terms in their audit reports (again, see Chapter 7). As a nonpartisan conscience out to improve government, "auditors feel that they have a mission to do." They "overwatch the government." When a government scandal breaks, the question GAO auditors ask themselves is "what has GAO been doing in that area?" It is, after all, "incumbent on auditors to point out solutions"; they should say "here is what ought to be done."

Evaluators are very critical of transgressors against their values of economy, efficiency, and effectiveness. The primary sinners against the values of economy and efficiency are agency managers. Although managers are also to blame for transgressions against the value of effectiveness, the chief wrongdoer from the auditor's viewpoint is the Congress.

Agency management is flawed because its attention is misdirected. According to the evaluators, managers attend to narrow, parochial concerns instead of focusing on economy and efficiency as they should. For instance, auditors are quick to point out that the armed services are constantly squabbling over responsibilities; in their minds interservice conflict and service parochialism blind the military to larger, more significant questions.

In the auditor's opinion, the Congress does not properly attend to the values of effectiveness and efficiency. If it did, legislators would seek to define expectations for governmental programs more carefully and reduce the overlap and duplication among agency responsibilities. To satisfy the auditors, congressmen would have to show more enthusiasm for oversight.

So auditors are an amalgam. They are perceived by the agencies and by themselves as fault-finders for the Congress. Clearly, this somewhat negative endeavor requires some form of self-justification. Consequently, they tend to conceptualize themselves as an elite with a mission to improve government. Improving government can take place when waste and mismanagement are exposed in evaluation reports. Thus they are "management consultants" to the executive and legislative branches. For them, this term is businesslike and professional sounding. The terms professionals use to describe themselves are important aspects of their ideology.

Public professionals outside the GAO value different things. They value their agency's programs and the institution which they helped create or sustain. Agency programs provide employment and status to public professionals. In fact the agency itself is a precipitate of a societal value, established to insure continuing federal attention to an issue. The professional groups which dominate that agency have not only a stake in the agency's health, but also a historical affiliation with its enveloping interest groups. Consequently, these public professionals can be expected to resist the invasion of outsiders, particularly auditors bent on finding fault with their proprietorship over the agency and its programs.[19] Auditing, therefore, is essentially political.

So what the evaluators say about themselves and write in their reports reflects their underlying norms and values and myths, that is, their ideology. Auditors value audit; they struggle to spread the acceptance of this value by various efforts to enhance the reputation and climate for audit at all governmental levels. Auditors also value involvement; their self-images convince them that they should have a strong impact on governmental output. Finally, they believe in businesslike government.

CHAPTER 7

GAO Reports and Their Impact
on Government

.

J ust as organizations have a primary ritual or repertoire, so too
do they have a principal form of output. For the U.S. Army, the
primary repertoire of the attack produces combat power on the
battlefield with the principal goal of defeating the enemy or, in this age
of containment, deterring the enemy from invading national or allied
territory. In the case at hand, the GAO's repertoire of evaluation produces
audit reports. These reports are issued to the Congress as a whole, to
committee chairmen, or to agency heads. The GAO prefers another way
of classifying its reports. That is, reports may be of three types: financial
audits, management audits or program audits.[1]

The impact of these evaluations on Congress and agencies is the final
measure of GAO professional behavior and effectiveness. This chapter
will first describe the types of audit reports and then consider their
collective impact on government.

EVALUATION REPORTS

A udit reports reflect the GAO's culture. The format and the three
types of GAO reports mirror the strategic principles propounded
by Lindsay Warren and embraced by his successors. Equally important
are the constraints and incentives built into the GAO's structure of planning mechanisms, hierarchical arrangements, and personnel system.

Auditors are productive. In Table 2, which lists their output since
1956, several trends are obvious. Since the early 1960s, the GAO has
averaged about 1,000 audit reports per year. The number of reports
to Congress has not varied considerably during this period. There has
been considerable increase in the number of congressionally-initiated

TABLE 2. Number of GAO Audit Reports Classified
by Fiscal Year and Addressee[1]

Fiscal Year	To Congress	To Committees Or Members	To Agencies	Total
1956	137 [2]		192	329
1957	130 [2]		219	349
1958	194 [2]		259	453
1959	238 [2]		471	709
1960	148	76	551	775
1961	126	68	703	897
1962	152	119	548	819
1963	196	141	481	818
1964	293	197	520	1010
1965	411	167	315	893
1966	181	146	600	927
1967	161	177	625	963
1968	157	231	765	1153
1969	177	204	642	1023
1970	203	321	644	1168
1971	173	287	515	975
1972	150	329	469	948
1973	152	352	405/40[3]	949
1974	145	408	322/204[3]	1079
1975	199	433	411	1043
1976[4]	301	638	441	1380
1977	330	439	313	1082
1978	349	490	297	1136
1979	285	399	299	983
1980	288	425	221	934
1981	256	464	256	976

1. Data obtained from the *Comptroller General's Annual Reports.* Data not available prior to 1956.
2. Data include Reports to Congress, Reports to Committees, and Reports to Individual Addresses.
3. The second figure indicates reports from the GAO's Office of Federal Elections, the predecessor to the Federal Elections Commission.
4. This year includes a 15-month transition period to the new Fiscal Year.

reports, from 76 in 1960 to 464 in 1981. The reports to agencies have generally declined during this period, with only 256 reports being issued in 1981. Clearly the GAO finds the Congress a more suitable place to submit its reports, a trend which reflects the acceptance of the strategic principle of responsiveness to Congress.

The number of audit reports produced each year is significant. GAO evaluators report more than auditors in any other Western country. Most other supreme audit organizations report to the legislature on only several occasions each year; these reports are generally summaries of the observations that the auditors have collected throughout that period.[2] For the GAO evaluators, producing reports is the stuff for status and promotion. When queried whether they would prefer one outstanding report or three or four acceptable reports, most auditors preferred more reports.

With few exceptions each report details one or more deficiencies. A complete deficiency or finding would include a statement of *condition* in an agency or program, the *criteria* against which to judge what the agency or program should be, the *effect* which is an assessment of the difference between the condition and the criteria, and the *cause* of the difference between the condition and the criteria.[3]

By the time a report is issued, the agency has provided its comments and girded itself for subsequent assaults. Consequently much of the GAO-agency strife has been played out. The report itself, depending on its salience to Congress and the news media, may also generate secondary and tertiary interactions as the news media covers the report, the GAO testifies on the report to Congress or supplies questions from its reports to House and Senate Appropriations Committee staff members, and as congressional committees and individual congressmen use the report for their own purposes. These purposes include, but are not limited to, the three activities described by David Mayhew which congressmen use in their reelectoral quests: advertising, credit claiming, and position taking.[4]

Report Format.   Like Joseph's coat, audit reports come in many colors. There are blue-cover reports to the Congress. To be associated with a successful blue-cover report is thought to enhance an evaluator's career. Success of a report is generally measured in terms of congressional use. If the report contributes to committee hearings as demonstrated by committee member reference to the report or if evaluators are called to testify before the committee because of an audit, then those associated with the report are remembered for their efforts. Other measures of success for reports include reference to them in the *Congressional Record* or in newspaper stories. Finally, to be associated with a report to which the Comptroller General refers with pride is also prestigious.[5]

There are also gray-cover reports. These are reports requested by committee chairmen or by a member of Congress acting on his own behalf. Evaluators feel that such reports are tainted by congressional politics.

Audits with white covers are awarded the least prestige in the report pecking order. These reports are intended for distribution only to agency officials and are based upon auditing initiated by the GAO. Generally speaking, these reports do not contain findings or deficiencies considered significant enough to warrant a blue-cover report to the Congress. Such reports represent audit work that did not bear fruit. They are issued primarily because too many resources have been invested to warrant scrubbing the audit.

Other aspects of the audit report format are also important. Each report has a title, a cover summary, and a digest. The report title is meant to convey a message.[6] A content analysis of GAO report titles is instructive. In an examination of all the blue-cover reports for the fifteen-month period ending September 30, 1976, most titles contained words or phrases suggesting that the agency being investigated was inadequate.[7] For instance, the program or agency administration "needs fundamental change," "remains inadequate," or "needs improved controls." Audit report titles also suggest that "more can be learned" or "more must be done." Auditors are quick to point out suggestions that "can help" or "ways to improve" or "actions required." The titles also propose that government can certainly be made better. Better results "should be obtained" or "can be achieved." Auditors typically find that "more could be done" or that something "should be changed."

The titles of GAO reports reflect the underlying values of the auditors. The concern for economy, efficiency, and effectiveness in government are evident in the recurrence of words implying failure and demanding action. From the evaluators perspective, more businesslike government could be ushered in with only a little more effort on everyone's part.

The cover summaries and the digests contained in each report are also significant. The cover summary appears below the title and usually contains three or four sentences which review the auditors' principal conclusions and findings.[8] The digests are three- or four-page summaries which can be easily torn out of each report. The wire service reporters find the digests provide an easy story which is readily accepted by their editors, primarily because of the GAO's reputation.[9] As interviews with committee staff members suggested, not everyone is willing to wade through a sixty- or seventy-page GAO report. Audit reports tend to be read only if a staffer has had a hand in planning them. Consequently, auditors feel that the digest provides an incentive for others to review their work.

Thus, the format of audit reports reflects GAO design. The colors of the report covers are important symbols that carry considerable professional meaning for the auditors. The cover summaries and digests are internal responses to external disregard of reports whose content seems so often obscure. The report titles betray the inherent tension of trying to reconcile the search for deficiencies with the congressional-imposed dictum to provide balanced reporting. The symbols and tensions of the dominant professional group, the modes of responding to external pressures, and the role of the leadership are all manifested in the reports and mirror the culture of the GAO.

Financial Audits. This and the subsequent two subsections will describe each type of evaluation, provide examples, and then generally discuss the content of that type of report.[10] We will then draw some conclusions about the overall thrust of GAO reports.

As practiced in the late 1970s, financial evaluations were assessments of accounting and auditing systems and reviews of agency financial practices. According to the 1950 Budget and Accounting Procedures Act, the GAO must "prescribe the principles, standards, and related requirements for accounting to be observed by each executive agency"; the Act also requires the GAO to "review the accounting systems of the executive agencies."[11] In practice this mandate and the various forms of financial audit are a search for failures to comply with GAO audit standards or congressional demands.

Accounting system approval was not a popular matter with the agencies, although Elmer Staats and Congress gave it considerable attention in the 1970s. The Comptroller General was queried frequently by the House and Senate Appropriations Committee on the GAO's efforts and success in approving these systems. Agencies found this attention misplaced. One senior bureaucrat commented that accounting system approval was an insignificant requirement that forced his department to generate paperwork. "In a changing world, by the time we get information to them [GAO], the system has evolved." An executive-level appointee agreed and observed that "no one in government has followed this requirement—it's been on the books for twenty years."[12]

The first example of a financial audit involves the review of auditing systems. In 1974 the Department of the Army found its internal accounting controls were not functioning properly. During the period

1974 to 1976, the Army Audit Agency (AAA) conducted many reviews of these systems. At the request of Congressman George Mahan, then Chairman of the House Appropriations Committee, the GAO did a report. Relying heavily on AAA reports, the auditors confirmed the inadequate nature of the Army's financial management system. As a result of this report, GAO auditors then decided to review the internal arrangements for audit within the Department of the Army. Its review was conducted at AAA headquarters and in its district offices in the United States and in Germany. The report found numerous deficiencies, the most salient of which were that the Army had placed restrictions on AAA by excluding certain areas and activities from internal audit and that AAA was subordinate to the Army Inspector General and therefore did not report immediately to the Secretary of the Army as required by GAO audit standards. The report also criticized the Army for not having an effective followup system to insure recommendations made by AAA auditors were promptly implemented.[13]

This report prompted both a congressional hearing and subsequent reports on the Air Force and Navy audit organizations. Congressman Jack Brooks, Chairman of the House Committee on Government Operations, convened a hearing to determine what followup action the Army had taken on the GAO's report. As an Army deputy assistant secretary testified, the Army was already reviewing its audit arrangements as a result of its accounting system difficulties and was in the process of correcting many of the faults reported by the GAO.[14] The GAO also undertook evaluations of the Navy Audit Service and the Air Force Audit Agency. Substantially the same deficiencies were found in each organization.[15]

A second example details several evaluations of agency financial practices. After passage of the Foreign Military Sales Act in 1968, the GAO increased its audit presence in this area. In reports issued in 1974 and 1975, the Defense Department and the services were criticized for not recovering full costs from foreign governments for training pilots and navigators. The GAO auditors were particularly critical that Iran had not been required to reimburse the U.S. government fully for its students at a time when the Iranians were demanding maximum prices for their oil exports. As a result, the Defense Department instructed the services to do more careful cost accounting to insure that indirect base operations support costs were included in billing foreign governments. These instructions produced sudden increased training costs for foreign governments which, in the eyes of senior military officers, hurt

U.S. relationships with its allies. As a result, the Department then decided to reduce its tuition rates.[16]

This last move prompted Congressman Mahan to request another GAO report. The 1976 evaluation criticized the Defense Department for its inconsistent pricing and billing policies and for undercharging foreign governments a total of $55 to $75 million in 1975. This report generated considerable press attention. By auditor standards it was a successful report.[17]

Thus one salient recurring deficiency found by financial audits is the failure of internal audit. Still another is failure to achieve savings where they are possible. During the last half of the 1970s, numerous GAO reports found fault with the arrangements for internal audit and the failure of agency managers to save money.[18] Both of these recurring deficiencies clearly assail the auditor's ideology. They mean that the values of economy and a vibrant climate for audit are not properly celebrated by executive agencies.

Management Evaluations.   Differentiating management from program audits is sometimes difficult. The evaluators themselves either seemed confused about the differences or were unabashedly inclined to label management audits as program evaluations. For the evaluators, the GAO's internal system of rewards follows the discovery of deficiencies, and deficiencies can be uncovered in the review of either agency management or programs. The distinction between the two forms thus seemed to be of more importance to the GAO leadership than to the individual auditor.

Yet management audits are distinct in that they emphasize efficiency. That is, such audits focus on agency procedures and the proper use of resources. Evaluators engaged in management evaluations are enjoined to be alert to fraud, abuse, and inadequate internal management controls.[19]

One example of such an audit involved the GAO in a nationwide grain scandal. By 1974 the Department of Agriculture's Agricultural Marketing Service (AMS) had received numerous complaints from foreign grain merchants about U.S. grain shipments. It therefore began to investigate the handling procedures at the port of New Orleans, where it then uncovered serious problems in weighing, classifying, and transporting of grain. Eventually AMS officials realized its staff was inadequate to the task and so turned the matter over to the Department's Office of Investigations. Soon the Federal Bureau of Investigation and

United States attorneys in New Orleans were involved, and indictments were brought against private grain inspectors licensed and supervised by AMS.[20]

This development was first reported by James Risser in the *Des Moines Register* on May 4, 1975.[21] His subsequent investigations and stories attracted reporters from the *New York Times* and the *Washington Post* and also prompted Congressman Edward Mezvinsky of Iowa to request a GAO report. His request was followed in June by another call for a GAO report from House Agriculture Committee Chairman Tom Foley of Washington and Senate Agricultural Committee member Hubert Humphrey of Minnesota. This request asked for a GAO report by February 15, 1976.[22] Both houses then began hearings in July and August on grain inspection procedures.

The GAO assigned 40 evaluators to the task; the evaluators interviewed 89 grain operators and state officials domestically, questioned 83 buyers and government officials abroad, tabulated data from 2,400 questionnaires, and visited 29 inspection agencies and 55 inspection points in the United States. The GAO's report, issued on February 12, 1976, found "serious weaknesses in the national grain inspection system," noting also that the system "operated without effective controls, procedures or lines of authority" and was not responsive to AMS supervision as required by law. The report went on to recommend that grain inspection be nationalized and supervised by the Department of Agriculture.[23]

As soon as the GAO report was released, the Senate Committee held another round of hearings and in its report substantially adopted the auditors' recommendations. The House was not as sanguine about these recommendations. Ultimately the conference committee agreed that all grain destined for international markets would be subject to inspection by a newly formed Federal Grain Inspection Service, whereas domestic market inspection would remain in the hands of private grain inspectors who would be more carefully supervised by the Department of Agriculture.[24] In the end the GAO report on management deficiencies seemed to convince the Senate Agriculture Committee that extensive changes were needed.

Very few management audits get such extensive attention. Yet the grain inspection audit is similar to other management evaluations in the kind of deficiencies discovered. In fact, four clusters of deficiencies recur in these evaluations, each of which can be exemplified by numerous reports. The fact that auditors find common faults in agency programs further substantiates the repertorial nature of their craft.

The first cluster of organizational deficiencies concerns overlap and duplication. These findings criticize agencies for overlapping jurisdictions, duplication of effort, and a lack of uniformity in management. A favorite target for overlap and duplication studies is the Department of Defense. For instance, in a 1973 report, auditors found fault with the fragmentation of DOD training arrangements; they noted that in twelve different medical and technical specialties, sufficient overlap in training occurred to warrant interservice training arrangements. A 1976 report noted that efforts of the DOD and the National Oceanic and Atmospheric Administration to inhibit overlap of warning dissemination systems had not been sufficient.[25]

Another cluster of findings emphasizes the virtues of detailed planning and thorough coordination. In 1969 and 1972 reports on the Water Pollution Abatement Program, auditors found that the responsible federal agency failed to insure that the states obtaining federal grants had developed proper pollution control plans. The auditors discovered in a 1975 report that the Department of Agriculture "has not developed the detailed plans or made the studies that should have preceded procurement [of an automatic data processing system]."[26]

The third managerial sin is failure to collect adequate information or install reliable administrative systems, systems which contain established, written rules. Agencies are criticized for not "collecting data" or for having "no reliable or complete reporting system," as in the 1972 audits of the Narcotic Addiction Treatment and Rehabilitation Programs. The FDA was found at fault for not "developing written procedures," for not requiring the "submission of consent forms," or for not obtaining "data on the extent of metabolite residues in food."[27]

There is a certain irony in the auditors' recurring complaints about both the absence of agency documentation and the need for more written procedures. In an era of deregulation, government agencies are under attack for their rigidity and lack of responsiveness. Citizens and corporations complain loudly about the paperwork required to obtain grants or to justify compliance with federal regulations.[28] And yet the same agencies find themselves assaulted by congressional auditors for failure to "establish uniform guidelines" or for "no reliable or complete reporting system."

Certainly in the case of grain inspection, the administrative system needed a complete overhaul. But in most other audits examined, there was not an absence of controls, but rather, from the auditor's perspective, insufficient controls. This perspective is not shared by most agency officials, for whom the evaluators' call for more controls seems excessive. Furthermore the demand for more documentation and written procedures strikes the outsider as a call designed to ease their audit burden; that is, the more paper, the easier it is to discover criteria and thus deficiencies in management. Thus, auditors promote paperwork and regulations, the stuff of big government.

Not only do they promote paperwork and regulations, they also discourage governmental responsiveness. By insisting upon detailed planning and coordination in government agencies, auditors are calling for more centralized control. Centralized control is the antithesis of responsiveness.

Finally, auditors repeatedly criticize agencies for failing to properly monitor the private sector as required by law or to enforce the provisions of federal statutes. The Equal Opportunity Commission was enjoined to "improve the monitoring of employer compliance" in eliminating employment discrimination. The Consumer and Marketing Service (CMS) of the Department of Agriculture and the Food and Drug Administration (FDA) were often cited for their negligence in the enforcement of statutes. In reports dated 1969, 1970, and 1971, CMS was criticized for its weak enforcement of standards at poultry and meat-packing plants. At least three other audit reports were critical of the FDA for failure to enforce regulations in such areas as the food-manufacturing industry, the production of medical diathermy devices, and the protection of human test subjects.[29]

This emphasis upon the inadequacy of agency surveillance and enforcement reflects a certain political naiveté in the auditors. Federal agencies are not negligent simply because they fail to enforce federal statutes in the areas of consumer affairs or general governmental regulation. The use of the term "negligence" in preference to others presupposes that federal agencies understand their responsibilities under the law, had the resources to carry out those responsibilities, and could expect support from the Administration and Congress in enforcement of the law.

Most regulatory agencies, of course, possess none of those attributes. Government laws are notoriously vague; in the realm of consumer protection against carcinogenic drugs, the meshing of scientific criteria with governmental laws becomes an almost impossible task. Federal regulatory agencies are frequently too undermanned to enforce federal laws. For instance, the CMA and FDA have available inspectors numbering only in the hundreds to contend with private activities across a continent with thousands of firms involved daily in multiple transactions. Finally, those agencies involved in surveillance and enforcement of regulatory statutes often find themselves in the midst of political firestorms over which they have no control. Those who are regulated seek to weaken, capture, or control the regulators. Without the support of political administrators or congressmen, the regulators are helpless. Federal regulation no longer wins much support among politicians; consequently, federal regulatory agencies are severely constrained.[30]

Program Evaluations.   Program evaluations assess effectiveness. That is, they seek to determine whether the desired results or benefits, as established by Congress or by the body of professional opinion, are being achieved. These audits also consider whether a program is being administered in an efficient way and its expenditures used in an economical manner.

Several examples illustrate these objectives. The first involves a computer system for the Veteran's Administration (VA). Under pressure from veterans and the congressional veterans' affairs committees, the VA sought to update its outmoded payment system by purchasing a new computer system called Target. This new program was enthusiastically supported by VA Administrator Max Cleland soon after he was installed in the Spring of 1977. Disposed to make many changes in the agency, Cleland felt that the Target program would reduce overhead, maintain better records, and provide for more accurate benefit payments.

Several members of Congress were not as enthusiastic about the program and so requested a GAO cost-benefit study. The GAO report of July 20, 1977, called Target a "risky venture" whose costs and benefits had not been thoroughly evaluated. Furthermore, the VA had not adequately considered alternative ways of meeting its needs for processing veterans benefits.[31] So in GAO's view, the Target program was not an economical use of resources.

Another GAO program evaluation involved the sale of a sophisticated radar plane called AWACS (Airborne Warning and Control System). In June, 1977, President Carter notified Congress of his program to sell seven AWACS to Iran to secure its borders from the Soviet Union; this notification was required by the 1973 Foreign Aid Authorization Act. Alerted by press reports in May that such a sale would be proposed, six senators, including John Culver and Thomas Eagleton, requested that the GAO analyze the program in terms of the risk that it might compromise the secret equipment aboard each aircraft.

In July, the GAO issued its report. Based on data provided by the Pentagon and intelligence assessments from the Central Intelligence Agency, the evaluators concluded that the sale of AWACS to Iran would indeed risk the U.S. lead over the Soviet Union in electronic warfare and therefore not yield the results claimed by the President. Furthermore the GAO found that the administration had not considered alternative radar systems which could meet Iran's security needs, nor had it accurately assessed the total cost to Iran of an AWACS-based defense.[32]

As is clear from these reports, to evaluate effectiveness is to apply the same conceptual framework employed in the discovery of any finding—cause, criteria, and effect. The conceptual framework of a "system" dominates the thinking of program auditors. They have found only the President has the authority "required to establish a unified Government telecommunications system." In another evaluation, the auditors recommended that the Interior Department should develop a "systematic coal-drilling program."[33]

The criteria used in effectiveness audits are the program goals or cost-benefit calculations. In reviewing the development of oil and gas resources on the Outer Continental Shelf, auditors found that the Secretary of the Interior should more "clearly define Shelf leasing goals and specify how these goals will be met and how they relate to overall national energy goals and plans." The Environmental Protection Agency (EPA) was advised to "establish criteria or guidance for setting research priorities" in federal progrms which reviewed the effects of air pollutants. As illustrated in the Target evaluation, costs and benefits are also favorite criteria. In reviewing the implications of deregulating the price of natural gas, the auditors felt that "the additional supplies of gas likely to result from deregulation must be weighed against the additional costs to consumers."[34]

The "cause"—why the condition and criteria are not the same—in program evaluations is laid both on agency management and the Congress. Agency management is told to establish more consistent criteria in order to clarify vague laws—that is the agencies are told to legislate. In the 1975 audit cited above, the Secretary of the Interior was told to "clearly define shelf leasing goals," and the EPA was told that it should prescribe criteria for "setting research priorities."

Evaluators urge Congress to enact more legislation either to clarify statutory language or provide more resources to achieve the goals prescribed by existing laws. The evaluators are more circuitous in faulting the Congress than in blaming the agencies. Reports contain sections which suggest "Matters for Consideration by the Congress" or "Issues for Consideration by the Committees on Appropriations." Such "Matters" and "Issues" call for more law and more money. For example, a 1974 audit of federal programs for educating the handicapped advised that "the Congress should consider amending pertinent legislation . . . and eliminating formula allocation factors." Another 1974 audit advised the Appropriation Committees that "EPA may need funds above the current level of 40–50 million dollars to meet the 1985 national goals of eliminating the discharge of pollutants to navigable waters."[35]

An even more significant demonstration of this subtle fault-finding of the Congress can be found in the growth of legislative recommendations. The 1921 Budget and Accounting Act required the Comptroller General to "make recommendations looking to greater economy or efficiency in public expenditures."[36] The recommendations provided prior to 1973 were limited. Before this date, most recommendations called for tightening legislation which applied to small segments of the government or the private sector. For instance, in the 1926 *Annual Report*, John McCarl noted that seven statutes should be modified, one of which dealt with the hiring of passenger vehicles. With the advent of the culture of oversight, the Comptrollers began to cautiously make more far-reaching legislative recommendations to Congress. By 1965 Joseph Campbell noted that in that year, ten recommendations had been accepted by Congress and seventeen more should be acted upon.[37]

The 1973 audit recommendations to the Congress reiterated in the *Annual Report* were still more numerous and significant. Of the thirty-five recommendations, one suggested the enactment of a national foreclosure law, while another proposed an expansion of FDA authority. Forty-eight such recommendations were made in 1975; Congress was encouraged to "provide additional financial and tax incentives" for one program, to "establish a national program for energy conservation," and to consider "several (GAO-initiated) legislative alternatives to encourage greater use of home dialysis" for treating chronic kidney failure. By 1977, these recommendations had grown to seventy-four in number.[38]

One can conclude, therefore, that GAO evaluation reports have promoted bigger government, an outcome which must be considered as an unintended consequence of the evaluators' efforts. That is, GAO financial, management, and program evaluations encourage growth in the size and scope of the state. The recurring deficiencies discovered in financial audits prompt calls for larger, more intrusive internal audit organizations and more extensive cost-accounting systems. Faults found in management audits emphasize the insufficiency of agency documentation and procedures, thereby promoting more paperwork and regulations. Also the recurring deficiencies of inadequate planning and poor enforcement demand more centralized control, thereby inhibiting government responsiveness to the public at large. Finally, program evaluations encourage agencies and the Congress to legislate more precise regulations and laws, as well as encouraging the Congress to provide more resources to achieve the value of effectiveness.

One can argue that the internal financial and management controls promoted by GAO evaluators are necessary to insure that tax dollars are properly spent. That may be true in some or even many of the cases where the auditors find deficiencies. But that is not the point. From the perspective of effective management, more controls are not necessarily welcomed. Most administrative appointees and career officials feel that they are perfectly capable of assuring economy, efficiency, and effectiveness in their agencies and are accountable to the Congress and to the public for doing so.

Again from their point of view, agency officials feel that their responsibility to manage is often hindered by constant GAO oversight, because Congress is more disposed to accept GAO findings than to listen to agency positions. For example, after twenty-eight years in government, during which he served as the Deputy in four cabinet-level agencies, Frank Carlucci recently observed that it was "becoming more difficult to accomplish a mission in government." As he went on to say,

> we put a premium on over-the-shoulder watchers, whether they're congressional staffers, investigative reporters, the Freedom of Information Act, White House supervisors, *or more auditors, more inspectors*—all of which are good things—but we have to keep them in balance. We have to put an equal premium on the guy who accomplishes his mission, takes a risk, and we have to reward him commensurate with his achievement. We do not do that in government.[39]

All this, of course, does not prove that GAO reports do in fact establish bigger government. It only speaks to the disposition of the reports to do so. In the next sections, we will discuss what impact GAO reports have on Congress and the executive branch, and why.

THE GAO AND CONGRESS

The two cultures through which the GAO has passed reflect the dilemmas in the relationship between the GAO and Congress. During the McCarl era and the culture of control, the GAO tried to dominate bureaucratic behavior from the legislative branch. With the culture of oversight, the Office pursued a new strategy in which it sought to maintain cognizance over executive branch agencies and to respond to congressional needs for information and evaluation of public policy and administration.

As these two cultural epochs suggest, to influence existing public policy and administration, Congress must both oversee and control. To oversee, it must gather information to find out what has happened in a policy arena as a result of laws Congress has enacted. It must discover, through investigations and hearings, what executive branch appointees and bureaucrats have done and are doing. Control is the assertion of congressional will. Congress, relying on the information gained in oversight, must come to a collective judgment on what should be done within a policy area and then insure its desires are carried out. The devices for carrying out this judgment include its power to authorize, to appropriate, and to budget.[40]

Oversight and control of existing policy and administration are not central to congressional concerns. As Richard Fenno has taught us, members of Congress value three things: reelection, influence in their chamber, and influence in some area of public policy.[41] Reelection, perforce, is valued over everything else. It is not assured. Members of Congress live in a contentious environment which generates great uncertainty. Regardless of the fact that many members seeking a return to Office are in fact reelected, there are sufficient exceptions to convince each one that he or she could be defeated in a forthcoming contest.[42]

To seek influence in the chamber and over some area of public policy, members of Congress specialize and initiate. They find one or perhaps two areas that will both satisfy their interests and call attention to their activities, thereby enhancing their prospects for reelection. Traditionally, members have found that the greatest payoffs lie in initiating new legislation. Such legislation can be used to satisfy constituencies, to gather support and respect from colleagues in the chamber, and to transform policy in the member's chosen field.

Oversight and control of existing public policy and administration, or what I will call review, can be dangerous. Review can stir up interest groups or the folks back home in unexpected and potentially harmful ways.[43] Thus, to investigate medicare may suggest to the retired community that hostility is intended toward a program on which that community is heavily dependent. Furthermore, the details and varied impacts of any program are so complex that members are reluctant to invest the time and effort to learn them. Members will venture into such terrain under some conditions. Where they feel at risk electorally and they see potential for publicity, they may become involved. Also where a national scandal unfolds which may embarrass the Congress or its committees or harm key constituencies, as in the grain example, members will investigate and propose changes. A few members, such as Congressman Les Aspin and Senator William Proxmire, have emphasized oversight and control in areas where they have particular expertise. Both appear to have found both personal satisfaction and electoral rewards for their efforts.[44]

In spite of these factors, oversight and control of existing policy and administration continue to be exercised on Capitol Hill. Committees are the primary actors in these activities. Until the advent of the budget committees, the appropriations committeees dominated the review of existing programs. However, even their efforts have primarily been focused not on established programs, but on new ones. The budget committees have recently eclipsed the traditional dominance of the appropriations committees and have become more salient in the committee pecking order.[45] These committees are not disposed to detailed review, but rather are preoccupied with fiscal policy and shaping targets for general categories of expenditures.

Review of existing programs is no more important in other committees either. The government affairs committees do conduct oversight hearings, but in no coherent fashion. The legislative or authorization committees generally see oversight and control as threatening to the programs and policies which they have so carefully fostered.

Thus, at best, oversight and control of existing public policy and administration are latent functions, which members of Congress and committees occasionally do exercise. When they do, their information comes from a plethora of sources, most of which are outside the legislative branch.[46] Lobbyists, analysts in private think tanks, consultants with policy expertise and bureaucratic experience, and scholars in universities can be found to confer with members or testify before Congress for virtually any government program. Executive branch officials and ranking bureaucrats are still another source of information.

Most of the work done in oversight is done by congressional staffers. Given the growth in the federal government and the broadened responsibilities of legislators, less preferred functions are done by the staff. As one committee staff director pointed out, the "nitty gritty of oversight is done by staffers," who do this work "with the tacit support of congressmen. They expect that you will follow up on things."[47]

From this discussion, one must infer that the GAO has not significantly promoted businesslike government through oversight. Certainly, as in the grain scandal or AWACS examples described above, the GAO can play a role. But that role is decidedly a subsidiary one in which the GAO supports congressional staffers who have become the barons of legislative oversight of existing policy and administration.[48]

The reasons for such a subsidiary GAO role are fourfold. First, members of Congress and GAO evaluators value different things. Members of Congress value reelection and influence, not efficiency and effectiveness in government. Second, with the growth of congressional staffs, members must focus more and more of their time on their own enterprises; little time is left to follow the findings developed by GAO evaluators. Third, the action in Congress has shifted from the appropriations process to the budget process. The budget committees are principally served by the Congressional Budget Office, not the GAO. What the GAO finds in its audits may potentially save the government millions of dollars, whereas the more pressing budget issues deal with billions of dollars of deficit. Fourth and finally, members of Congress and their staffers do not find their preferred sources of information in the legislative branch. Outsiders can provide details and analyses more quickly than GAO evaluators, who are dominated by an arduous fault-finding repertoire.

This conclusion that reports are not crucial in promoting businesslike government through congressional oversight in substantiated by the details of how Congress actually relies on the GAO. Office evaluations are at once a symbol of executive accountability, a form of oversight, an occasional bludgeon to achieve programmatic ends, and sometimes a tool for electoral activities. The Office serves, first, as a symbol to the Congress that executive branch decision making is accessible to legislative review. Enabled by its unique statutory access to and cognizance over agency personnel and programs, the auditors can provide congressional committees with details of organizational behavior and program performance. Clearly, much of the GAO-related legislation since the second World War can be considered as a concerted effort to open up the executive branch to congressional scrutiny through the audit.

The Congress also has recently provided for audit of previously sacrosanct agencies. For instance the Internal Revenue Service and the Bureau of Alcohol, Tobacco and Firearms had long been accorded independence from the legislative audit. In the 1977 battle to bring these agencies to heel, the House Government Operations Committee pointed out that without GAO review, "Congress has no independent assurance that [these agencies] are carrying out operations in an efficient, effective and economical manner."[49]

Thus the GAO serves as a comforting symbol to Congress that "continuous watchfulness"—using the terms of the 1946 Legislative Reorganization Act—is being exercised over the executive branch. So public institutions are important symbols not only to their clientele outside of government but to their constituents within the government. They provide reassurance that certain functions are being discharged and thereby permit Congress and political executives charged with those functions to pursue other, preferred activities.

The legislative audit is itself a form of oversight. In numerous statements, members of Congress have fully conceded that part of their oversight responsibility has devolved to the GAO. The House Appropriations Committee has called the Office a "highly essential instrument of legislative oversight in checking the efficiency of government programs and the propriety of government expenditures." Members of the Senate Committee on Government Operations have labeled the GAO as "one of the Legislative Branch's principal oversight agencies."[50] This concession of responsibility is not in consonance with the original congressional designs for the modern GAO. The 1946 Legislative Reorganization Act, which first detailed congressional responsibility for oversight of executive agencies, envisioned that GAO audit reports would serve as a stimulus for oversight and did not conceive that the legislative audit would be itself a form of oversight.[51]

Congressional disinterest in oversight is significant, for it highlights an alteration in congressional role expectations in an era of big government. In essence it suggests that Congress has conceded this responsibility to others. Unfortunately for the Congress—and the nation— abandonment of sustained oversight to the accountants will not insure executive accountability. Despite GAO's broad mandate, its reviews are not influential with agency professionals unless backed up by congressional involvement.

When members or staffers do wish to intervene, the GAO provides a convenient bludgeon to express displeasure or to stir up interest groups attentive to agency programs. Where congressional staff or members of Congress are dissatisfied with agency management or program performance, the GAO—with its preoccupation with fault finding—can be employed to dig up deficiencies to embarrass administrators. As Herb Roback, the late staff director of the House Committee on Government Operations, observed, critical GAO reports "put agency heads and program managers on notice that improvements are expected if future authorizations and funding are to be allowed."[52]

The GAO can also help build support for new legislative initiatives. Just as policy evaluation shapes the climate of opinion surrounding an issue and serves to mobilize government action,[53] so too can GAO evaluations recognize the existence of a particular problem and thereby involve program and agency constituencies to support a legislative solution. As exemplified above in the grain scandal report, such evaluations are usually employed in tandem with other techniques for coalition-building such as hearings and press releases. The GAO evaluations by themselves seldom, if ever, generate widespread concern over an issue.

Finally, the GAO can be a useful tool for electoral activities. Any congressionally-initiated evaluation invariably occasions at least two press releases—and hopefully a press conference. The request for an evaluation report permits the member of Congress to claim credit for putting the GAO onto a serious problem faced by the government and to take a position on the evils of this or that program, the swollen nature of government, or the inefficiency of agency management. Once the GAO has provided the member with a report, it waits for forty-eight hours or so before releasing the report to the public in order to permit the legislator to issue another press release or hold a press conference again claiming credit and taking a position.

These press releases frequently get media attention, especially in the trade press. For instance, *The Army Times* and its sisters, *The Navy Times* and *The Air Force Times*, are very attentive to releases which concern the military. Senator Proxmire and Congressman Aspin can almost always expect attention from these publications when they release GAO reports. Local newspapers are also attentive to press releases from local members of Congress. This media attention can then be reprinted in the legislators' newsletters, just in case the folks back home did not see it the first time.

THE GAO AND GOVERNMENT

This book has emphasized an important theme which typifies the personality of the legislative audit. That is, the auditors are partisans of economy, efficiency, and effectiveness in government. This partisanship reflects the frequently repeated congressional demand that the GAO work to make the government more businesslike.

In a capitalist society, after all, it should come as no surprise that "practical business policy" would be applied to the affairs of government. Yet clearly many of the norms which the auditors and businessmen share are irrelevant to the operations of government and inconsistent with the values of a democratic state. Democratic governments operate through advocacy and bargaining. As Harold Seidman has pointed out, "Economy and efficiency are demonstrably not the prime purposes of public administration. . . . The basic issues of Federal organization and administration relate to power: who shall control it and to what ends?"[54]

Furthermore, post-industrial societies are forced to confront complex social and economic issues for which there may be no solutions. For such issues, costs cannot be calculated until what can and cannot be done is determined, and such a determination is usually in itself costly.[55] Equally disturbing to the auditors' businesslike norms, experimentation to determine what can be done is likely to overlap and duplicate efforts in other agencies. Finally, experimentation is seldom effective during the initial phases of the policy process[56] and is thereby subject to GAO criticism.

Executive branch operations are also conditioned by the motivations and resources of public officials whose aspirations differ considerably from those in the private sector. Political appointees and bureaucrats are not likely to adhere to GAO values, nor be swayed by GAO reports. Effective management in the public sector is significantly different from effectiveness in the private sector. To mention several of the differences, agency executives must, unlike their counterparts in business, accept goals and operate through structures established by other organizations, rely on personnel over whose careers they have little or no control, and apply limited resources to objectives which are truly massive in scope.[57] In such an environment, public managers can only expect to survive through political skills, not through studied adherence to the businesslike norms of economy, efficiency, and effectiveness.

Furthermore, GAO evaluation reports do not fit the needs of public managers. These managers must attend to a universe of claimants: congressional demands, shifts in direction and policy as propounded by presidents, pressure from clientele groups for continued or more support, resistance from public interest groups opposed to agency programs, and shifting attention from the press. Thus GAO evaluation reports are but one of the many clamorers for attention in the public manager's universe, and a minor one at that. Only when these reports are used by claimants more central to the manager's concerns is he or she likely to take a serious and sustained interest. Therefore, we are left with an ironic outcome. Although evaluation reports encourage government growth, agency managers and legislators don't take them seriously enough to insure that the evaluators consistent call for more resources and program rationalization are usually achieved.

The auditors' values are also inconsistent with democratic values. The political system which has evolved out of the American Constitution is in itself rife with redundancy: separated branches which share power; federalism in which local governments, states, and the federal government compete for influence and resources; overlapping terms of office; and a multitude of other arrangements which serve to check legislative and executive power.[58] The American system celebrates pluralism and consensus. In fact, as Theodore Lowi has argued, the government seeks to create groups where none exist.[59] In turn these groups strive to establish government bureaus and then agencies to defend their interests,[60] thereby insuring an even less businesslike government. For a democratic government, good decisions gain consensus and ignore such external criteria as economy, efficiency, and effectiveness in government.[61]

We are left with one last hope for promoting businesslike government, that is, that somehow the GAO watchdog can attract enough attention that needed changes will be made. As Mary Douglas and Aaron Wildavsky have suggested, watchdogs can "stop people from doing some bad things."[62] But if more is wanted—and clearly many observers have hoped for more from the GAO[63]—then watchdogs need to be endowed differently. They need the power to force change, not to just watch and bark.

To do more, the GAO watchdogs or evaluators need more than the power to publicize. Publicity can on occasion catch the attention of those endowed with the constitutional authority to enforce change.

That is, publicity can interest presidents, members of Congress, judges and political appointees. Yet more often each of these actors has other more immediate concerns which relate to survival and perpetuation or enhancement of their own influence. Unless the watchdog's bark can somehow be joined with the bite of authority, his warning will be lost in the political storms which rage at the centers of institutional power. In essence the warning is drowned out in the legislative branch by each member's concerns for reelection, influence in the chamber, and public policy results.

But to give the GAO more than the power to publicize—at this juncture there is little left to give the GAO in terms of access to government policy making and administration—is to deny members of Congress the tools they need to pursue their preferred ends. For the GAO to be able to force change in executive bureaucracies, the Office would need the power to control, which is the power to legislate. Such a concession by Congress is unthinkable.

Thus we are faced with an apparent irony. The GAO and its profesional auditors have successfully adapted themselves to a dynamic, almost whimsical environment that can simultaneously call for more opinions about the viability of agency management systems as in the Lipscomb Report and then later criticize the GAO for asserting opinions in its reports and making recommendations as in the Holified Report. And yet in spite of this adaptation, the auditors' craft is *not used* by either the Congress or agency managers *to promote more efficient or effective government.* We are then left with a muddle: has the GAO transformed itself successfully or not? What indices are we to use to assess organizational success? The last chapter will seek to resolve these and other remaining questions.

SUMMARY, PART III

L indsay Warren, Joseph Campbell, and Elmer Staats were the architects and engineers for the culture of oversight. During this epoch, they and their elites imposed a new strategy of reporting on the GAO. That strategy was composed of five components: responsiveness to Congress, cognizance over agency operations, professionalization of the audit staff, evaluation of agency operations, and precision in reporting. To police that strategy, to insure predictability and to maintain organizational values, a structure was necessary. By the last half of the 1970s, that structure included: a flat organizational hierarchy and a large institutional staff, elaborate planning mechanisms to coordinate GAO output and monitor environmental developments, and a fully rationalized personnel system which promoted in the auditors a strong sense of organizational identification.

Out of this strategy and structure came an organizational culture which consisted of redesigned rituals and a new ideology. The dominant ritual in the GAO was the evaluation repertoire which was performed by four types of auditors. Line auditors conducted and auditor managers supervised the evaluations; then staff auditors reviewed the evaluations, and auditor advocates marketed them.

The evaluation repertoire itself was devoted to discovering, recording, and reporting deficiencies to Congress. These deficiencies were found in agency financial systems, management routines, and programs. Regardless of the matter under review, all evaluations were found to be alike. They employed unwritten rules and shortcuts handed down from auditor to auditor over decades of auditing. To contend with agency resistance to their fault-finding repertoire, the auditors used a variety of techniques to manage conflict and tactics to circumvent or confront executive branch managers.

Another facet of culture is ideology. The evaluators' ideology was composed of norms for auditor dress and for behavior around agency managers, and their myths included a sense of superiority and a belief in the ability of government to be more businesslike. Finally, the ideology was composed of several core values, which included: the importance of audit for government; the necessity of auditor involvement in agency affairs; and the concern for economy, efficiency and effectiveness in management and programs.

Out of an organization's strategy, structure, and culture comes an output by public professionals. For the public professionals in the GAO, this output was evaluation reports. These reports promoted bigger government by recommending more resources be applied to financial and managerial systems as well as to many programs; they also called for more regulations and more law to rationalize agency operations. In spite of this promotion, the evaluation reports had only a modest impact on Congress and minimal influence with agency managers in promoting more efficient and businesslike government. This was so because the dominant values of GAO auditors, as reflected in their reports, were inconsistent with congressional values and with the values of agency program managers.

Congress did use the GAO, but not to promote businesslike government as the auditors would have liked. That is, the Congress found the

GAO useful principally as a symbol that executive agencies were being overwatched. Congress also used the Office as a bludgeon and as an electoral device. The evaluators and the reports they wrote could be used to coerce executive agencies into conformance with congressional wishes. The reports could also be used to advertise to constituents a position which members felt would be useful in their quests for reelection. As we will argue in the final chapter, these are more meaningful measures of organizational effectiveness, and thus the GAO's transformation must be measured as highly successful.

CHAPTER 8

Conclusion

.

Thus by 1981, the General Accounting Office had changed profoundly from the organization it was in 1940 when Lindsay Warren assumed his duties as Comptroller General of the United States. In 1940, the audit was strictly a technical affair centralized in GAO headquarters offices and involving virtually no professionals. It was the GAO's green-eyeshade era, in which clerks arduously compared vouchers with strict interpretations of congressional intent. By 1981, professional GAO auditors, most of whom were recruited as accountants, conducted decentralized evaluations of agency finances, management, and programs.

The pace of change during this forty-year period would at first seem to be rapid. During much of Lindsay Warren's tenure, changes in the size of the Office were pronounced as the organization swelled to 14,219 and then contracted to 5,913 by his departure.[1] During both the Warren and Staats eras, new legislation expanding the mandate of the Office was enacted frequently.

Yet these essentially surface alterations are not change in the sense we have discussed here. As we have used the term, organizational change means alterations in culture and output. Which is to say that the rituals and ideology of public professionals, as well as their products, must be transformed if true change is to be achieved. Using these deeper and more enduring measures, we can say that the GAO changed in an incremental fashion over this forty-year period. The dominant ritual, the evaluation repertoire, shifted slowly, with new tactics and techniques added each year to circumvent and confront agency resistance. The ideology of oversight was constructed cautiously as, for example, the principles of reporting and cognizance took hold and emphasized such values as the importance of audit and of evaluator presence in agency affairs. Finally, the evaluation reports themselves began slowly to build a body of recommendations for Congress to make agency management and programs more businesslike.

Although year-to-year change was gradual, in the end it had accumulated significantly. There was very little backsliding in the three eras which constituted this forty-year epoch. Given the very different personalities of the three Comptrollers who presided over each of these eras, this lack of backsliding would at first appear surprising. To address this issue, we must first review why the GAO had changed at all. Both of these issues suggest still a third. That is, given all this change, can the GAO as an organization be considered successful by 1981?

ASSESSING ORGANIZATIONAL SUCCESS

The theory articulated in Chapter 1 noted that organizations either change in response to environmental alterations or become ineffectual. The propositions developed there and at the beginning of succeeding chapters argued that environmental shifts build up over time and that most organizations tend to change only when the disparities between the environment and organizational output become dramatic. Furthermore, dissonance between an organization and its environment is necessary for change, but not sufficient. Also important for cultural change are leaders, agency elites, and flexible technologies.

This framework fits developments in the GAO. As discussed in Chapter 3, environmental shifts did build up during the 1930s and 1940s and continued into the late 1970s. These included new accounting and evaluation technologies, the New Deal and a permanently mobilized national security apparatus that expanded the state, and numerous changes in Congress spurred in part by these developments. These shifts forced the GAO to change and keep pace with its environment or face organizational irrelevance. Furthermore, Congress prodded the GAO along through numerous laws and nonstatutory demands that promoted strategic and structural changes. To cite one of many possible examples, House committees pushed Campbell to increase the number of GAO supergrade positions.

Institutional leaders were also crucial in changing the GAO. As the propositions developed in Chapter 3 emphasized, leaders have an important role in generating strategies, agendas, and structures. The most successful for the GAO were Warren and Staats. Although Campbell figured prominently in professionalizing the Office, he failed to recognize the continuing shifts in the GAO's environment. For instance, he did not see that congressional expectations for the GAO were shifting in the 1960s and that new evaluation technologies (such as the planning, programming, and budgeting system) had to be considered by the Office. His failure to "watch outward" led to the Holifield Hearings, which created organizational chaos as dispirited career elites found the core technology under assault. This failure may be ascribed to the fact that the entire Office leadership retreated into the core technology without even considering whether that technology was relevant to Congress.[2] When organizations fail in such a fashion, the blame is properly laid at the feet of appointed leaders.

Warren and Staats, on the other hand, spent much of their time "watching outward." Both realized that change in organizational output was imperative and insured that organizational shifts occurred to insure that change was achieved. Yet their efforts went beyond these shifts. Warren became the most visible spokesman for a continued congressional presence in the budget process by insisting that executive-centered calls for reform by the Brownlow and Hoover Commissions were a serious mistake. Staats was prominent in testifying before congressional committees on the proper direction for congressional staff and budget reform in the 1970s, promoting legislation for independent inspector generals in each federal department and agency, and seeking to improve the quality of auditing in state and local governments. In essence both Comptrollers were watching out to assess and test environmental developments to insure the GAO was not surprised by external events. Thus one measure of capable leadership is whether leaders transcend their organizations to play roles in shaping the environment, rather than awaiting environmental developments and seeking only to respond to them.

As with environmental shifts and leaders, core technologies and elites are also crucial for organizational change. As the principal mediators between leaders and organizational professionals, elites serve to protect the core technology and insure shifts in organizational structure are implemented. Although buffeted by the Holified Hearings, the core technology of auditing (or evaluation as Staats preferred to call it) unfolded in a slow, coherent fashion during the epoch of oversight. Evolution insured continued organizational viability in the face of the "bloomin' buzzin' confusion"[3] which, to uninitiated professionals, characterizes organizational environments. The auditing repertoire was a comforting ritual which told the GAO auditors what to do and how to do it even in the face of demands for broader audits of management and programs. Without such a ritual, the auditors could not have coped with change.

Elites must also manage structural change. The career elite established a planning mechanism in the Warren era and the personnel system during Campbell's era. In the 1970s, the executive elite and career counter-elite were charged with adapting planning mechanisms and the personnel system to the strategic principles refined by Staats.

So change in the GAO occurred because the environment demanded it, two highly competent leaders were on hand to promote it, and elites were available to implement it. Clearly, as we discussed in Chapter 5, there was considerable resistance to the changes wrought by appointed and career leadership. The green-eyeshade auditors of the control era, the investigators, and the lawyers were opposed to change. This recalcitrance was overcome in the end, because the Congress promoted change, and appointed leaders were able to find support within the institution and the outside profession of commercial auditing. Without environmental pressure, new leadership, internal institutional support, and a new technology to address organizational needs, change in the fundamental sense of transformed professional behavior is not possible.

For most public organizations most of the time, the felicitous congruence of each of these four factors—environmental pressure, leadership, internal support, and new technology—is seldom achieved. Any one or even two of these factors would seem insufficient for fundamental organizational change, that is, the transformation of professional behavior. Without environmental pressure, change is unlikely to be considered. Without energetic leadership, there is no recognition of the need for change. Without internal support, the ever-present institutional friction cannot be overcome. And without new technology, there is no new direction available for the institution. Therefore, it seems clear that once organizations have come to be dominated by professional repertoires and ideologies, they are very resistant to change.

We can now address the issue of why professional change in the GAO seemed to compound in one direction. Simply stated, backsliding was inhibited by environmental shifts and demands. One may not necessarily agree that congressional or technological changes over this forty-year period were linear. Certainly there were developments such as the Holifield Hearings which suggested that the GAO should retrench into financial auditing.

Yet overall one can see that environmental trends for the GAO ran to increasing complexity and disaggregation. Evaluation technology grew more sophisticated and rich over this epoch, as operations research was developed in World War II, systems analysis skills added in the 1960s, and new technologies devised by the social science and business administration communities were added in the 1970s. Another trend was the continuing disaggregation of Congress as party leadership and committee power were eroded by the activities of subcommittees and individual members. These trends promoted GAO adherence to the strategy of reporting espoused by Lindsay Warren, by reinforcing the strategic principles of responsiveness to Congress, evaluation, and professionalization.

Laws also inhibited organizational backsliding. The expanding body of enabling legislation over this period was built one law atop the other such that the aggregate was consistent. These laws continued to echo the 1921 Budget and Accounting Act's emphasis on the GAO as the keeper of the flame for businesslike government. They also emphasized and reemphasized the five principles laid down by the prophet Lindsay Warren.

Our final task in this section is to assess organizational success of the GAO. In the last chapter, I essentially argued that Congress and agency managers were not reliant on GAO audit reports to *promote efficiency in government*. That is, the dominant organizational output was not used in a fashion which promoted businesslike government. What we have not discussed were the trends in usage of these reports or the suitability of this measure of efficacy. The trends appear positive. Very little use had been made of GAO audit reports or recommendations in the 1930s. By 1981, GAO efforts occasionally were important in congressional deliberations as in the examples of the grain scandal and AWACS. Although this trend occurred in the face of extensive environmental turbulence, it cannot be considered sufficient to label the GAO as a successful organization.

However, in combination with other facets of GAO performance and with the transformation of the Office, one must label the GAO a successful organization. It would seem that successful organizations do not necessarily end up serving the purposes for which they were apparently intended, but ultimately do occupy an ecological niche which assures long-term survival.[4] As we noted in Chapter 7, the avowed purpose of the GAO to promote businesslike government is inconsistent with congressional values and needs. Consequently, one should not be surprised that elements in Congress adapted the Office to their own ends.

Congress needs a variety of tools to use in its constitutionally mandated struggle with the executive branch and the presidency. Demands for more businesslike government are but small arms in the congressional arsenal. Larger guns include those used to coerce executive agencies and to maintain electorates independent of the president. Thus GAO reports were employed to bludgeon executive agencies into compliance with congressional ends. They also were used by members of Congress to emphasize their independence from the program of the President, thereby protecting them from reliance on presidential coattails during elections. We must then conclude that by this standard of success—whether agency output is useful to its environment—the GAO has been successful. That is, it has admirably served the political needs of the Congress. The other measure of success—whether an agency achieves its mission as that mission is defined by internal ideology (for the GAO, whether it has promoted businesslike government)—is essentially irrelevant to outsiders who look to the organization to serve their own purposes. Thus external expectations about performance are not necessarily consistent with internal organizational aspirations.

Finally that the GAO was able to maintain its organizational essence over this forty-year period is in itself a measure of success. If the fundamental prize in any organization is its character,[5] then GAO leaders and elites were successful in maintaining that character more or less intact over these four decades. Simultaneously, they also managed to enhance the organization's mandate such that its responsibility for overseeing established agencies and programs was expanded. Thus Peter Smith is correct when he asserts that change succeeds in organizations when the "requisite skills, resources, procedures and motivation are present," and there exists "a prior history of external pressure and internal tension, coupled with the use of both external and internal change agents."[6]

Therefore to assess success in public organizations, one must focus on the environment. One measure of success is the extent of environmental use of organizational products. Such a measure should not, however, focus on whether elements in the task environment use organizational output in a fashion consistent with internal ideology, which in the GAO's case was to promote businesslike government. Rather one should consider whether that output serves environmental purposes, as elements in that environment construe the proper purposes for the organization. For the GAO, Congress perceives that the auditors are to serve in its political battles with such rivals as the President and bureaucratic agencies.

Another measure of organizational success is the internal reaction to environmental changes. Here one should focus on core rituals and ascertain whether those rituals have been modified to fit new environmental demands. Finally, one can measure organizational mandates over time. Where environmental actors have enriched an organization's mandates or substantially broadened them, then the organization can be said to have been successful.

The reader at this point might reasonably object that the GAO is a special case. That is, the theory and supporting propositions developed here may nicely unravel the GAO, but not other organizations with more complex core technologies and demanding external environments. To address this objection, the case of another organization will be developed briefly. In the final sections of the book, we will compare developments in these two organizations, critique the theory, and then return to our opening point about the importance of organizational studies.

A SECOND CASE: THE ARMY IS TRANSFORMED

U p to the Spanish American War, the United States Army and its parent, the Department of War, had not changed much. In fact its organization looked very much like that of September 4, 1792, when the field Army was established under the new Constitution. Even the War of 1812 and the Civil War had imposed no permanent changes either on Army organization or relationships between the Regular Army and the National Guard units controlled by the states. Following the Civil War, a period of isolation from a more liberal American society had begun the process of reform and professionalization, as the officer corps busied itself with chasing Indians, assessing the military implications of the Civil War, and studying military developments in Europe.[7]

This internal professional reform movement was not sufficient to transform the Army. Environmental prods and new leadership were also needed. The immediate spark was the Spanish American War, which overwhelmed the Army's logistical and support system. A public scandal ensued over the lack of planning, preparation, and coordination within the Department of War.

To partially relieve the tension, President McKinley appointed the Dodge Commission to investigate. The Commission found that Congress had imposed extensive restrictions on War Department bureaus which thereby constrained the Secretary of War from coordinating them in wartime.[8] In fact the story of War Department reform from 1899 to 1947 is of Congress reluctantly relinquishing control and then reneging on administrative improvements it had previously supported. The Department was, to use James Hewes words, a "hydra-headed holding company."[9] The Commission recommended changes using the modern industrial corporation as a model.

The Commission's recommendations were symptomatic of deeper forces at work in America which were to transform the Army during this period. New organizational forms had evolved to cope with industrialization, and the Dodge Commission was only one of several sources calling for the application of these corporate forms to public agencies. In addition, as American economic power flourished, U.S. political elites came to realize that the nation would eventually be forced to play a role in international affairs. Managing new American colonies in Cuba, Puerto Rico, and the Philippines after the Spanish-American War was but the first manifestation of this trend. Not only was the Army unsuited to the demands of administering these colonies—a task it was chosen to do, it was also incapable of defending American economic interests abroad. In comparison to new military organizations on the Continent, the Department of War and the Army seemed positively ossified.[10]

Strategy in the Culture of Preparedness   To these new challenges came a new generation of appointed leadership composed of progressive conservatives who understood and sympathized with professional line officers (officers of infantry, cavalry, and artillery, as opposed to technical officers of ordnance, quartermaster, and other support services) and their demands for military preparedness. The messiah for the modern Army was Elihu Root, and his most noted apostles were Henry Stimson and Leonard Wood. Root had been a highly successful lawyer in New York City when President McKinley appointed him as Secretary of War. A skilled conciliator, he was regarded by McKinley and Theodore Roosevelt as their strongest cabinet member.[11]

Henry Stimson started his successful law career in Root's firm. He was selected as Secretary of War by President Taft in 1911 and served until 1913. During World War I, he saw action as an artillery colonel.

After the War he was an Ambassador to Nicaragua, Governor General in the Philippines, and Herbert Hoover's Secretary of State. He returned to the War Department as Secretary in 1940 and ended his public service there in 1945.[12]

Root's other apostle was a soldier, but a rather curious mix of professional and politician by careerist standards. A Harvard Medical School graduate, Leonard Wood joined the Army as a contract surgeon and rose through the ranks. Later he helped Roosevelt organize the Rough Riders, fought in Cuba, and was promoted by McKinley from Medical Corps captain to Regular Army brigadier general. Roosevelt appointed him Chief of Staff in 1910 where he remained until 1914. Then as commander of the eastern region at Governor's Island, New York, he lectured and published widely on the need for military preparedness and universal military training.[13]

The strategy and structure for the culture of military preparedness were designed by Elihu Root and brilliantly articulated in his reports as Secretary of War and in several memos on issues such as officer education. They were popularized by the books, articles, and speeches of Wood, whom Russell Weigley has described as "the great evangelist of a citizen Army."[14] The structure was implemented by Stimson during his two tours as Secretary of War and throughout the period 1899–1947 by the career line officers who either helped originate or came to share their vision.

The strategy for this culture involved four principles.[15] First the organization should be weaned from congressional dominance—with its preconception of the "military-as-pork-barrel"—and given the central purpose of preparing for war. Second the size of the standing Army should be increased and consolidated into a few posts to enhance training. The forty-nine posts, consisting of only about 650 men each, spread over twenty-four states and territories served the needs of an Indian-fighting Army perhaps, but not one which would expect to fight a foreign power with brigade and division-sized units.

The third tenet was managerial. It sought explicitly to subordinate the Army to civilian control and impose a clear hierarchy on the Department of War, making it more responsive to central direction from civil and military authority. Finally, to resolve the established tension between the standing and citizen armies, the new strategy sought to professionalize the National Guard and integrate it and other reserves into the active Army in peacetime for effective functioning of the "two armies" during time of war.

The legal mandates to legitimize the new strategy and structure included the General Staff and Militia Acts of 1903. They first established a General Staff Corps to be headed by a Chief of Staff who would serve "under the direction of the President or of the Secretary of War." Officers of the General Staff were to be line officers who could serve no more than four years in Washington. The principle of universal military obligation and the professionalization of the National Guard were contained in The Militia Act. It declared that all able-bodied men were to constitute a Reserve Militia and that the National Guard was to be the Organized Militia and a reserve for the Regular Army. The Guard had to meet higher standards of training and readiness, standards which were to be set by Regular line officers.

Structuring for Preparedness.   The composition of the professional elite before 1899 differed during peace and war. During peacetime, line officers dominated the field Army, while technical officers, with their permanent assignments to Department of War bureaus, dominated events in the Capital. During wartime, career line officers vied with National Guard officers and with officers who had political appointments for top commands.[16]

To resolve this strife, Root and Stimson chose line officers as the elite profession and general officers of the line and General Staff as the career elite. Technical and Guard officers were subordinated at the highest level to this career elite. This was done by eliminating permanent assignments of technical officers to Washington and empowering the new Chief of Staff to supervise all elements in the Army to include the bureaus. In turn, the Chief was subject to the direction of the Secretary of War. By involving line officers in the affairs of the Guard, line ascendancy was further enhanced.

The personnel system also changed. In recruiting, higher goals were set. To meet the needs of colonial administration, Root enlarged the forces for Philippine occupation; the Army leadership thereafter argued for and received a larger standing Army. In the period 1871 to 1897, the force varied between 26,000 and 29,000 men; after 1900 it never fell below 64,000 men.[17] At West Point, course standards and admission requirements were stiffened, and a large-scale building program instituted.

The training and socialization processes for officers were also changed. The Army school system was reestablished after the War and refined. In a 1901 War Department order, Root required that all large posts establish or reestablish schools to instruct officers in the theory and practice of war; in time these schools became branch-specific courses of instruction to teach tactics to company grade officers. Officers who performed well at these schools were to be sent on to more advanced schools such as Fort Leavenworth, called at first the Army School of the Line and later the Command and General Staff College. Thereafter, officers were to attend the Army War College, which Root himself initiated to train officers in the art and science of war.

To resolve the enduring debates over the relationship between the Regular Army and the National Guard and over military training for citizens, Root and his apostles sought not only to include Guard officers in Army schools, but also to train civilians. While still Chief of Staff, Wood organized summer training camps for college youths and later stimulated the Plattsburgh idea to train business and professional men. Wood, ever the evangelist, also argued that citizen soldiers could be trained in six months for military service. This idea was not widely accepted by the line professionals, but was ultimately demonstrated by Wood himself during World War I.[18]

The new leadership also assailed the procedures for promotion. Heretofore promotion was based on seniority, with many years required for officers to rise to the grade of lieutenant colonel or colonel. Root and Stimson both felt that promotion should be based on merit, that is by demonstrated performance and potential in the service. Their proposals were not to be implemented immediately, but in time they were accepted.

Hierarchical changes included not only the institution of a General Staff and the Chief of Staff, but also the consolidation of small Army units into four divisions, the creation of a Joint War-Navy Board and an Army League to promote war preparedness. As the Army's "board of directors," the General Staff, as developed by Root and reorganized by Wood, was to plan and coordinate all Army activities in preparing for war. These responsibilities translated into the functions of gathering information, coordinating personnel and technical matters, and preparing mobilization plans for war.[19]

In their efforts to reduce the number of "hitching post forts" spread across the United States, Stimson and Wood found congressional resistance too intense. Intent on protecting the largess from these small posts, Congress became so aroused that it called for Wood's removal as Chief of Staff, and both Stimson and Root were needed to persuade

President Taft to keep him. If they could not rearrange the Army into larger garrisons to permit troop maneuvers and speedy assembly in consonance with mobilization needs, Stimson and Wood turned to temporary concentrations and paper solutions. Wood organized a maneuver division in Texas. The ninety days required to assemble this force and the required gutting of regiments throughout the country for filling the division was both an embarrassment to the officer corps and an opportunity for the leadership. Both Stimson and Wood wrote articles emphasizing the nation's "helplessness to meet with trained troops any sudden emergency."[20]

Stimson then asked the War College to organize the Army around a divisional structure, a plan that called for four divisions. Stimson called in the Army's career elite and "hashed out" the procedures for such a radical shift. The plan was to be implemented almost immediately, when Stimson ordered the mobilization of the Second Division in southern Texas to meet the threat posed by the Mexican Civil War.

The new leadership also sought to reach out during this period. Recognizing the importance of coordination and joint planning with the Navy, Root pursuaded that Department to form a Joint Army and Navy Board which survived until the early stages of World War II, when it was replaced by a more vibrant mechanism. The final significant organizational change for the culture of preparedness was the creation of an Army League. Although not an organ of the government, the League was created in 1912 with the active support of Wood and his friend Frederic Huidekoper to promote military preparedness and a stronger Army.[21]

Out of this epoch dominated by the culture of preparedness came both the ascendancy of line officers in Army affairs and a new preoccupation with readiness. Certainly technical officers continued to be important in the bureaus, but by the end of World War II their position was clearly subordinate to the Chief of Staff and the General Staff. Root's, Stimson's, and Wood's reforms and proposals for reform were to be established and refined by successive Chiefs of Staff and by thoughtful professionals such as Brigadier General John McAuley Palmer.

The new status of the line officer was, of course, entirely satisfactory not only to this new elite profession but to the Army itself. By the arrangements of this new compact, the officer corps could be reasonably assured that civilian meddling in professional Army affairs would be reduced, for after all the Army was now firmly subordinate to civilian control by the Secretary of War. Yet, as Paul Hammond has pointed out, such subordination also meant that the Secretary of War was in many ways a captive of his Chief of Staff. Indeed the Chief was responsible for the activities of the entire Army to include the General Staff, the bureaus, and the field Army.[22]

This limitation aside, the Army did acquit itself well during this era. The real test of this new Army was not World War I, although Pershing and the American Expeditionary Force did conduct themselves with distinction, but rather World War II, when the efforts of Root and his apostles had been absorbed. In spite of being hamstrung by citizen indifference to military affairs and congressional reductions during the interwar years, the Army was called upon to prosecute a global war. A thoroughly professional and energetic corps of line and technical officers were to distinguish themselves not only in planning and coordinating the War, but in fighting it with daring and imagination. They were supplemented by Guard and citizen-dominated units that were integrated successfully into the Army and performed effectively.[23] Yet this success was tarnished by the fact that mobilization and commitment of forces to battle was a slow process. Also the Army was not able to convince the Congress or national elites of the importance of readiness. That development was to occur in the Army's next epoch, when the Cold War culture came to be dominant.

ORGANIZATIONAL CATASTROPHE AND CREATIVE LEADERSHIP

Clearly the cultural theory is useful in understanding a range of public organizations. It suggests the importance of critical periods in organizational development as well as the role of leaders and elites in addressing such periods.

Thus there would seem to be parallels among organizations in what Philip Selznick has called the "critical" experiences of institutions. Such experiences affect the organization's ability to "uphold its distinctive aims and values."[24] These experiences often involve catastrophes, as perceived by the organization's task environment, constituencies, or the public at large. Catastrophes modify elite rigidity, congressional resistance, and presidential recalcitrance. Career elites frequently spike change not only because altering organizational performance threatens their position, but also because their success, and therefore their sense of the institution, grew out of that performance.[25] Thus Adjutant General Ainsworth resisted Leonard Wood's efforts to assert control over the bureaus; later, after Stimson had dismissed him, Ainsworth allied himself with Wood's congressional opponents because he was convinced that reform efforts were antithetical to the Army's best interests.[26]

Congress resists organizational change as well. Its resistance can originate from either constitutional or parochial concerns. Congress opposed the Brownlow Committee's call to modify the GAO's mandate before World War II, because of its constitutional responsibility for appropriations. More parochial resistance to change was evident when the Congress strongly opposed the consolidation of the Army's "hitching-post forts" to permit maneuvers of larger forces.

Finally, presidential recalcitrance is frequently modified only by organizational catastophe. President McKinley recognized soon after the Spanish-American War began that Root's predecessor, Secretary of War Russell Alger, was mediocre and impulsive. Disposed to support his appointee in spite of these weaknesses, McKinley was only moved to dismiss him when public outcry over the Army's performance became intense.[27] It would seem that elected and appointed leaders are frequently unwilling to make dramatic performance change, and catastrophe is a necessity for spurring it.

Leadership is crucial to reviving institutions in the face of catastrophe or in volatile task environments. Such leadership requires the ability to improvise creatively. Creativity is needed to recognize the necessity for changing organizational rituals and ideologies as a precursor to transforming professional behavior. Creativity is also needed to recognize the utility of obstacles imposed by the task environment and by internal conflict as opportunities for promoting cultural change.[28] In the cases of the GAO and the Army, Warren and Root recognized that "operator" behavior had to change, that public and congressional calls for reform promoted such change, and that internal tensions between accountants and lawyers and between line and technical officers were useful prods to action.

Creativity is diagnostic, prescriptive, and mobilizing. Developments in an organization's environment must be given subjective meaning; in other words, they must be interpreted in terms of their implications for the organization and its professionals.[29] Thus Warren could argue that the Brownlow Committee proposals were a call for a new ritual and a new ideology, both of which would direct auditors to report to Congress instead of seeking to exercise control over the executive branch.

Prescription and mobilization entail the design of a course of action—a course we have described as composed of strategy and structure—

to mollify the task environment and to enlist internal support so as to impose that course of action. Root designed a new strategy to resolve the conflict between line and technical officers and then established line officers in the General Staff to insure his strategy was successful. Leaders must also improvise throughout their tenures by experimenting with strategic principles and structural components. Such improvisation recognizes the transient nature of organizational environments and the necessity to impose modifications to address external change. Thus Elmer Staats spent his entire fifteen-year term modifying the principles originally designed by Warren. As late as 1980, he was still reworking the principle of cognizance by promoting a bill to permit the GAO to seek agency documents through court injunctions; also in 1980, he created the Office of Program Evaluation to provide a structural spokesman for the principle of evaluation.

Another facet of improvisation is the search for legitimacy. If organizational change is to be lasting, then the dominant element in the organization's task environment must pass laws or issue orders or regulations confirming such changes. Warren, Staats, and Root all recognized this necessity; their terms were accentuated by public laws which legitimized the changes they made.

In comparing the relative success of GAO and Army leaders, one must conclude that longevity and flexibility promote more immediate organizational success. With the fifteen-year term and broad organizational mandate of the Comptroller General, Warren and Staats could design new strategic principles and structural components and then be around long enough to oversee their implementation. Root, like most political leaders in the executive branch, was Secretary of the Army for a much briefer period. His authority was circumscribed by statutory limitations and a suspicious Congress. The culture which Root sought to impose took some forty-five years and two world wars to become fully established.

DRAWBACKS TO THE CULTURAL THEORY

This theory and its supporting propositions are not without problems. My reservations about them are fivefold.

Level of Abstraction. The theory is perhaps too abstruse. It operates at a level of generalization which may not reveal enough to satisfy all students of organizational behavior. Such students may find that in trying to explain a great deal about organizational development, it ends up explaining nothing. That is, by its focus on environmental earthquakes, grand organizational strategy, structural atmospherics, and the impact these elements have on organizational culture and professional behavior, it tries to do too much.

And yet this cultural theory identifies significant issues which must be addressed in the study of public organizations. The theory attempts to integrate issues into a coherent filter which can be used to strain the rich and dynamic world of organizational affairs. All filters are selective and imprecise. As Herbert Kaufman has observed, "All discussions of organizational theory have an elusive character."[30]

Sequencing. I am not necessarily convinced that strategy precedes structure. One old Washington adage goes, "Show me your programs and I will tell you your policies." Thus structure may be positioned, and then strategies erected around them. Political leaders are masters of rationalizing action and are known to employ specialists in organizational intelligence to buttress their rationalizations.[31]

Of course this may be but another variant of the chicken and egg problem. Regardless of which comes first, both strategy and structure would seem to precede cultural change. Rituals, values, myths, and norms are highly resistant to change. They can be altered only through slaughter,[32] attrition, or inducement. Professional groups in organizations can be eliminated by wholesale firing—a highly improbable course of action given government personnel procedures—or by resignation or retirement. The attrition process is, of course, a slow one. It took several decades for the GAO to entirely rid itself of the investigators who populated the Investigations Division during McCarl's day. Thus the only effective short-term approach is offering inducements to professionals for changing the organization's rituals and ideology. Such inducements must grow out of changes in philosophy and personnel management, which is to say strategy and structure.

Imprecision.   As with any theory which organizes thought, terms are a problem. The term "professional" as often reflects aspiration as reality; all occupations wish to be considered professions. That is, they wish to base individual action on some scientific expertise, to be perceived as applying that science to social needs, and to share a sense of corporativeness.[33] Firemen have fire science and want to be thought of as professional firemen. Military officers at West Point talk of a cadet's behavior as "very professional" or, the worst condemnation imaginable, "terribly unprofessional." In time, through subtle negotiation and quiet agreement, a wide variety of behavior comes to be called "professional," some of which seems not at all related to the science from which it presumably flowered.

Another objection to the term is that not all employees of public organizations are now or always have been professionals. One can argue that career bureaucrats who occupy organizational villages are not really professionals, that many who are important tribesmen are essentially technicians who possess neither an advanced degree nor even an undergraduate one, and that in the past these villages were clearly dominated by clerks and pseudo professionals—those who pretended to possess some expertise, but were in fact charlatans (for example "colonels" who would purchase regiments during the Civil War).

Other terms are equally imprecise. Output, culture, rituals, and ideology can as easily confuse as clarify. When political scientists speak of output, they are usually thinking of David Easton's systems model which defines output as "a transaction between the political system and its environment." Such output, according to Easton, may be either verbal statements or performance.[34] The cultural model used here argues that the one common feature of all such output is behavior by government professionals. Deciding whether particular professional behavior is output, organizational maintenance, or professional rivalry is not always clear even to the initiated. Thus all that is agency output is produced by professional behavior, but all behavior by professionals is not necessarily agency output.

To offer a weak defense, any theory must rely on terms and invariably such terms are reductionistic. The term "professional" may not apply to every government employee, but the observer of American public organizations must concede that most bureaucrats seem to fit the standard. That is, they are highly skilled and educated, for the most part dedicated to the public good as they have been led to understand that good by public laws and agency regulations, and committed to their agency. Furthermore, we have tried to define our terms throughout, noting, for example, that ideology was composed of values, norms, and myths and that myths were beliefs about the world which may or may not be accurate.

Operationalizing the Theory. Applying the theory to a public organization is hard work which requires intensive research. I felt comfortable applying it to the GAO after conducting over two hundred interviews and working through hundreds of hearings, reports, documents, pamphlets, regulations, and orders. In the case of the Army, I was able to draw on more than a dozen books for support in describing what I have called the culture of preparedness. But then I have been in the

Army for twenty-two years and could see the impact of past developments on organizational design.

Identifying a cultural epoch is difficult. One may base its beginning on an organizational catastrophe like the Spanish American War for the Army, but one is not always convinced that an epoch may end in a catastrophe. Or for that matter, one is not certain what a catastrophe really is. To use the Army again as an example, it would appear that the Cold War, which required a large standing force, was the ending of one epoch and the beginning of a new one for the Army. From the Army's point of view, many more soldiers on active duty may not be "catastrophic" (although as taxpayers we may see it that way!).

The discovery of the leadership's strategy is more art than science. As defined here, strategy is "an institutional design which develops over time." It involves a plan or series of decisions which political executives make during their tenure about organizational goals and output. Since these decisions in the case of Lindsay Warren were made over a period stretching from 1940 to 1954, Warren could not have articulated his strategy at any single point in his tenure, because he had no way of knowing what tomorrow would bring. So strategy must be inferred. My inferences about Warren's strategy grew out of his decisions, his testimony before Congress, his speeches and his annual reports.

Too Retrospective. Finally the theory looks back, not forward. It is heavily reliant on what has happened over time in organizational design to explain current organizational behavior. It does not appear to provide propositions to forecast future organizational developments or professional behavior. In other words, it is not a "model" in the strict sense social scientists use that term.

Yet it does provide a host of propositions about why professionals in organizations behave as they do and how to assess the success of their repertoire. Other propositions about organizational development, the importance of leaders and strategies, the role of structure, and the central nature of personnel management in conditioning professional behavior are also advanced. One might also argue that the "strict sense" in which social scientists have used the word "model" is indeed too demanding, too strict. Predicting behavior of a collective as complicated as an established organization sets demands upon us which discourage even the most hardy student of institutional behavior.

TOWARD THE STUDY OF ORGANIZATIONAL POLITICS

Despite these drawbacks, this cultural theory emphasizes the study of professional behavior and organizational politics. By identifying a number of significant propositions about organizational affairs, it invites comparison within and across organizations. Synchronic and diachronic comparisons can be drawn on how various leaders have addressed catastrophe, what professional cadres were chosen as the elite and why, and how hierarchical design influences organizational output. The efforts in this chapter to discover such parallels suggest what can be done. Out of such comparison may grow more definitive propositions about organizational behavior.

Finally this theory promotes the study of individual professions and the organizations they dominate, a task political scientists have not emphasized. As the limitations discussed above suggest, the study of professional and organizational politics and evolution is, to borrow from Max Weber, the "slow boring of hard boards."[35] Organizations are made of oak, not pine. Their professionals have established multiple defenses to discourage the woodcutter from access to the core.

However difficult, the task is important. Organizations are perhaps the only stable force on the American political landscape, and, as such, they are at times the focus and at other times the determinants of government politics. Presidents and their political executives strut on the stage for less than a decade. Members of Congess may last two, sometimes even three decades. Dominant political agendas survive for perhaps one-half a century. Some government agencies can, however, trace their lineage to at least the founding of the republic. The GAO's roots lie in the creation of the Office of the Auditor General in 1776; the United States Army dates back to 1775.

The presence of enduring organizations on the national scene structures the debate about governmental purpose. President Ronald Reagan's proposals for the elimination of the Departments of Energy and Education were not frivolous. Rather they reflected serious misgivings about institutionalizing such responsibilities at the federal level. Energy was a matter for the marketplace, and education for state and local government. Whatever his rationale, Reagan's proposals have sparked controversy in Congress and among constituent groups. Other recent examples of debate about organizations include those arising over the performance of such agencies as the Central Intelligence Agency, the Federal Bureau of Investigation, and the Food and Drug Administration, as well as over decisions made by the Department of Interior and the Federal Trade Commission. Political controversy over government organizations is endemic to American politics.

Not only do organizations provide the focus for governmental politics, they are also at times the determinants for political action. The study of bureaucratic politics is popular in the field and even more popular for journalists, commentators, and other observers. As one author has defined it, bureaucratic politics is players in positions, each possessing various goals, interests, stakes, and stands. These players collide over issues and bargain; the outcome is a result of this interplay.[36] One critic of this framework and of those who have applied it argues that it doesn't properly account for the differences in power and access among the players; presidents, for example, are in a quite different league from newly elected members of Congress.[37] Of more importance, much of what most of these players do is conditioned by the organizations they represent.

The players emphasized in studies of bureaucratic politics are elected and appointed officials. Presidents and legislators may have some discretion in their choice of stands, but more often than not their interests and stakes are organizational. The growth of staff resources in Congress means that each member not only represents a district or state, but also the small organization he or she has created.[38] Legislators do not lightly or consistently ignore the advice of their legislative and administrative assistants—to do so is to risk losing them. Presidents have similar problems with their assistants in the White House Office and with the organizations in the Executive Office of the Presidency which represent Administration interests. Clearly such organizations are ephemeral, but their impact on elected officials is real.

An even stronger case can be made for political executives appointed by the president and confirmed by Congress. The behavior of these executives is in fact conditioned by organizational culture. Although they have a role to play in cultural design, their flexibility is at best circumscribed and more frequently nonexistent. Once they have accepted the existing culture or (in those rare cases) had the opportunity to totally redesign it, they come to the stage hitched to their organizations. Successful executives stay hitched or lose support not only in their organizations, but soon thereafter from enveloping constituencies and key members of Congress. To lose such support is to lose influence and thus the ability to play in the game.

There is flexibility in the harness. Not much, but some. The most successful political executives find that latitude, exploit it, and indelibly leave their mark on the organization and the government as a whole. Warren and Root were such executives. Political executives as bureaucratic players are conditioned by their "little bands of professionals." What executives say and do usually reflects the bargains they have struck with career elites and professional cadres in their organizations. Certainly the President, through various clearance devices, can shape what executives do, but Presidents seldom are able to initiate action. Government organizations initiate much of the action in American institutional politics.

Graham Allison's call that "we must move to a conception of happenings as events whose determinants are to be investigated according to the canons that have been developed by modern science" has been only partly realized.[39] We have been preoccupied with the study of bureaucratic politics. What we need now are more studies of organizational politics.[40] The framework developed here is, one hopes, a beginning that invites improvement, alteration, or elimination in favor of more refined ones.

Notes

PREFACE

1. Joseph Cooper, Organization and Innovation in the House of Representatives," in *The House at Work*, ed. J. Cooper and G.C. MacKenzie (Austin: Univ. of Texas Press), 323–26.
2. Frederick C. Mosher, *The GAO: The Quest for Accountability in American Government* (Boulder, Colo.: Westview Press, 1979); and Joseph Pois, *Watchdog on the Potomac: A Study of the Comptroller General of the United States* (Lanham, Md.: Univ. Press of America, 1979).

CHAPTER 1

1. Harold Seidman, *Politics, Position and Power*, 2nd ed. (New York: Oxford Univ. Press, 1975), 221–98.
2. Daniel Mazmanian and Jeanne Nienaber, *Can Organizations Change?* (Washington, D.C.: Brookings Institution, 1979).
3. John Tierney, *Postal Reorganization* (Boston: Auburn House, 1981).
4. Mosher, *The GAO*.
5. Ann Robinson, review of Frederick Mosher's *The GAO* in *Journal of Public Policy* 1 (Feb. 1981), 148–50.
6. Comptroller General, *Annual Report, 1981* (Washington, D.C.: U.S. Government Printing Office, 1981), 1. Hereafter cited as *CGAR* with the year covered by the report.
7. *Ibid*, 10.
8. James Q. Wilson, *The Investigators* (New York: Basic Books, 1978), 9.
9. Herbert Kaufman, *The Forest Ranger: A Study in Administrative Behavior* (Baltimore: Johns Hopkins Univ. Press, 1960), 91–200.
10. Frederick Mosher, *Democracy and the Public Service* (New York: Oxford Univ. Press, 1968), 103–10.
11. "Corporate Culture: The Hard to Sell Values That Spell Success or Failure," *Business Week* (Oct. 27, 1980), 143–60.
12. Mary Douglas and Aaron Wildavsky, *Risk and Culture* (Berkeley: Univ. of California Press, 1983).

13. Terrence Deal and Allan Kennedy, *Corporate Cultures: The Rites and Rituals of Corporate Life* (Reading, Penn.: Addison-Wesley, 1982).
14. *Ibid.*; Robin Williams, *American Society*, 3rd ed. (New York: Knopf, 1970), 25–36; and Milton Singer, "The Concept of Culture," *International Encyclopedia of the Social Sciences*, ed. David Sills, III (New York: Free Press, 1968), 527–42.
15. A.M. Pettigrew, "On Studying Organizational Culture," *Administrative Science Quarterly* 22 (Dec. 1979), 570–81. Similar conceptions about the existence of a bureaucratic culture being contained within a distinct era are suggested in somewhat different terms by James Thompson, *Organizatons in Action* (New York: McGraw-Hill, 1967), and Philip Selznick, *Leadership in Administration* (New York: Harper & Row, 1957). For example, James Thompson talks of "co-alignment" in time and space between a complex organization and its environment. "Survival rests on the co-alignment of technology and task environment with a viable domain, and of organization design and structure appropriate to that domain" (Thompson, 147–48).

    Philip Selznick enjoins us to study the critical experiences of institutions. Such experiences affect institutional ability "to uphold its distinctive aims and values." The study of institutions "requires a genetic and developmental approach, an emphasis on historical origin and growth stages. There is a need to see the enterprise as a whole and to see how it is transformed as new ways of dealing with a changing environment evolve (Selznick, 136, 141)."

    Selznick conceives of bureaucratic culture as organizational character. He sees four attributes to character: it is a historical product; it is an integrated product in that there is a discoverable pattern to the ways in which the institution is organized; it is functional in that the institution reconstructs itself to solve problems; and it is dynamic in that the institution generates new strivings, needs and problems (Selznick, 38–42).
16. For uses of strategy and structure as concepts see Alfred Chandler, *Strategy and Structure* (Cambridge: MIT Press, 1962), and Samuel Huntington, *The Common Defense* (New York: Columbia Univ. Press, 1961), esp. 123–35 and 426–39.
17. This concept of strategy is a composite portrait drawn from the following sources: Chandler, p. 13; Matthew Holden, "Imperialism in Bureaucracy," in *Bureaucratic Power in National Politics*, ed. Francis Rourke, 2nd ed. (Boston: Little, Brown, 1972), 198; and James Thompson and William McEwen, : "Organizational Goals and Environment," *American Sociological Review* 23 (1958), 25.
18. Selznick, 25–28, 61–64. In this book I use the terms leadership, political executives, and political appointees as synonymous. My ideas on the latitude of political executives are drawn from the following sources: Hugh Heclo, *A Government of Strangers* (Washington, D.C.: Brookings Institution, 1977), 103–104; James Q. Wilson, "The Changing FBI—The Road to ABSCAM," *The Public Interest* 59 (Spring 1980), 9; and Harvey Sapolsky, *The Polaris System Development* (Cambridge: Harvard Univ. Press, 1972), especially 19–60. Also see Chester Barnard, *The Functions of the Executive* (Cambridge: Harvard Univ. Press, 1968).
19. My thinking about character has been influenced by James David Barber, *The Presidential Character*, 2nd ed. (Englewood Cliffs, N.J.: Prentice-Hall, 1977) and Edgar Puryear, *Nineteen Stars: A Study in Military Character and Leadership*

(Washington, D.C.: Coiner Publications, 1971).

20. Thompson, 51; Chandler, 14; Seidman, 150; and Selznick, 56–61. These authors provide different ideas about what issues are crucial in structuring an institution. My list selects matters which recur in theirs and is also based upon my GAO interviews and my experience in the Army.

21. Seidman, 301.

22. Selznick, 114–15, 138.

23. Thompson, 25–28, 142–54; and Herbert Simon, *Administrative Behavior*, 2nd ed. (New York: Macmillan, 1957), 96, 228–31.

24. Mosher, *Democracy*, 129–30, 146–55.

25. Morris Janowitz, *The Professional Soldier* (New York: Free Press, 1960), 101, 127–39.

26. For instance, in the Army, officers attend specialty courses (called Basic Courses) just after commissioning. After about five years, they attend their specialty Advanced Courses. If selected, they then attend the Command and General Staff College 10–12 years after commissioning and the War College 16–22 years into their service. Most other bureaucratic professions do not have this extensive a training system, but Office of Personnel Management sponsored courses as well as agency courses are available. On the Army, see Janowitz, 139–45. On the history of this scheme, see Chapter 8.

27. Michael Malbin, *Unelected Representatives* (New York: Basic Books, 1980), 9.

CHAPTER 2

1. "Control" is the authority to decide upon the legality of government expenditures. See U.S. Commission on Organization of the Executive Branch of Government (Hoover Commission), *Budgeting and Accounting* (Washington, D.C.: U.S. Government Printing Office, 1949), 56. See also Wallace Earl Walker, "The General Accounting Office and Information for Congressional Review," M.S. thesis, Massachusetts Institute of Technology, 1973, 20–21.

2. Polybius, *The Histories of Polybius*, trans. Evelyn S. Shuckburgh, I (Westport, Conn.: Greenwood Press, 1974).

3. Sir Ivor Jennings, *Parliament*, 2d ed. (London: Cambridge Univ. Press, 1967), 283–90; "Post Audit Controls," *The Watchdog* (Nov. 1947), 10.

4. O.R. McGuire, "The Comptroller General of the United States," as reprinted in U.S. Congress, Senate, Senator Logan, 74th Cong., 2d sess., January 13, 1936, *Congressional Record*, 80, No. 1, p. 313.

5. Darrell Smith, *The General Accounting Office: Its History, Activities and Organization* (Baltimore: Johns Hopkins Press, 1927), 2–11; and Fred Powell, ed., *Control of Federal Expenditures: A Documentary History, 1775–1894* (Washington, D.C.: Brookings Institution, 1939), 14–18.

6. McGuire, 313 and Smith, 15–26.

7. Daniel Selko, *The Federal Financial System* (Washington, D.C.: Brookings Institution, 1940), 413; and Harvey Mansfield, *The Comptroller General* (New Haven: Yale Univ. Press, 1939), 55–57.

8. Woodrow Wilson, "The Study of Administration." *Political Science Quarterly* 2 (June 1887), 197–222.

9. Seidman, 252; Mosher, *Democracy*, 72; and Louis Fisher, *Presidential Spending Power* (Princeton: Princeton University Press, 1975), 31.
10. Mansfield, 60.
11. Leonard White, *The Republican Era: 1869–1901* (New York: Macmillan, 1958), 113–14.
12. Edward S. Corwin, *The President: Office and Powers, 1787–1957*, 4th ed. (New York: New York Univ. Press, 1957), 237, 311, 468; and Alexander L. George and Juliette L. George, *Woodrow Wilson and Colonel House* (New York: Dover, 1968), 143–56.
13. Legislative Reference Service, "Relations of the General Accounting Office to Congress," manuscript prepared at the Library of Congress, April 12, 1944.
14. Mansfield, 68; and Smith, 61.
15. U.S. Congress, House, Representative James Good, Speech on the Budget and Accounting Act, 67th Cong., 1st sess., May 5, 1921, *Congressional Record*, 67, No. 2, p. 1080.
16. U.S. Congress, House, Representative James Good, Speech on the Budget and Accounting Act, 66th Cong., 1st sess., Oct. 17, 1919, *Congressional Record*, 66, No. 7, p. 7085, emphasis added.
17. *Budget and Accounting Act*, (1921) Sect. 41–44. Also see Alexander S. Pow, "The Comptroller General and the General Accounting Office of the United States," Ph.D. diss., New York Univ. 1960.
18. Representative Good, Oct. 17, 1919, *Congressional Record*, pp. 7085–86; and Good, May 5, 1921, *Congressional Record*, p. 1090.
19. As one of McCarl's Division Chiefs testified to the Senate in 1937 about GAO-Congress relationships,

> I . . . feel very much like a son whose father, when he reached the age of majority, fixed upon him certain responsibilities, gave him certain things to do, told him to go ahead . . . and report to him from time to time as to how he was doing them, and then . . . the father paid no attention whatever to the reports, and the son came to the conclusion that it was not worth while [sic] reporting.

(J.D. Dent as quoted in Mansfield, 268).
20. Assistant Comptroller General Frank Weitzel as quoted in J.D. Brown, "The U.S. General Accounting Office's Changing Focus as the Federal Government's Auditor," Ph.D. diss., George Washington Univ., 1973, p. 99.
21. Raymond Clapper, "Between You and Me," *Washington Post*, April 1, 1935; and Charles Cutler, "He Says 'No' to Presidents," *American Magazine* (1937). These and many other articles were contained in a historical file in the GAO's Law Library; page numbers were not included.
22. Mansfield, 71.
23. *CGAR, 1930*, 16–17, emphasis added.
24. Mansfield, 2.
25. *Budget and Accounting Act*, (1921) sect. 41, 44, 47, 49.
26. Mansfield, 156; and *CGAR, 1928*, 37.
27. *CGAR, 1923*, 29.
28. Interview II 25; and Mansfield, 72–3, 176–77.

29. *CGAR, 1923,* 39, emphasis added.
30. *CGAR, 1932,* 59; and Smith, 156–67. The list of titles is not exhaustive, but rather meant to be indicative of the general responsibilites of clerks serving in the GAO at this time.
31. Dwight Waldo, *The Administrative State* (New York: Ronald Press Co., 1948), p. 195.
32. E.L. Normanton, *The Accountability and Audit of Governments* (New York: Praeger, 1966), 112, 258; "Office of the Future?," *GAO Management News,* May 3, 1976, 1; and Interviews II 27, III 17, and II 61.
33. These and other anecdotes on McCarl's disallowances can be found in the following sources: Gerald G. Schulsinger, "The General Accounting Office: Two Glimpses." Inter-University Case Program, Number 35 (Birmingham: Univ. of Alabama Press, 1956); and Vermont Royster, "While Government is Watchful of Each Penny and Nickle, Its Waste of the Dollar Puts Us in a Pickle," *Wall Street Journal,* (May 1949).
34. "Full Check-up of Emergency Units Sought," *Washington Star,* June 6, 1934.
35. Richard E. Brown, *The GAO* (Knoxville: Univ. of Tennessee Press, 1970), 26–39.
36. *CGAR, 1937,* 111.
37. President's Committee on Administrative Management, *Report of the President's Committee on Administrative Management in the Government of the United States* (Washington, D.C.: U.S. Government Printing Office, 1937), hereafter referred to as the Brownlow Committee, so named for the Chairman, Louis Brownlow.
38. Charles S. Hyneman, *Bureaucracy in a Democracy* (New York: Harper, 1950), 374; also see 373–81. Lastly see Lucius Wilmerding, *The Spending Power* (Archon Books, 1971).
39. U.S. Congress, Senate, Select Committee on Government Organization, *Government Organization,* S. Rept. 1236, 75th Cong., 1st sess., 1937 and U.S. Congress, House, Extension of Remarks of Representative Fred Vinson on the General Accounting Office, Aug. 16, 1937, *Congressional Record,* 53, No. 10, pp. 2449–53.
40. Wellington Brink, "Lindsay Carter Warren: Whip Over Public Spending," as contained in U.S. Congress, House, Extension of Remarks of Congressman Graham A. Barden, 79th Cong., 2d sess., May 9, 1946, *Congressional Record,* 17, No. 11, pp. A2560–A2562; and "Footnotes on the Headlines," *New York Times,* Aug. 4, 1940, sec. IV, p. 2.

CHAPTER 3

1. Heclo, 103–104. On the need for simplicity, a recent National Academy of Public Administration report concluded that complicated bureaucratic procedures impede performance. See "Federal Agencies Get Plans for Improving Management," *New York Times,* November 28, 1983, B9.
2. Wilson, "The Changing FBI," 9.
3. See Chapter 8.

4. Fred Greenstein, "Eisenhower as an Activist President," *Political Science Quarterly* 94 (Winter 1979–80), 581.

5. Seidman, 126; and Heclo, 171–207.

6. Erwin Hargrove, "The Task of Leadership: The Board Chairmen" in *TVA: Fifty Years of Grass-Roots Democracy*, ed. Erwin Hargrove and Paul Conkin (Urbana: Univ. of Illinois Press, 1984), 89–121.

7. Normanton, 103.

8. See for example U.S. Congress, House, Committee on Expenditures in the Executive Departments, *Investigation of Procurement and Buildings, Hearings* on the General Accounting Office's Audit of Wartime Freight Vouchers, Part 7, 80th Cong., 2d sess., 1948, p. 941.

9. U.S. Bureau of the Census, *Historical Statistics of the U.S., Colonial Times to 1957* (Washington, D.C.: U.S. Government Printing Office, 1960).

10. Chandler, 391; and Mosher, *Democracy*, 73.

11. Hoover Commission, 35–43.

12. U.S. Congress, House, Committee on Expenditures in the Executive Departments, *Budgeting and Accounting Procedures Act of 1950*, 81st Cong., 2d sess., 1950, H. Rept. 2556, p. 5; and U.S. Congress, Senate, Committee on Expenditures in the Executive Departments, *Budget and Accounting Procedures Act of 1950*, 81st Cong., 2d sess., 1950, S. Rept. 2031, p. 4.

13. Richard Neustadt, *Presidential Power* (New York: John Wiley, 1960), 2, 191.

14. Jack Riley, "Tar Heel of the Week—Lindsay C. Warren" as appearing in U.S. Congress, Senate, Extension of Remarks of Senator Clyde Hoey, Aug. 29, 1950, *Congressional Record*, pp. A6483–A6484; "Lindsay Carter Warren," *The National Cyclopedia of American Biography*, 1952 (Volume H), pp. 282–84; and "Watchdog on Washington's Waste," *Reader's Digest*, Aug. 1952, p. 124.

15. Lindsay Warren, "Statement on the Reorganization Bill Before the House Committee on Expenditures in the Executive Departments," Jan. 25, 1949, p. 8.

16. U.S. Congress, Senate, Senator Clyde Hoey's Speech on Lindsay Warren, April 1, 1954, *Congressional Record*, pp. 4062–66.

17. *CGAR, 1943*, 4; Riley, A6484 and Lindsay Warren, "Will the Wasters Win Again," as appearing in U.S. Congress, Senate, Extension of Remarks of Senator Herbert O'Conor, May 17, 1949, *Congressional Record*, p. A3141.

18. Brink, A2560–A2562; Riley; and *CGAR, 1943*, 4.

19. Jerry Kluttz, "The Federal Diary," *Washington Post*, January 19, 1952; "GAO Shake-up Terminates 400," *Government Employees Exchange*, Feb. 13, 1952; Allen Voss, "Ellsworth H. Morse, Jr.: Assistant Comptroller General of the United States," *GAO Review* (Winter 1978), 1–12; Robert Wallace, *Congressional Control of Federal Spending* (Detroit: Wayne State Univ. Press, 1960), 162; U.S. Congress, Senate, Senator Ribicoff, Speech on "Retirement of Adolph T. Samuelson, Assistant Comptroller General," 94th Cong., 1st sess., July 9, 1955, *Congressional Record*, 121, No. 107, p. S12135; and Interviews II 25, II 36, II 40, and II 61.

20. Warren's strategy was inferred from a careful reading of the *CGAR*'s from 1940 to 1954 (*CGAR, 1954* was most useful). This section also relies on articles about him and by him which appeared in numerous newspapers and in the *Congressional Record*, some of which are cited above.

21. *CGARs* as follows: *1950*, 61; *1954*, 8; and *1948*, 4; Interviews II 86 and II 88;

U.S. Congress, House, Committee on Expenditures in the Executive Branch, *The General Accounting Office: A Study of Its Functions and Operations*, 81st Cong., 1st sess., 1949, H. Rept. 1441, p. 29.

22. *CGAR, 1951*, 28–9.
23. Normanton, 269.
24. *CGAR, 1952*, vi.
25. *CGAR, 1949*, iii; and *CGAR, 1946*, iii.
26. See the following sources: *CGAR, 1940*, 3; *CGAR, 1945*, 62; Lindsay Warren, "Statement Before the Senate Committee on Expenditures in the Executive Departments, on S. 2054," Feb. 27, 1950, 5; "Improvement Made in U.S. Accounting Office Under the Direction of Warren," *Washington, N.C. Daily News*, Apr. 2, 1954, p. 5; *CGAR, 1950*, 5–6; and Interview III 10.
27. *The Budget and Accounting Procedures Act, U.S. Code*, 1970 ed., Title 31, secs. 65, 66, and 67 (1950)).
28. *Federal Loan Agency Administration*, Public Law 4, U.S. Code Congressional Service (1945), 3–4; and *Government Corporation Control Act, U.S. Code*, 1970 ed., Title 31, secs. 850 and 856 (1945).
29. U.S. Congress, House, Committee on Expenditures in the Executive Departments, *Reorganizations in Executive Branch*, 79th Cong., 1st sess., 1945, H. Rept. 971, p. 6; *Legislative Reorganization Act, U.S. Code*, 1970 ed., Title 31, sec. 60 (1946); and Interview II 61.
30. *Anti-Kickback Act, U.S. Code*, 1970 ed., Title 41, sec. 51 (1946); *Armed Services Procurement Act, U.S. Code*, 1970 ed., Title 41, sec. 153 (1947); and *Contracts Negotiated Without Advertising—Examination of Contractors' Books and Records*, Public Law 245, U.S. Code Congressional Service (1951), 713, 2569–73.
31. U.S. Congress, Senate, Committee on Expenditures in the Executive Departments, *Federal Property and Administrative Services Act of 1949*, 81st Cong., 1st sess., 1949, S. Rept. 475, p. 1.
32. U.S. Congress, House, Committee on Government Operations, *The General Accounting Office*, 84th Cong., 2d sess., 1956, H. Rept. 2264, p. 15. This report was prepared primarily at the behest of Representative Glenard Lipscomb of California, hereafter cited as *Lipscomb Report.*
33. Luther Huston, "Lindsay Warren Set Savings Key," *New York Times*, May 3, 1954; Mary Ann Pardue, "Warren Has Anniversary," *Raleigh News and Observer*, Nov. 1, 1953, sec. IV, p. 14; and letter to Major General Lewis B. Hershey from Comptroller General Lindsay Warren (B-115334), April 30, 1954.
34. *CQ Almanac, 84th Congress, 1st session, 1955* (Washington: Congressional Quarterly News Features, 1955), 195; and *CQ Almanac, 97th Congress, 1st session, 1981* (Washington: Congressional Quarterly, 1981), 255.
35. Gary Orfield, *Congressional Power* (New York: Harcourt and Brace, 1975).
36. John Saloma, *Congress and the New Politics* (Boston: Little, Brown, 1969); Samuel Huntington, "Congressional Responses to the Twentieth Century," in *The Congress and America's Future*, ed. David Truman, (Englewood Cliffs, N.J.: Prentice-Hall, 1965); Joseph Harris, *Congressional Control of Administration* (Garden City, N.Y.: Anchor Books, 1964); and Morris Ogul, *Congress Oversees the Bureaucracy* (Pittsburgh: Univ. of Pittsburgh Press, 1977).
37. Lawrence Dodd and Richard Schott, *Congress and the Administrative State*

(New York: John Wiley and Sons, 1979); and James Sundquist, *The Decline and Resurgence of Congress* (Washington: Brookings Institution, 1981).

38. Harrison Fox, Jr., and Susan Hammond, *Congressional Staffs* (New York: Free Press, 1977), 171; and Malbin, 252–53.

39. Robert Salisbury and Kenneth Shepsle, "Congressional Staff Turnover and the Ties-That-Bind," *American Political Science Review* 75 (1981), 381–96.

40. Sundquist, 326.

41. Michael Kirst, *Government Without Passing Laws* (Chapel Hill: Univ. of North Carolina Press, 1969).

42. Arthur Maass, *Congress and the Common Good* (New York: Basic Books, 1983), 262, 138–41.

43. U.S. Congress, House, Committee on Government Operations, House of Representatives, 87th Cong., 2d sess., 1962, p. 1. Numerous other hearings were held on such agencies as the Small Business Administration, Department of Interior, Civil Service Commission, Post Office, Civil Aeronautics Board, and Federal Aviation Agency.

The interpretation in this section was influenced by Leo Herbert who has observed,

> Whereas top management in Government, including the Congress, had previously emphasized how well the agencies spent and controlled their appropriations, now it began to emphasize how efficiently the managers performed. Because of this emphasis on efficient management, and to supply the need, the professional staff members of the GAO developed the capability to evaluate deficiencies in management—any type of management—for any activity they might encounter. They became experts in determining deficiencies because the environment demanded it.

See his "A Perspective of Accounting," *The Accounting Review* 46 (Jul. 1971), 437. Herbert was then Director of the Office of Personnel Management for the GAO.

44. *Lipscomb Report*, 25–9.

45. U.S. Congress, Joint Committee on Defense Production, *Defense Production Act: Progress Report No. 32, Hearings* before the Joint Committee on Defense Production, 84th cong., 1st sess., 1955, pp. 159, 172, 160. Hereafter cited as the auditors came to know it: The Zink Stink.

46. U.S. Congress, Senate, Committee on Government Operations, *Nomination of Joseph Campbell, Hearings* before the Committee on Government Operations, 84th Cong., 1st sess., 1955, pp. 2–7; Interview II 61; and Peter Edson, "GAO Does Its Best, but Government Waste is Enormous," *Knoxville News-Sentinel*, June 19, 1962.

47. Among the many *New York Times* articles consulted, note the following: "Democrats Support Cole as Controller," *New York Times*, Feb. 24, 1954; "Cole Backed for Warren Post," *New York Times*, Apr. 2, 1954; and "Senate Fight Due Over Controller," *New York Times*, Dec. 19, 1954. Also see Letter to Senator John L. McClellan from Maurice Stans, President of the American Institute of Accountants, as contained in *Nomination of Joseph Campbell*, 19–20.

48. Interviews, especially II 9, II 27, II 36, II 48, II 88, III 17 and IV 54. Also

see "Watchdog Widens Role," *Business Week*, March 19, 1960, pp. 109–16; James McCartney, "Taxpayer's Dedicated Watchdog Nips Away at Waste in Washington," *Chicago Daily News*, Dec. 29, 1962; and Lawrence Stern, "GAO Sleuthing Pays Big Dividends," *Washington Post*, Feb. 10, 1963.

49. Joseph Campbell, as quoted in Ladislas Farago, *It's Your Money* (New York: Random House, 1969), 236. Also see U.S. Congress, House, Committee on Appropriations, *Independent Offices Appropriations for 1964, Hearings* before a Subcommittee of the Committee on Appropriations, House of Representatives, 88th Cong., 1st sess., 1963, p. 216. Hereafter all Appropriations Committee Hearings on the GAO will be cited as *HAC, 1964, Hearings*, p. 216.

50. U.S. Congress, House, Committee on Government Operations, *Comptroller General Reports to Congress on Audits of Defense Contracts, Hearings* before a Subcommittee of the Committee on Government Operations, House of Representatives, 89th Cong., 1st sess., 1965, p. 42. Because these Hearings were held by Representative Chester Holifield (D, Calif.), they will be cited hereafter as *The Holifield Hearings*.

51. Many Interviews, including II 9, II 27, II 33, II 56, II 88, and III 17.

52. *The Holifield Hearings*, 646 and U.S. Congress, House, Committee on Government Operations, *Defense Contract Audits*, 89th Cong., 2d sess., 1966, H. Rept. 1344, pp. 4, 8, 9 (hereafter cited as *The Holifield Report*).

53. Many Interviews and *The Holifield Report*, 5.

54. Paul Montagna, *Certified Public Accounting: A Sociological View of a Profession in Change* (Houston: Scholar Book Co., 1974), 19, 32, 86–7.

55. *The Holifield Report*, 1–14.

56. U.S. Congress, Senate Committee on Government Operations, *The Accounting Establishment, A Staff Study* prepared by the Subcommittee on Reports, Accounting and Management of the Committee on Government Operations, 95th Cong., 1st sess., 1977, pp. 1618 and 1638; "Accountants: Cleaning Up America's Mystery Profession," *U.S. News and World Report*, Dec. 19, 1977, pp. 39–42; and Deborah Rankin, "Tough Senate Study on Auditing Practice Ends on Softer Note," *New York Times*, Nov. 14, 1977.

57. See Neil Churchill and William Cooper, "Auditing and Accounting—Past, Present and Future," in *Eric Louis Kohler: Accounting's Man of Principle*, ed. William Cooper and Yuji Ijiri (Reston, Va.: Reston Publishing, 1979), 226; Roger Wilkins, "Mayors are Taking a New Look at Problems of America's Cities," *New York Times*, Apr. 9, 1979; William Cooper and Yuji Ijiri, "Accounting and Accountability Relations," in *Eric Louis Kohler*, 204–6; and Jacob Birnberg and Natwar Gandi, "Toward Defining the Accountant's Role in the Evaluation of Social Programs," *Accounting, Organizations and Society* (1976), 5–10.

58. Herbert Roback, "Program Evaluation By and For the Congress," *The Bureaucrat* 5 (Apr. 1976), 11–12; and U.S. Congress, Senate, Senator Roth speech on "Public Program Analysis and Evaluation for the Purposes of the Executive and the Congress," 92d Cong., 2d sess., June 8, 1972, *Congressional Record*, 13, No. 16, pp. 20179–20180.

59. "Biography: Elmer B. Staats," supplied by the General Accounting Office; U.S. Congress, Senate, Committee on Government Operations, *Nomination of Elmer B. Staats, Hearings*, 89th Cong., 2d sess., 1966; "Presidential Appointments,"

Washington Post, Feb. 13, 1966; Louis Brandt, "New Head of General Accounting Office Has Long Experience in Budget Bureau," *St. Louis Post Dispatch*, Feb. 20, 1966; and entries in *The Congressional Record*.

60. Interview II 11.
61. Lyndon Johnson, "Remarks at the Swearing In of Elmer Staats as Comptroller General of the United States" (Mar. 8, 1966), *Public Papers of the President: Lyndon Baines Johnson*, I (Washington, D.C.: U.S. Government Printing Office, 1967), 287–88.
62. Heclo, 164–66; and Hugh Heclo, "OMB and the Presidency—The Problem of 'Neutral Competence,' " *The Public Interest* 38 (Winter 1975), 80–98.
63. Elmer Staats, "Management or Operational Auditing," *GAO Review* (Winter 1972), 27.
64. *CGAR, 1968*, 12; and *CGAR, 1969*, 12.
65. "Statements before Congressional Committees by the Honorable Elmer Staats," supplied by the Office of the Comptroller General, Aug. 1976.
66. For a few of the many examples see the following: U.S. Congress, Senate, Committee on Government Operations, *Capability of the GAO to Analyze and Audit Defense Expenditures, Hearings*, 91st Cong., 1st sess., 1969, p. 170; Eric Redman, *The Dance of Legislation* (New York: Simon & Schuster, 1973), 204; and William Selover, "Congressional Watchdog—Protecting the Tax Dollar," *Christian Science Monitor*, Mar. 11, 1968. For testimonials from three noted scholars (Alton Frye, Harvey Mansfield, Sr., and Roy Crawley) on GAO's responsiveness to Congress, see U.S. Congress, Joint Committee on Congressional Operations, *Congressional Research Support and Information Services, Hearings*, 93d Cong., 2d sess., 1974, pp. 79, 103, 109.
67. See the following articles, all authored by Elmer Staats: "Future of the American City," *GAO Review* (Spring 1978), 1–5; "Acquisition Management Needs Realistic Forecasting to Close the Confidence Gap," *Defense Management Journal* (Apr. 1974), 20–3; "The GAO—How Its Work Affects Local Government," *Governmental Finance* 2 (Aug. 1973); Intergovernmental Relations: A Fiscal Perspective," *Annals* (1974), 33–9; "GAO Audit Standards: Development and Implementation," *Public Management* (Feb. 1974), 2–7; and "The Nation's Stake in Congressional Budget Reform," *The National Public Accountant* (Dec. 1975), 3–7.
68. Elmer Staats, "New Problems of Accountability," Speech before the American Society of Public Administration, n.d., 2; reprint provided by the Information Office, U.S. General Accounting Office and Elmer Staats, "Public Confidence in Government," *The Conference Board Record* (Jan. 1973), 21.
69. Staats, "Intergovernmental Relations," 36.
70. The campaign to bring these sacrosanct agencies to heel was extensive. Much of the work was done by the Senate Committee on Government Operations and by Representative Wright Patman. For more details see Wallace Earl Walker, "The Bureaucratic Politics of Fault Finding: The Cultures of Auditing in the General Accounting Office," Ph.D. diss., Massachusetts Institute of Technology, 1980, p. 293, note 17 and p. 300, note 80.

On GAO monitoring of campaign contributions see *CGAR, 1972*, 27–31; *CGAR, 1975*, 9–10, 295–96; and Linda Charlton, "Inquiry Into Democratic Break-In Strips General Accounting Office of Some of Its Anonymity," *New York*

Times, Sep. 3, 1972.
71. U.S. Congress, Senate, Senator Prouty on "Economic Opportunity Amendments of 1967," 90th Cong., 1st sess., Sept. 29, 1967, *Congressional Record*, 113, No. 20, pp. 27378–89.
72. See U.S. Congress, House, Committee on Rules, *Legislative Reorganization Act of 1970*, H. Rept. 91-1215, 91st Cong., 2d sess., 1970, p. 18.
73. U.S. Congress, Senate, Committee on Rules and Administration, *Congressional Budget Act of 1974*, S. Rept. 93–688, 93rd Cong., 2d sess., 1974, p. 67.
74. U.S. Congress, House, Committee on Government Operations, *GAO Act of 1979*, H. Rept. 96–425, 96th Cong., 1st sess., 1979 and *CGAR, 1978*, 11.
75. This section on Staats's strategy was distilled from thirty-five interviews. The interviewees included nearly all the GAO division and office directors and members of the executive elite who saw Staats daily. Also the *CGARs* from 1966 to 1981 were useful, as were Staats's many publications, some of which were cited above.
76. U.S. Congress, Senate, Committee on Government Operations, *Government Economy and Spending Reform Act of 1976, Hearings*, 94th Cong., 2d sess., 1976, p. 126.
77. *CGAR, 1966*, 22; and *CGAR, 1981*, 89.
78. "Elmer Staats Defines GAO Role, Scope," *Washington Star*, Jan. 10, 1977.
79. Interviews II 64, III 23, and IV 3. Also Roger Sperry *et al., GAO, 1966–1981: An Administrative History* (Washington, D.C.: U.S. Government Printing Office, 1981), 63, 65–7.
80. U.S. Congress, Senate, Committee on Government Operations, *Nomination of Robert F. Keller, Hearing*, 91st Cong., 1st sess., 1969.
81. *CGAR, 1977*, 2; U.S. Congress, House, "Executive Level Positions for General Accounting Office," 92d Cong., pp. 28891–92; U.S. Congress, Senate, "General Accounting Office Positions," 92d Cong., 1st sess., Dec. 3, 1971, *Congressional Record*, 117, No. 34, pp. 44485; GAO Memorandum dated Jan. 25, 1972, to all employees from Elmer Staats, entitled "Strengthening GAO's Organization to Meet the Demands of the 1970s," and GAO Memorandum dated May 6, 1976, to all employees from Elmer Staats, entitled "Organizational Changes."
82. *CGAR, 1971*, 8; *CGAR, 1972*, 2-3; *CGAR, 1978*, 1; *CGAR, 1966*, 16; GAO Memorandum dated Dec. 13, 1976, to the Assistant Comptroller General and Division and Office Directors from the Task Force on Treatment of Policy Issues, entitled "Problem Solving Working Paper for the Williamsburg Meeting"; GAO Memorandum dated Oct. 19, 1976, to the Comptroller General from the Directors of the Office of Program Planning and the Office of Policy, entitled "Communication"; and GAO Memorandum dated Nov. 24, 1976, to the Directors Conference Attendees from the Executive Secretary of the Conference Committee, entitled "December Directors' Conference."

CHAPTER 4

1. Herbert Kaufman, *The Limits of Organizational Change* (University: Univ. of Alabama Press, 1971), 5–46, 68–91.
2. Karl Mannheim, as quoted by Reinhard Bendix, "Bureaucracy," *International Encyclopedia of the Social Sciences*, II, 214.

3. Kaufman, *Limits*, 52.

4. *Ibid.*, 84.

5. Talcott Parsons notes that all social systems must solve the following problems: environmental adaptation, goal achievement, integration of subunits and value maintenance. My construction here is reliant on Parsons. See Peter Blau, "Organizations: Theories of Organizations," *International Encylcopedia of the Social Sciences*, II, 214.

6. Seidman, 14.

7. Melville Dalton, *Men Who Manage* (New York: John Wiley and Sons, 1956); and Harold Wilensky, "Organizations: Organizational Intelligence," *International Encyclopedia of the Social Sciences*, 11, 319–34.

8. Larry Gamm, "Planning in Administration," *Policy Studies Journal*, (Autumn 1976), 72–3; and Charles Madge, "Planning, Social: Introduction," *International Encyclopedia of the Social Sciences*, 12, 125–29.

9. *CGAR, 1941*, iv.

10. Rather than risk the possibility of embarrassing the authors of these reports, who are still alive, I will give them an anonymous letter designation. A, "An Analysis of the Operations and Organization of the Accounting and Bookkeeping Division," Sept. 1950 (document from the GAO Law Library); A, "An Analysis of the Operations and Organization of the Claims Division," Oct. 1951 (document from the GAO Law Library); a letter to the Comptroller General from A, Dec. 29, 1950, found in the GAO Law Library; and a letter to the Comptroller General from B, May 5, 1954, found in the GAO Law Library.

11. A, "Report on Survey: Office of Investigations," Nov. 30, 1951 (document from the GAO Law Library); and a letter to the Acting Comptroller General from B, Nov. 19, 1954, found in the GAO Law Library.

12. A letter to the Comptroller General from A, Apr. 25, 1952; and a letter to the Comptroller General from B, Apr. 28, 1954, both found in the GAO Law Library.

13. A letter to the Comptroller General from C, May 2, 1954, found in the GAO Law Library.

14. The Comptroller General pointed out in desperation in 1944 that the records received by the GAO over the period 1934–1944 exceeded in bulk all those accumulated during the government's history, *CGAR, 1944*, 9–11.

15. Selznick, 113.

16. *CGAR, 1956*, 1–2, 216; *CGAR, 1958*, 228; *CGAR, 1959*, 244; and *CGAR, 1965*, 360.

17. Interviews II 50, III 19 and III 24; *The Lipscomb Report*, 46–47; *CGAR, 1956*, 3; *CGAR, 1957*, 3; and *CGAR, 1965*, 355–56.

18. Numerous interviews, including I 12, II 4, II 72, and II 86.

19. Roy Kirk, "Implementing the Lead Division Concept," *GAO Review* 10 (Fall 1976), 17–24; and several Memorandums, including GAO Memorandum dated Feb. 3, 1975, from Elmer Staats to Heads of Divisions and Offices, entitled "Implementation of the Lead Division Concept"; and GAO Memorandum dated Sept. 16, 1975, from Elmer Staats to Heads of Divisions and Offices, entitled "Further Guidance on Program Planning."

20. U.S. GAO Program Planning Staff, "Proposed Conceptual Design of an Integrated Management Information System for the U.S. General Accounting Office," Sept.

1968; and U.S. GAO, Comptroller General's Order Number 2.17, "Data Processing Center," Feb. 9, 1970.

21. *CGAR, 1969,* 261; *CGAR, 1970,* 9; *CGAR, 1971,* 7; *CGAR, 1972,* 2; *CGAR, 1974,* 187–88; and *CGAR, 1975,* 213, 215, 219.

22. GAO Memorandum dated Aug. 30, 1971, to the Comptroller General from the Chairman of the Organization Planning Committee, entitled "Proposals for Reorganization of the General Accounting Office."

23. GAO Memorandum dated Jan. 25, 1972, to All Employees from Elmer Staats, entitled "Strengthening the GAO to Meet the Demands of the 1970s"; and numerous *CGARs,* including *1971,* 9; *1972,* 2–3; *1974,* 39; and *1976,* 74, 85.

24. U.S. Congress, House, Select Committee on Congressional Operations, *General Accounting Office Services to Congress: An Assessment,* H. Rept. 95-1317, 95th Cong., 2d sess., 1978, p. 12.

CHAPTER 5

1. U.S. Congress, House, Representative Wright Patman, Speech on the Honorable Joseph Campbell, 89th Cong., 1st sess., Aug. 3, 1965, *Congressional Record,* VXI, No. 14, p. 19255.

2. *CGAR, 1981,* p. 10. The remaining 28% were as follows: attorneys (3%), personnel management and other support professionals (6%) and clerical and technical (19%).

3. Campbell, as quoted in James McCartney, "Taxpayers' Dedicated Watchdog Nips Away at Waste in Washington," *Chicago Daily News,* Dec. 29, 1962.

4. *CGAR, 1961,* 243–44; *CGAR, 1962,* 229–30; *CGAR, 1963,* 263–64; *CGAR, 1964,* 305–10.

5. Interviews II 67, II 72, II 73, and II 86.

6. Interviews II 57, II 67, II 72, II 73, II 79, II 86, III 4, III 5, III 12, and III 29.

7. *HAC, 1962, Hearings,* 331; *HAC, 1963, Hearings,* 51; and *HAC, 1966, Hearings,* 442.

8. *CGAR, 1964,* 393–98.

9. Interview III 13.

10. This section is reliant upon thirteen interviews, especially II 50, II 71, II 86, III 3, and III 27.

11. *CGARs* as follows: *1962,* 234; *1963,* 270; *1964,* 312, and *1965,* 203-4.

12. Montagna, 86–87.

13. *HAC, 1964, Hearings,* 182.

14. Montagna, 43–45.

15. This section is also heavily reliant on interviews, especially II 10, II 11, II 13, II 16, II 17, II 20, II 40 and III 13.

16. Montagna, 45–54.

17. Ellsworth Morse, "The Case for Accepting GAO Experience," *Journal of Accountancy* (June 1960).

18. *CGAR, 1964,* 311–13.

19. See, for example, U.S. GAO, "Employee Responsibilities and Conduct Manual" (Washington, D.C.: U.S. General Accounting Office, 1966).

20. Interview II 72; *HAC, 1961, Hearings*, 787; *HAC, 1966, Hearings*, 440; and *CGAR, 1969*, 382.

21. Interviews II 72, II 86, and III 29.

22. Interview III 23.

23. Interviews II 7, II 72, II 78, and III 15.

24. Interviews II 86, II 90, and III 15.

25. *HAC, 1961, Hearings*, 725, 733; *HAC, 1961, Hearings*, 725, 733; *HAC, 1962, Hearings*, 331; *HAC, 1963, Hearings*, 51; *HAC, 1966, Hearings*, 440; U.S. Congress, House, Committee on Post Office and Civil Service, *Positions in the General Accounting Office*, 87th Cong., 1st sess., 1961, H. Rept. 575; and U.S. Congress, Senate, Committee on Post Office and Civil Service, *Supergrade Positions in the General Accounting Office*, 87th Cong., 1st sess., 1961, S. Rept. 988.

26. *The Holifield Report*, 4–5.

27. Kaufman, *Forest Ranger*, 166–67; and Interview II 39.

28. This section is based on eighteen interviews.

29. U.S. Congress, House, Committee on Post Office and Civil Service, *Separate Personnel System for the General Accounting Office, Hearing* before the Subcommittee on Civil Service, 95th Cong., 2d sess., 1978, p. 9.

30. *HAC, 1976, Hearings*, 627. This section is based on 23 interviews.

31. U.S. GAO Youth Advisory Committee, "Youth Advisory Committee Report to the Deputy Comptroller General, 1975–1976," Aug. 6, 1976.

32. *CGAR, 1966*, 119–21; *CGAR, 1972*, 154–56; and U.S. GAO, Office of Personnel Management, *Training Newsletter*, April 1–June 30, 1976.

33. For example the *GAO Review* in the Spring, 1972, issue contained articles on engineering applications to the program audit, use of Delphi techniques in program auditing, use of questionnaires in gaining information on federal programs, new GAO responsibilites in federal campaign reporting, and details on the new GAO reorganization. The Winter, 1978, issue contained articles on computer-assisted auditing, a program audit on needs of the aged, studying the impact of regulatory agencies, and supplying information to Congress on federal programs.

34. This section is based on nineteen interviews such as II 16, II 26, II 86, III 4 and III 26.

35. Elmer Staats, "Career Planning and Development: Which Way is Up?," *GAO Review* 10 (Fall 1976), 1–6.

36. Heclo, *Government*, 125.

37. *CGAR, 1967*, 147; and U.S. GAO, "1975 GAO Honor Awards Ceremony" (pamphlet).

38. L. Howard Bennett, "A Report on the Equal Employment Opportunity Program in the General Accounting Office (Headquarters)" (Washington, D.C.: U.S. General Accounting Office, Mar. 25, 1974). This section is dependent on the following interviews: II 2, II 26, II 69, II 86, and III 14.

39. Bennett; Michael Bernstein, "GAO Bias is Charged," *Washington Daily News*, Mar. 19, 1971; "Anti-Bias Protestors Rally Outside 4 Federal Agencies," *Evening Star*, Mar. 22, 1971; Letter dated Feb. 28, 1964, to Joseph Campbell from Representative Charles Diggs (D, Michigan); Letter dated Oct. 6, 1972, to Robert Hampton (Chairman of the Civil Service Commission) from Eliot Stanley of the Citizens Advocate Center; Letter dated Nov. 3, 1972, to Representative Ronald

Dellums (D, California) from Elmer Staats; U.S. Congress, House, Representative Ronald Dellums on "The Need for Hiring Standards at the GAO," 92d Cong., 2d sess., Oct. 18, 1972, *Congressional Record*, 118, No. 28, pp. 37404–46; U.S. Congress, House, Representative Shirley Chisholm (D, NY) on "Discrimination at the GAO," 92d Cong., 2d sess., Oct. 18, 1972, *Congressional Record*, 118, No. 28, pp. 37426–67; and U.S. Congress, House, Representative John Conyers (D, Michigan) on "General Accounting Office Minorities Program," 92d Cong., 2d sess., Oct. 18, 1972, *Congressional Record*, 118, No. 28, 37432–23.

40. For example, see *HAC, 1976, Hearings*, 554; and *HAC, 1980, Hearings*, 1819. On the Senate side, see for example U.S. Congress, Senate, Committee on Appropriations, *Legislative Branch Appropriations for 1978, Hearings* before a Subcommittee of the Committee on Appropriations, 95th Cong., 1st sess., 1977, p. 158, hereafter cited as *SAC, 1978, Hearings*.

41. *HAC, 1980, Hearings*, 1852–53.

42. U.S. Congress, Senate, Committee on Government Operations, *General Accounting Office Act of 1974, Hearings*, 93rd Cong., 2d sess., 1974, p. 194. See also Erwin Knoll, "The Half-Hearted GAO: Congress Gets What It Wants," *Progressive*, 25 (May 1971), 23.

43. GAO Memorandum dated July 22, 1974, to the Assistant Comptroller General for Management Services from Chairman of the EEO Advisory Council, entitled "Employee Career Development System"; "GAO-Wide Training Program Set to Eliminate Functional Racism," *GAO Management News*, May 2, 1977, 1; and William Godfrey, "Some 'Nonwhite' Afterthoughts on Functional Racism," *GAO Review*, 13 (Summer 1978), 53–7.

44. *HAC, 1980, Hearings*, 1852.

45. Carl Von Clausewitz, *On War*, ed. and trans. Michael Howard and Peter Paret (Princetown, N.J.: Princeton Univ. Press, 1976), 119.

46. Kaufman, *Limits*.

47. John Steinbrunner as quoted in Morton Halperin, *Bureaucratic Politics and Foreign Policy* (Washington, D.C.: Brookings Institution, 1974).

48. U.S. Congress, House, Committee on Expenditures, *Investigation of General Accounting Office Audits of Wartime Freight Vouchers*, 80th Cong., 2d sess., 1948, H. Rept. 2457, p. v.

49. Interview III 17 and III 18.

50. U.S. GAO, *Comprehensive Audit Manual* (Washington, D.C.: U.S. Government Printing Office, 1960), 13–2. Emphasis added.

51. *HAC, 1980, Hearings*, 1824, 1935; Inderjit Badhwar, "Buzz Off, Says Staats," *Federal Times*, Nov. 1, 1979; Inderjit Badhwar, "New GAO Hiring System Called Costly," *Federal Times*, Mar. 19, 1979; and Inderjit Badhwar, "At GAO Anyway, Racist Policies Thrive," *Federal Times*, Apr. 16, 1979.

52. Wilensky, 331.

53. Ben Twight, *Organizational Values and Political Power* (University Park, Penn.: Pennsylvania State Univ. Press, 1983), 17.

54. Amitai Etzioni, *Modern Organizations* (Englewood Cliffs, N.J.: Prentice-Hall, 1964), 68; and Kaufman, *Limits*, 15.

55. Kaufman, *Limits*, 18.

CHAPTER 6

1. N.H. Gerth and C. Wright Mills, eds., *From Max Weber* (NY: Oxford Univ. Press), 59–61, 323–34. Unless otherwise noted this chapter is based principally upon interviews. The quoted material without attribution are the words of GAO evaluators themselves or close observers of the GAO in the bureaucracy, the Congress, or the news media. Also useful in this chapter, particularly in detailing the audit process, were General Accounting Office, *Comprehensvie Audit Manual*, I and II (Washington, D.C.: GAO, 1972) and General Accounting Office, *Report Manual* (Washington, D.C.: GAO, 1976). For more details on these interviews see Walker, "Bureaucratic Politics," 347–53 and 401–408.

   The late Professor Jeffrey Pressman of MIT suggested that perhaps the best way to talk about the GAO auditor-evaluators was to let them talk for themselves. Since the auditors are doing the talking, we will shift to the present tense for ease of description. Such a shift does not mean that what they told me in 1976 and 1977 necessarily applies to the present; although as my overall argument suggests, the current ritual almost certainly is very similar to what I describe here.

2. See the following reports of the U.S. Comptroller General: "Financial Operations of the Five Service Academies, FPCD-75-117" (Feb. 6, 1975); "Academic and Military Programs of the Five Service Academies FPCD-76-8" (Oct. 31, 1975); and "Student Attrition at the Five Federal Service Academies, FPCD-76-12" (Mar. 5, 1976).

3. The consultants for the LMFBR study included the following: Dean Abrahamson, Environmentalist, School of Public Affairs, University of Minnesota; Professor Manson Benedict, Nuclear Engineer, MIT; Hans Bethe, Nuclear Physicist and Nobel Prize Winner; Ralph Lapp, Nuclear Physicist and author of books on science; John Taylor, General Manager, Breeder Reaction Division, Westinghouse Corporation; and Charles Luce, Chairman of the Board, Consolidated Edison of New York. See U.S. Comptroller General, "The Liquid Metal Fast Breeder Reactor: Promises and Uncertainties, OSP-76-1" (July 31, 1975).

4. The use of consultants is much like the use of contract arrangements employed by executive agencies. As Seidman notes, "Contracting may broaden the base of public support by fostering alliances with politically influential organizations and groups in the private community" (Seidman, 292).

5. Mosher, *Democracy*, 99–133.

6. Interview II 18; also see Graham Allison, *The Essence of Decision* (Boston: Little, Brown, 1971), 83–85; and Arnold Meltsner, *Policy Analysts in the Bureaucracy* (Berkley: Univ. of California Press, 1976) and "Bureaucratic Policy Analysts," *Policy Analysis* (Winter 1975), 128.

7. Comptroller General, *Standards for Audit of Government Organizations, Programs, Activities, and Functions* (Washington, D.C.: GAO, 1972); Darwin Casler, *The Evolution of CPA Ethics* (East Lansing, Mich.: Michigan State University Graduate School of Business Administration, Occasional Paper No. 12, 1964); and Robert Rasor, Operational Auditing: Training Booklet Number 1 (n.p.: R. Rasor, 1973; booklets were developed by contract for GAO training).

8. *HAC, Hearings, 1978*, 42–43; and *CGAR, 1977*, 1–3.

9. Select Committee on Congressional Operations, viii, 16–20.

10. Normanton, 267.
11. *Comprehensive Audit Manual, I,* 8–17.
12. Heclo, *Government,* 169.
13. Harold Fine, "A Readability Analysis of Twenty-Nine Audit Reports of One Federal Agency," Master's Thesis, George Washington Univ., 1972, 51–64; and Laura Hunter "The Language of Audit Reports" (Washington, D.C.: U.S. General Accounting Office, 1957).
14. *Report Manual,* 7–4, 7–5.
15. Martin Fitzgerald, "The Expanded Role of the General Accounting Office in Support of a Strengthened Congress," *The Bureaucrat,* 3 (Jan. 1975), 393.
16. Jeffrey Pressman and Aaron Wildavsky, *Implementation* (Berkeley: Univ. of California Press, 1973), 109.
17. U.S. General Accounting Office, "A Summary of Observations on Postal Service Operations from July, 1971 to January, 1976" (Washington, D.C.: GAO, GGD-76-61, March 5, 1976). Hereafter all audit reports will be cited by their title, GAO number (GCD-76-61) and their date.
18. "Why the Army Should Strengthen Its Internal Audit Function, FGMSD--77-49" (July 26, 1977); "The Naval Audit Service Should Be Strengthened, FGMSD-78-5" (November 11, 1977); and "The Air Force Audit Agency Can Be Made More Effective, FGMSD-78-4" (Nov. 11, 1977).
19. Seidman, 14–37.

CHAPTER 7

1. Comptroller General, "Standards for Audit of Governmental Organizations, Programs, Activities and Functions" (Washington, D.C.: GAO, 1981), 3.
2. Normanton, 131.
3. *Report Manual,* 13–8.
4. David Mayhew, *Congress; The Electoral Connection* (New Haven: Yale Univ. Press. 1974), 61–73.
   On the concern voiced by congressional committees for member use of the GAO see the following: Committee on Government Operations, *Capability of the GAO to Analyze and Audit,* 178; and *HAC, Hearings, 1978,* 58.
5. These points on reports were inferred from numerous interviews of auditors. Almost all mentioned some use of a report by Congress, its committees, or members of Congress. Their views on the pecking order of reports were generally consistent.
6. *Report Manual,* 9–5.
7. *CGAR, 1977,* 229–313.
8. *Report Manual,* 9–6.
9. Interviews IV 41 and IV 53.
10. I asked each of the Audit Division Directors as well as many Deputy and Associate Directors to name "good" GAO audit reports. I chose about twelve of these to pursue through interviews of senior people in the agencies covered. In some cases these people were political appointees and in other cases senior career professionals In each case at least three non-GAO people were interviewed on each report.
    Also I studied approximately seventy-five audit reports, primarily given to me

based on this process. Further, I reviewed the digests and titles of several hundred more. This of course is not a sample representative of the GAO's total effort, but certainly would qualify as a reasonable cross-section of what they think is their best work.

My conclusions about the impact of these reports, which follows in this chapter, reflects the agency people I talked to on these reports and other reports they had observed as well as commentary, both oral and written, from members of Congress, congressional staffers and scholars.

11. *Accounting and Auditing Act of 1950, U.S. Code*, Title 31, sec. 66 (1950).

12. Interviews IV 23 and IV 20; *CGAR, 1969* through *CGAR, 1977*.

13. "Why the Army Should Strengthen Its Internal Audit Function, FGMSD-77-49" (July 26, 1977); and Interviews IV 4, IV 17, IV 19, IV 20, IV 21, IV 22, IV 23, and IV 46.

14. U.S. Congress, House, Committee on Government Operations, *Internal Auditing by the Department of the Army, Hearing*, 95th Cong., 1st sess., 1977.

15. "The Air Force Audit Agency Can Be Made More Effective, FGMSD-78-4" (Nov. 11, 1977); and "The Naval Audit Service Should Be Stengthened, FGMSD-78-5" (Nov. 11, 1977).

16. Interviews IV 19, IV 36, IV 37, and IV 40.

17. "Millions of Dollars of Costs Incurred in Training Foreign Military Students Have Not Been Recovered, FGMSD-76-91" (Dec. 14, 1976); and numerous newspaper clippings to include: Tom Raum, "Pentagon Is Hit on Arms Sale Training Costs," *Washington Post*, Dec. 18, 1976; and George Anthan, "Foreign Pilot Training Hits U.S. Taxpayer," *Des Moines Register*, Dec. 25, 1976.

18. *CGAR, 1975* thru *CGAR, 1979*.

19. "Standards for Audit," 3.

20. Many of the details of this case came from the following interviews: IV 5, IV 12, IV 18, IV 27, IV 41, IV 42, IV 45, and from John Manchir and Larry Goldsmith, "Assessment of the National Grain Inspection System," *GAO Review* (Fall 1976), 7–14.

21. "Anatomy of a Pulitzer," *Des Moines Register*, 1976.

22. Letter from Congressman Edward Mezvinsky to Elmer Staats dated May 22, 1975, and letter from Congressman Thomas Foley and Senator Hubert Humphrey to Elmer Staats dated June 24, 1975.

23. "Assessment of the National Grain Inspection System, RED-76-71" (Feb. 12, 1976).

24. U.S. Congress, Senate, Committee on Agriculture, Nutrition and Forestry, *Grain Inspection Reform Act of 1976*, S. Rept. 94-757, 94th Cong., 2d sess., 1976.

25. "Opportunities for Increased Interservice Use of Training Programs and Resources, B-17573" (Nov. 27, 1973); and "Need to Control Federal Warning System Proliferation, LCD-76-105" (Apr. 9, 1976). Numerous other reports could be cited in this and subsequent categories.

26. "Water Pollution Abatement Program: Assessment of Federal and State Enforcement Efforts, B-166506" (Mar. 23, 1972); and "Improved Planning—A Must Before a Department-wide Automatic Data Processing System Is Acquired for the Department of Agriculture, LCD-75-108" (June 3, 1975).

27. "Narcotic Addiction Treatment and Rehabilitation Programs in San Francisco and Alameda Counties, California, B-166217" (July 24, 1972); "Narcotic Addiction

Treatment and Rehabilitation Programs in the County of Los Angeles, B-166217" (July 21, 1972); "The Food and Drug Administration's Financial Disclosure System for Special Government Employees: Progress and Problems, FPCD-76-99" (Jan. 24, 1977); "Federal Control of New Drug Testing Is Not Adequately Protecting Human Test Subjects and the Public, HRD-76-96" (July 15, 1976); and "Use of Cancer-Causing Drugs in Food Producing Animals May Pose Public Health Hazard: The Case of Nitrofurans, MWD-76-85" (Feb. 25, 1976).

28. U.S. Congress, Senate, Committee on Government Operations, *Paperwork Review and Limitation Act of 1976, Hearings*, 94th Cong., 2d sess., 1976.

29. "The Equal Employment Opportunity Commission Has Made Limited Progress in Eliminating Employment Discrimination, HRD-76-147" (Sep. 28, 1976); "Enforcement of Sanitary, Facility, and Moisture Requirements at Federally Inspected Poultry Plants, B-163450" (Sep. 10, 1969); "Weak Enforcement of Federal Sanitation Standards at Meat Plants by the Consumer and Marketing Service, B-163450" (June 24, 1970); "Consumer and Marketing Services Enforcement of Federal Sanitation Standards at Poultry Plants Continues to Be Weak, B-163450" (Nov. 16, 1971); "Dimensions of Unsanitary Conditions in the Food Manufacturing Industry, B-164031(2)" (April 18, 1972); "Federal Control of New Drug Testing is Not Adequately Protecting Human Test Subjects and the Public, HRD-76-96" (July 15, 1976); and "Stronger Measures Needed to Insure that Medical Diathermy Devices are Safe and Effective, HRD-76-153" (Sep. 2, 1976).

30. Seidman, p. 31. Interviews IV 7, IV 11, IV 27 and IV 42.

31. "Veterans Administration Justification of Costs and Benefits of Proposed Computer System (Target), HRD-77-98" (July 20, 1977). This example based on the following interviews: IV 26, IV 31, IV 38, IV 43, IV 44 and IV 51. Also numerous newspaper clippings were provided by these interviewees.

32. Pat Towell, "Case Study: Carter and Congress on AWACS," *Congressional Quarterly* (Sep. 3, 1977), 1857–63.

33. "Review of Status of Development Toward Establishment of a Unified National Communications System, B-166655" (July 14, 1969); and "Role of Federal Coal Resources in Meeting National Energy Goals Needs to be Determined and the Leasing Process Improved, RED-76-79" (Apr. 1, 1976).

34. "Outlook for Federal Goals to Accelerate Leasing of Oil and Gas Pressures on the Outer Continental Shelf, RED-75-343" (Mar 19, 1975); "Federal Programs for Research on the Effects of Air Pollutants, RED-76-46" (Dec. 11, 1975); "Implications of Deregulating the Price of Natural Gas, OSP-76-11" (Jan. 14, 1976).

35. "Federal Programs for Education of the Handicapped: Issues and Problems, B-164031(1)"; (Dec. 5, 1974); and "Research and Demonstration Programs to Achieve Water Quality Goals: What the Federal Government Needs to Do, RED-74-184" (Jan. 16, 1974).

36. *Budget and Accounting Act of 1921, U.S. Code*, Title 31, sec. 3122 (1921).

37. *CGAR, 1926*, 1–16; and *CGAR, 1965*, 33–43.

38. *CGAR, 1973*, 262, 266; *CGAR, 1975*, 15, 17, 21; *CGAR, 1977*, 15–22. To provide a better appreciation of the growth of these recommendations since 1965—the year of the Holifield Hearings—data gathered from the *Annual Reports* are noted below. It is important to emphasize that these recommendations for legislation grow out of audit reports themselves and should be distinguished from

recommendations that the GAO auditors and lawyers make on pieces of legislation already introduced into Congress and provided to GAO for comment. Each recommendation listed grew out of that year's auditing; the data do not include recommendations made in prior years and restated.

Year	Number of Recommendations
1965	17
1966	9
1967	15
1968	8
1969	10
1970	13
1971	16
1972	20
1973	35
1974	32
1975	48
1976	45
1977	74

39. Philip Boffey, "Carlucci: Thoughts on Government and Leaving It," *New York Times*, Jan. 4, 1983, emphasis added. Also see Sundquist, 33.
40. My thinking here was influenced by Sundquist, 315–43.
41. Richard Fenno, *Congressmen in Committees* (Boston: Little, Brown, 1973).
42. Mayhew, 33–37
43. Seymour Scher, "Conditions for Legislative Control," *Journal of Politics* (1963), 531–33; and Stephen Bailey, *Congress in the Seventies* (New York: St. Martin's, 1970), 84. Also see Sundquist, 327.
44. Interviews I 12, II 47, and IV 39. Also see, for example, Richard Madden, "Aspin Gets Leverage With Press Releases," *New York Times*, Feb. 3, 1976; and Steven Roberts, "Proxmire Thrives in His Chosen Role as Senate Maverick," *New York Times*, Sep. 19, 1977.
45. Among those who have discussed this development, perhaps the first was Allen Schick. See his "The Appropriations Committees in Congress," a paper prepared for delivery at the American Political Science Association meeting, San Francisco, Sep. 2–5, 1975.
46. Allen Schick, "The Supply and Demand for Analysis on Capitol Hill," Congressional Research Service paper, June, 1975. Also see James Thurber, "The Evolving Role and Effectiveness of the Congressional Research Agencies," *The House at Work*, 300. Thurber notes there, "No students of Congress have shown the four congressional support agencies to be important sources of information for members and legislative assistants." Yet, Thurber's data suggest that members and staffers do rank all four support agencies high for supplying information. Frankly, I am skeptical of these findings based upon my research and upon some personal experience working with staffers.
47. Interview IV 31. Confirmed by II 65, IV 18, and IV 40, and U.S. Congress, House, Select Committee on Committees, *Committee Organization in the House, A Panel Discussion*, 93rd Cong., 1st sess., 1973, 267–69. In this discussion then

Representative John Culver (D, Iowa) and others agreed that increased oversight meant that committee staffs would need to perform that function. Oversight has increased, and the staff does most of the work.

48. Thurber, 306. Here Thurber and I agree.
49. U.S. Congress, House, Committee on Government Operations, *GAO Audits of the Internal Revenue Service and the Bureau of Alcohol, Tobacco, and Firearms,* H. Rept. 95-480, 95th Cong., 1st sess., 1977, p. 5.
50. U.S. Congress, House Committee on Appropriations, *Legislative Branch Appropriation Bill,* FY 1968, H. Rept. 323, 90th Cong., 1st sess., 1967, p. 16; and U.S. Congress, Senate, Committee on Government Operations, *Legislative Oversight and Program Evaluation, Hearings,* 94th Cong., 2d sess., 1976, p. 5.
51. Thomas Henderson, "Congressional Oversight of Executive Agencies" (Gainesville: University of Florida Monograph Number 40, 1970), 50-51.
52. Herbert Roback, "Program Evaluation by and for the Congress," *The Bureaucrat* 5 (Apr. 1976), 29.
53. Martin Rein and Sheldon White, "Can Policy Research Help Policy?," *The Public Interest* (1977), 126, 130-35.
54. Seidman, 27-28.
55. Thompson, 15.
56. Alice Rivlin has proposed such experimentation. See her *Systematic Thinking for Social Action* (Washington, D.C.: Brookings Institution, 1971), 91-108.
57. Joseph Bower, "Effective Public Management," *Harvard Business Review* (March-April, 1977).
58. Martin Landau, "Redundancy, Rationality, and the Problem of Duplication and Overlap" in *Bureaucratic Power in National Politics,* 2d ed., ed. Francis Rourke (Boston: Little, Brown, 1972), 348.
59. Theodore Lowi, *The End of Liberalism* (New York: W.W. Norton, 1969), 83.
60. Seidman, 150-51, 224.
61. Charles Schultze, *The Politics and Economics of Public Spending* (Washington: Brookings Institution, 1968), 52.
62. Douglas and Wildavsky, 138.
63. For example, see Fisher, 263; Ogul, 177; Thomas Cronin, *The State of the Presidency* (Boston: Little, Brown, 1975), 311; and Ira Sharkansky, "The Politics of Auditing, in *The New Political Economy,* ed. Bruce Smith (New York: John Wiley, 1975), 312-13.

CHAPTER 8

1. Walker, "The General Accounting Office," 22.
2. Selznick, 78-79, 148.
3. A quote used frequently by Professor Dean Burnham of MIT and attributed to Mr. Dooley.
4. Kaufman, *Limits,* 8.
5. Selznick, 40-42.
6. Peter Smith, *Groups Within Organizations* (London: Harper and Row, 1973), 117.
7. This section is dependent for facts of the period 1792-1947 upon the books listed

below. The interpretation is, of course, mine. See the following: Russell F. Weigley, *History of the United States Army* (New York: Macmillan, 1967); Samuel Huntington, *The Soldier and the State* (Cambridge: Harvard Univ. Press, 1959); Walter Millis, *Arms and Men* (New York: G.P. Putnam's Sons, 1956); Paul Hammond, *Organizing for Defense* (Princeton: Princeton Univ. Press, 1961); James Hewes, Jr., *From Root to McNamara: Army Organization and Administration, 1900–1963* (Washington, D.C.: Government Printing Office, 1975); Otto L. Nelson, Jr., *National Security and the General Staff* (Washington: Infantry Journal Press, 1946); James Masland and Laurence Radway, *Soldiers and Scholars: Military Education and National Policy* (Princeton: Princeton Univ. Press, 1957); Philip C. Jessup, *Elihu Root*, Volume I, 1845–1909 (New York: Dodd, Mead, 1938); Richard Leopold, *Elihu Root and the Conservative Tradition* (Boston: Little, Brown, 1954); Henry Stimson and McGeorge Bundy, *On Active Service in Peace and War* (New York: Harper and Brothers, 1948); Elting Morison, *Turmoil and Tradition: A Study of the Life and Times of Henry L. Stimson* (Cambridge: Houghton Mifflin, 1960); Richard Current, *Secretary Stimson: A Study in Statecraft* (Archon Books, 1970); Hermann Hagedorn, *Leonard Wood* (New York: Harper and Brothers, 1931); Russell F. Weigley, *Towards an American Army: Military Thought from Washington to Marshall* (New York: Columbia University Press, 1962); and Wallace Earl Walker, "Emory Upton and the Army Officer's Creed," *Military Review* 61 (April 1981), 65–68.

8. Hammond, 10–12; and Hewes, 6–7.
9. Hewes, 5.
10. Hammond, 23; Hewes, 15; Millis, 131–210; Weigley, *History*, 314; and Morison, 155.
11. Weigley, *History*, 312–13; Leopold, 6, 174; and Jessup.
12. Current; Stimson and Bundy; and Morison.
13. Hagedorn; Weigley, *Towards*, 199–222; and Weigley, *History*, 327–78.
14. Weigley, *Towards*, 208.
15. The strategy I discuss here is based upon Root's principal efforts as Secretary and on efforts and interests of Wood and Stimson. It does not rely on any single author, but rather on a careful study of Weigley, *History*; Stimson and Bundy; Jessup; Leopold; Hammond; Hewes; Nelson; and Weigley, *Towards*.
16. Hammond, 9; Hewes, 8–9; and Hagedorn, 108–109.
17. Weigley, *History*, 566–69.
18. Weigley, *History*, 320–41; Leopold, 39; Masland and Radway, 83–85; and Jessup, 265–72.
19. Nelson, 246; Morison, 153–54; Huntington, *Soldier*, 251; Hammond, 85; and Hewes, 369.
20. Weigley, *History*, 334.
21. Morison, 167–68; Stimson and Bundy, 38–39; and Hammond, 7.
22. Hammond, 20–23, 30–31; and Hewes, 21.
23. Weigley, *History*, 379, 479–80.
24. Selznick, 136.
25. Nelson, 10.
26. Morison, 150–67; Stimson and Bundy, 33–37; and Weigley, 327–39.
27. Weigley, *History*, 306–12.

28. Jameson Doig, "Entrepreneurial Leadership in the 'Independent' Government Organization," a paper prepared for delivery at the American Political Science Association meeting, Sept. 1–4, 1983, p. 7; and Tom Cronin, "Thinking and Learning About Leadership," remarks, (Fall 1983), 21.

29. Robert C. Tucker, *Politics as Leadership (Columbia: Univ. of Missouri Press, 1981), 16–19.*

30. Kaufman, *Limits*, 118.

31. Wilensky; this idea suggested to me by Major Dan Kaufman.

32. Donald Warwick, *A Theory of Public Bureaucracy* (Cambridge: Harvard Univ. Press, 1978), 209–10.

33. These are Huntington's criteria for a profession. See his *Soldier*, 8–10.

34. David Easton, *A Systems Analysis of Political Life* (New York: John Wiley and Sons, 1965), 345–53.

35. Gerth and Mills, 128.

36. Allison, 163–82.

37. James Foster, "The Lessons of War: Vietnam in Historical Perspective," Ph.D. diss., Massachusetts Institute of Technology, 1975, pp. 62–136.

38. Salisbury and Shepsle, 394.

39. Allison, 255.

40. Letter to the author from Frances Rourke, Professor of Political Science, Johns Hopkins University dated Aug. 11, 1982; and Hal Rainey, "Organizational Theory and Political Science," a paper prepared for delivery at American Political Association meeting, Sept. 1–4, 1983, pp. 1, 4, 19–21.

Selected Bibliography

BOOKS, DISSERTATIONS, AND THESES

Abrahamson, Mark, ed. *The Professional in the Organization.* Chicago: Rand-McNally, 1967.

Allison, Graham, *The Essence of Decision.* Boston: Little, Brown, 1971.

Bailey, Stephen. *Congress in the Seventies.* New York: St. Martin's, 1970.

Barnard, Chester. *The Functions of the Executive.* Cambridge: Harvard Univ. Press, 1968.

Brown, J.D. "The U.S. General Accounting Office's Changing Focus as the Federal Government's Auditor." Ph.D. diss., George Washington Univ., 1973.

Brown, Richard E. *A History of Accounting and Accountants.* Edinburgh: T.C. and E.C. Jack, 1905.

Brown, Richard E. *The GAO.* Knoxville: Univ. of Tennessee Press, 1970.

Burnham, Walter Dean. *Critical Elections and the Mainsprings of American Politics.* New York: Norton, 1970.

Casler, Darwin. *The Evolution of CPA Ethics.* East Lansing: Michigan State Graduate School of Business Administration, Occasional Paper No. 12, 1964.

Chandler, Alfred. *Strategy and Structure.* Cambridge: MIT Press, 1962.

Chatfield, Michael. *A History of Accounting Thought.* Hinsdale: Dryden Press, 1974.

Clausewitz, Carl von. *On War.* Edited and translated by Michael Howard and Peter Paret. Princeton: Princeton Univ. Press, 1976.

Cooper, J., and MacKenzie, G.C., eds. *The House at Work.* Austin: Univ. of Texas Press, 1982.

Cooper, William, and Uji Ujiri, eds. *Eric Louis Kohler: Accounting's Man of Principle.* Reston: Reston Publishing 1979.

Corwin, Edward S. *The President: Office and Powers, 1787–1957.* 4th ed. New York: New York Univ. Press, 1957.

Cronin, Thomas. *The State of the Presidency.* Boston: Little, Brown, 1975.

Current, Richard. *Secretary Stimson: A Study in Statecraft.* Archon Books, 1970.

Daenecke, Eric. "A Study of the United States General Accounting Office With Emphasis on the Period Since 1938." Ph.D. diss., American Univ., 1950.

Dalton, Melville. *Men Who Manage.* New York: John Wiley & Sons, 1959.

Deal, Terrence, and Kennedy, Allan. *Corporate Cultures.* Reading: Addison-Wesley, 1982.

Dexter, Lewis A. *Elite and Specialized Interviewing.* Evanston: Northwestern Univ. Press, 1970.

Dodd, Larry, and Schott, Richard. *Congress and the Administrative State.* New York: John Wiley and Sons, 1979.

Douglas, Mary, and Wildavsky, Aaron. *Risk and Culture.* Berkeley: Univ. of California Press, 1983.

Downs, Anthony. *Inside Bureaucracy.* Boston: Little, Brown, 1967.

Farago, Ladislas. *It's Your Money.* New York: Random House, 1964.

Fenno, Richard. *Congressmen in Committees.* Boston: Little, Brown, 1973.
———. *Home Style.* Boston: Little, Brown, 1978.

Fine, Harold. "A Readability Analysis of Twenty-Nine Audit Reports of One Federal Agency." Masters thesis, George Washington Univ., 1972.

Fiorina, Morris. *Congress: Keystone of the Washington Establishment.* New Haven: Yale Univ. Press, 1977.

Fisher, Louis. *Presidential Spending Power.* Princeton: Princeton Univ. Press, 1975.

Foster, James. "The Lessons of War: Vietnam in Historical Perspective." Ph.D. diss., Massachusetts Institute of Technology, 1975.

Gilb, Corrine. *Hidden Hierarchies: Professions and Government.* New York: Harper and Row, 1960.

Hagedorn, Hermann. *Leonard Wood.* New York: Harper and Brothers, 1931.

Halperin, Morton. *Bureaucratic Politics and Foreign Policy.* Washington, D.C.: Brookings Institution, 1974.

Hammond, Paul. *Organizing for Defense.* Princeton: Princeton Univ. Press, 1961.

Hargrove, Erwin, and Paul Conkin, eds. *TVA.* Urbana: Univ. of Illinois Press, 1984.

Harris, Joseph P. *Congressional Control of Administration.* Garden City, N.Y.: Anchor Books, 1964.

Heclo, Hugh. *A Government of Strangers.* Washington, D.C.: Brookings Institution, 1977.

Heclo, Hugh and Aaron Wildavsky. *The Private Government of Public Money.* Berkeley: Univ. of California Press, 1974.

Henderson, Thomas. "Congressional Oversight of Executive Agencies." Gainesville: Univ. of Florida, Monograph Number 40, 1970.

Hewes, James, Jr. *From Root to McNamara: Army Organization and Administration, 1900-1963.* Washington: Government Printing Office, 1975.

Huntington, Samuel. *The Common Defense.* New York: Columbia Univ. Press, 1961.

———. *The Soldier and the State.* New York: Random House, 1964.

Hyneman, Charles S. *Bureaucracy in a Democracy.* New York: Harper, 1950.

Janowitz, Morris. *The Professional Soldier.* New York: Free Press, 1960.

Jessup, Philip. *Elihu Root, Volume I, 1845-1909.* New York: Dodd, Mead, 1938.

Kaufman, Herbert. *The Forest Ranger.* Baltimore: Johns Hopkins Univ. Press, 1960.

———. *The Limits of Organizational Change.* Univ. of Alabama Press, 1971.

Kirst, Michael. *Government Without Passing Laws.* Chapel Hill: Univ. of North Carolina Press, 1969.

Leopold, Richard. *Elihu Root and the Conservative Tradition.* Boston: Little, Brown, 1954.

Lowi, Theodore. *The End of Liberalism.* New York: W.W. Norton, 1969.

Maass, Arthur. *Congress and the Common Good.* New York: Basic Books, 1983.

MacNeil, Neil, and Harold Metz. *The Hoover Report.* New York: MacMillan, 1956.

Malbin, Michael. *Unelected Representatives.* New York: Basic Books, 1980.

Mansfield, Harvey. *The Comptroller General.* New Haven: Yale Univ. Press, 1939.

Masland, James, and Radway, Laurance. *Soldiers and Scholars: Military Education and National Policy.* Princeton: Princeton Univ. Press, 1957.

Mayhew, David. *Congress: The Electoral Connection.* New Haven: Yale Univ. Press, 1976.

Mazmanian, Daniel, and Nienaber, Jeanne. *Can Organizations Change?* Washington: Brookings Institution, 1979.

Millis, Walter, *Arms and Men.* New York: G.P. Putnam's Sons, 1956.

Montagna, Paul. *Certified Public Accounting: A Sociological View of a Profession in Change.* Houston: Scholars Book Co., 1974.

Morrison, Elting. *Turmoil and Tradition: A Study of the Life and Times of Henry L. Stimson.* Cambridge: Houghton Mifflin, 1960.

Mosher, Frederick. *Democracy and the Public Service.* New York: Oxford Univ. Press, 1968.

———. *The GAO.* Boulder, Colo.: Westview Press, 1979.

Nelson, Otto. *National Security and the General Staff.* Washington: Infantry Journal Press, 1946.

Neustadt, Richard. *Presidential Power.* New York: John Wiley, 1960.

Niskanen, William. *Bureaucracy and Representative Government.* Chicago: Aldine, 1971.

Normanton, E.L. *The Accountability and Audit of Governments.* New York: Praeger, 1966.

Ogul, Morris. *Congress Oversees the Bureaucracy.* Pittsburgh: Univ. of Pittsburgh Press, 1977.

Orfield, Gary. *Congressional Power: Congress and Social Change.* New York: Harcourt & Brace, 1975.

Pois, Joseph. *Watchdog on the Potomac.* Lanham, MD: Univ. Press of America, 1979.

Pow, Alexander S. "The Comptroller General and the General Accounting Office of the United States." Ph.D. diss., New York Univ., 1960.

Powell, Fred, ed. *Control of Federal Expenditures: A Documentary History, 1775-1894.* Washington, D.C.: Brookings Institution, 1939.

Pressman, Jeffrey and Aaron Wildavsky. *Implementation.* Berkeley: Univ. of California Press, 1973.

Puryear, Edgar. *Nineteen Stars: A Study in Military Character and Leadership.* Washington, D.C.: Coiner Publications, 1971.

Rivlin, Alice. *Systematic Thinking for Social Action.* Washington, D.C.: Brookings Institution, 1971.

Rourke, Francis. *Bureaucratic Power in National Politics.* 2d ed. Boston: Little, Brown, 1972.

Rushing, William and Mayer Zald, eds. *Organizations and Beyond.* Lexington, Mass: D.C. Heath, 1978.

Saloma, John. *Congress and the New Politics.* Boston: Little, Brown, 1969.

Sapolsky, Harvey. *The Polaris System Development.* Cambridge: Harvard Univ. Press, 1972.

Scherer, Frederic. *The Weapons' Acquisition Process.* Cambridge: Harvard Univ. Press, 1964.

Schulsinger, Gerald G. "The General Accounting Office: Two Glimpses." Inter-University Case Program, No. 35. Birmingham: Univ. of Alabama Press, 1956.

Schultze, Charles L. *The Politics and Economics of Public Spending.* Washington D.C.: Brookings Institution, 1968.

Seidman, Harold. *Politics, Position and Power.* 2d ed. New York: Oxford Univ. Press, 1975.

Selko, Daniel T. *The Federal Financial System.* Washington, D.C.: Brookings Institution, 1940.

Selznick, Philip. *Leadership in Administration.* New York: Harper and Row, 1972.

Smith, Darrell. *The General Accounting Office: Its History, Activities and Organization.* Baltimore: Johns Hopkins Press, 1927.

Smith, Peter. *Groups Within Organizations.* London: Harper and Row, 1973.

Sperry, Roger et al. *GAO, 1966-1981.* Washington, D.C.: U.S. Government Printing Office, 1981.

Stimson, Henry and McGeorge Bundy. *On Active Service in Peace and War.* New York: Harper and Brothers, 1948.

Sundquist, James. *The Decline and Resurgence of Congress.* Washington: Brookings Institution, 1981.

Thompson, James. *Organizations in Action.* New York: McGraw-Hill, 1967.

Tierney, John. *Postal Reorganization.* Boston: Auburn House, 1981.

Tobin, James, et al. *The American Business Creed.* Cambridge: Harvard Univ. Press, 1956.

Tucker, Robert C. *Politics as Leadership.* Columbia: Univ. of Missouri Press, 1981.

Twight, Ben. *Organizational Values and Political Power.* University Park: Pennsylvania State Univ. Press, 1983.

Waldo, Dwight. *The Administrative State.* New York: Ronald Press, 1948.

Walker, Wallace Earl. "The Bureaucratic Politics of Fault Finding." Ph.D. diss., Massachusetts Institute of Technology, 1980.

———. "The General Accounting Office and Information for Congressional Review." Master's thesis, Massachusetts Institute of Technology, 1973.

Wallace, Robert A. *Congressional Control of Federal Spending.* Detroit: Wayne Univ. Press, 1960.

Warwick, Donald. *A Theory of Public Bureaucracy.* Cambridge: Harvard Univ. Press, 1978.

Weigley, Russell F. *History of the United States Army.* New York: Macmillan, 1967.

———. *Towards an American Army: Military Thought from Washington to Marshall.* New York: Columbia Univ. Press, 1962.

White, Leonard D. *The Federalists.* Nw York: Macmillan, 1948.

White, Leonard D. *The Republican Era: 1869-1901.* New York: Macmillan, 1958.

Wildavsky, Aaron. *The Politics of the Budgetary Process.* 2d ed. Boston: Little, Brown, 1974.

Willoughby, W.F. *The Legal Status and Functions of the General Accounting Office of the National Government.* Baltimore: Johns Hopkins Press, 1927.

Wilmerding, Lucius. *The Spending Power.* Archon Books, 1971.

Wilson, James Q. *The Investigators.* New York: Basic Books, 1978.

ARTICLES

Bennett, L. Howard. "A Report on the Equal Employment Opportunity Program in the General Accounting Office (Headquarters)." Washington, D.C.: General Accounting Office, March 25, 1974.

Birnberg, Jacob, and Natwar Gandi. "Toward Defining the Accountant's Role in the Evaluation of Social Programs." *Accounting, Organizations and Society* (1976), 5–10.

Bower, Joseph. "Effective Public Management." *Harvard Business Review* 55 (March–April 1977), 131–40.

Burnham, Walter Dean. "Revitalization and Decay: Looking Toward the Third Century in American Politics." *Journal of Politics* (Aug. 1976), 146–72.

Charlton, Linda. "Inquiry into Democratic Break-In Strips General Accounting Office of Some of Its Anonymity." *New York Times*, Sept. 3, 1972, p. 38.

Doig, Jameson. "Entrepreneurial Leadership in the'Independent' Government Organization." A paper delivered to the American Political Science Association, Sept. 1–4, 1983.

Fenno, Richard. "The House Appropriations Committee as a Political System." *American Political Science Review* 56 (June 1962), 310–24.

Fisher, Louis. "Congressional Budget Reform: The First Two Years." *Harvard Journal of Legislation* 14 (April 1977), 413–57.

Fitzgerald, Martin. "The Expanded Role of the General Accounting Office in Support of a Strengthened Congress." *The Bureaucrat* 3 (Jan. 1975), 383–400.

Fox, Harrison, and Susan Hammond. "The Growth of Congressional Staffs." *Proceedings of the Academy of Political Science: Congress Against the President* 32, No. 1, pp. 112–24.

"The GAO: Watchdog Over Washington." *Dun's Review* (Feb. 1977), 6.

"GAO-Wide Training Program Set to Eliminate Functional Racism," *GAO Management News*, May 2, 1977, p. 1.

Greenstein, Fred. "Eisenhower as an Activist President." *Political Science Quarterly* 94 (Winter 1979–80), 575–99.

Heclo, Hugh. "OMB and the Presidency—the Problem of 'Neutral Competence'." *The Public Interest* 38 (Winter 1975), 80–98.

Herbert, Leo. "The Environment in Governmental Accounting in the Seventies." *GAO Review* (Fall 1972), 22–32.

———. "A Perspective of Accounting." *The Accounting Review* 46 (July 1971), 433–40.

Hunter, Laura Grace. "The Language of Audit Reports." Washington, D.C.: U.S. Government Printing Office, 1957.

Huntington, Samuel. "The Democratic Distemper." *Public Interest* 16 (Fall 1975), 9–38.

Kent, Ralph. "Changes and Challenges for the Accounting Profession." *Evaluating Governmental Performance.* Washington, D.C.: U.S. General Accounting Office, 1975, pp. 229–45.

Kirk, Roy. "Implementing the Lead Division Concept." *GAO Review* 10 (Fall 1976), 17–24.

Knoll, Erwin. "The Half-Hearted GAO: Congress Gets What It Wants." *Progressive* 25 (May 1971), 19–23.

Lawer, Neil. "Closing the Books on Fifty Years of Service." *Public Administration Review* 5 (Sept.–Oct., 1977), 575–76.

MacDonald, Scot. "Reorganization Along Functional Lines Makes Congress' GAO More Responsive." *Government Executive* 4 (June 1972), 54–57.

MacMahon, Arthur W. "Congressional Oversight of Administration: The Power of the Purse." *Political Science Quarterly* 58 (June 1943), 161–90.

McDiarmid, John. "Reorganization of the General Accounting Office." *American Political Science Review* 31 (June 1937), 508–16.

Meltsner, Arnold. "Bureaucratic Policy Analysts." *Policy Analysis* (Winter 1975), 115–39.

Morgan, Thomas D. "The General Accounting Office: One Hope for Congress to Regain Parity of Power With the President." *North Carolina Law Review* 51 (Oct. 1973).

Morse, Ellsworth. "The Case for Accepting GAO Experience." *Journal of Accounting* (June 1960).

———. "GAO Audits of Management Performance." *Journal of Accountancy* (Oct. 1961).

Polsby, Nelson, et al. "The Institutionalization of the House of Representatives." *American Political Science Review* 62 (March 1968), 144–68.

Rein, Martin and Sheldon White. "Can Policy Research Help Policy?" *The Public Interest* (1979), 119–36.

Roback, Herbert. "Program Evaluation By and For the Congress." *The Bureaucrat* 5 (April 1976), 11–36.

Russell, Gary. "The Coats Guard's Personality: A Product of Changing Roles and Missions." *U.S. Naval Institute Proceedings* (March 1976), 39–45.

Salisbury, Robert and Kenneth Shepsle. "Congressional Staff Turnover and the Ties that Bind." *American Political Science Review* 75 (1981), 381–96.

Saloma, John. "The Responsible Use of Power." Washington, D.C.: American Enterprise Institute, 1964.

Scher, Seymour. "Conditions for Legislative Control." *Journal of Politics* (1963), 526–51.

Sharkansky, Ira. "The Politics of Auditing." In *The New Political Economy*, edited by Bruce Smith. New York: John Wiley, 1975.

Singer, Milton. "The Concept of Culture." In *International Encyclopedia of the Social Sciences*, edited by David Sills, Vol. III, 527–42. New York: Free Press, 1968.

Staats, Elmer. "Acquisition Management Needs Realistic Forecasting to Close the Confidence Gap." *Defense Management Journal* (April 1974), 20–23.

———. "Career Planning and Development: Which Way Is Up?" *GAO Review* 10 (Fall 1976), 1–6.

Staats, Elmer. "Evaluating the Effectiveness of Federal Social Programs." Speech before the National Capital Area Chapter of the American Society for Public Administration, Jan. 17, 1973.

———. "Management or Operation Auditing." *GAO Review* (Winter 1972), 25–35.

———. "The Nation's State in Congressional Budget Reform." *The National Public Accountant* (Dec. 1975), 3–7.

———. "New Problems of Accountability." Speech before the American Society of Public Administration, n.d.

———. "Public Confidence in Government and the Need for Accountability." Address before the Executive Club of Chicago, Oct. 5, 1972.

———. "The United States General Accounting Office: Its Role as an Independent Audit and Evaluation Agency." Speech before the Australian Society of Accountants, Feb. and March, 1977.

Stoner, Floyd. "Federal Auditors as Regulators." In *The Policy Cycle*, edited by Judith May and Aaron Wildavsky. Beverly Hills: Sage, 1978.

Thompson, James, and William McEwen. "Organizational Goals and Environment." *American Sociological Review* 22 (1958), 23–31.

Voss, Allen. "Ellsworth H. Morse, Jr.: Assistant Comptroller General of the United States." *GAO Review* (Winter 1978), 1–12.

Warren, Lindsay C. "Our Biggest Ratholes Were Created By Law." *Saturday Evening Post*, June 12, 1954, p. 10.

———. "Will the Wasters Win Again?" In U.S. Congress. Senate. Senator Herbert O'Connor. Extension of Remarks. May 17, 1949. *Congressional Record*, A3141.

"Watchdog Widens Role." *Business Week*, March 19, 1960, pp. 109–16.

Wildavsky, Aaron. "The Political Economy of Efficiency: Cost-Benefit Analysis, Systems Analysis and Program Budgeting." *Public Administration Review* (Dec. 1966), 292–319.

Wilensky, Harold. "The Professionalization of Everyone." *American Journal of Sociology* 70 (Sept. 1964), 138–58.

Wilson, James Q. "The Bureaucracy Problem." *The Public Interest* (Winter 1967), 3–9.

———. "The Changing FBI—The Road to ABSCAM." *The Public Interest* (Spring 1980), 3–14.

———. "The Rise of the Bureaucratic State." *The Public Interest* (Fall 1975), 77–103.

Wilson, Woodrow. "The Study of Administration." *Political Science Quarterly* 93 (Fall 1878), 197–222.

Zeidenstein, Harvey. "The Reassertion of Congressional Power: New Curbs on the President." *Political Science Quarterly* 93 (Fall 1978), 393–410.

Zwerlding, Stephen. "GAO: Learning to Plan and Planning to Learn." *GAO Review* 10 (Fall 1976), 25–35.

GAO DOCUMENTS

GAO Memorandum dated January 25, 1972, to all employees from Elmer Staats, entitled "Strengthening GAO's Organization to Meet the Demands of the 1970s."

GAO Memorandum dated February 3, 1975, to Heads of Divisions and Office from Elmer Staats, entitled "Implementation of the Lead Division Concept."

GAO Memorandum dated May 6, 1976, to all employees from Elmer Staats, entitled "Organizational Changes."

GAO Memorandum dated May 10, 1976, to the Heads of Divisions and Offices from Elmer Staats, entitled "Establishment of a Pilot Program to Assess Assignments."

McCarl, J.R. Letter to messrs. Gary Campbell *et al.* September 28, 1934, as contained in GAO Law Library.

———. Letter to the "Officials and Employees of the General Accounting Office." June 30, 1936, as contained in GAO Law Library.

U.S. Comptroller General. *Annual Reports, 1921–1981.* Washington, D.C.: U.S. Government Printing Office.

———. "Examples of Findings from Governmental Audits: Audit Standards Supplement Series, No. 4." Washington, D.C.: U.S. General Accounting Office, 1973.

———. "Standards for Audit of Governmental Organizations, Programs, Activities and Functions." Washington, D.C.: U.S. General Accounting Office, 1972.

U.S. General Accounting Office. *Comprehensive Audit Manual.* Washington, D.C.: U.S. General Accounting Office, 1972.

———. "Employee Responsibilities and Conduct Manual." Washington, D.C.: U.S. General Accounting Office, 1966.

———. *Legislation Relating to the General Accounting Office.* Washington, D.C.: U.S. General Accounting Office, 1977.

———. *Recruiting Manual.* Washington, D.C.: U.S. General Accounting Office, 1963.

———. *Report Manual.* Washington, D.C.: U.S. General Accounting Office, 1976.

CONGRESSIONAL DOCUMENTS

U.S. Congress. House. Committee on Appropriations. [*Selected*] *Independent Offices Appropriations for 1937 to 1965, Hearings.* 74th–88th Congresses, 1936–1964.

———. Committee on Appropriations. *Legislative Branch Appropriations, 1966–1979.* H. Repts. 89th–95th Congresses, 1965–1978.

———. Committee on Appropriations. *Legislative Branch Appropriations for 1966 to 1980, Hearings.* 89th–96th Congresses, 1965–1980.

———. Committee on Expenditures in the Executive Departments. *Budgeting and Accounting Procedures Act of 1950.* H. Rept. 2556, 81st Cong., 2d sess., 1950.

———. Committee on expenditures in the Executive Branch. *The General Accounting Office: A Study of Its Functions and Operations.* H. Rept. 1441, 81st Cong., 1st sess., 1949.

———. Committee on Expenditures in the Executive Departments. *Investigation of (the) General Accounting Office Audit of Wartime Freight Vouchers.* H. Rept. 2457, 80th Cong., 2d sess., 1948.

———. Committee on Expenditures in the Executive Departments. *Investigations of Procurements and Buildings, Hearings* on the General Accounting Office's Audit of Wartime Freight Vouchers, part 7, 80th Cong., 2d sess., 1948.

———. Committee on Government Operations. *Availability of Information from Federal Departments and Agencies (Air Force Refusal to the General Accounting Office).* H. Rept. 234, 86th Cong., 1st sess., 1959.

———. Committee on Government Operations. *Comptroller General Reports to Congress on Audits of Defense Contracts, Hearings* before a Subcommittee of the Committee on Government Operations. 89th Cong., 1st sess., 1965.

———. Committee on Government Operations. *GAO Audits of the Internal Revenue Service and the Bureau of Alcohol, Tobacco and Firearms.* H. Rept. 95-480, 95th Cong., 1st sess., 1977.

———. Committee on Government Operations. *The General Accounting Office.* H. Rept. 2264, 84th Cong., 2d sess., 1956.

———. Committee on Post Office and Civil Service. *Separate Personnel System for the General Accounting Office, Hearing.* 95th Cong., 2d sess., 1978.

———. Committee on Rules. *Legislative Reorganization Act of 1970.* H. Rept. 91-1215, 91st Cong., 2d sess., 1970.

———. "GAO Legislation of 1974." 93rd Cong., 2d sess., 1974. *Congressional Record,* 120, No. 22, 28999–29001.

———. Representative Blanton. Speech on the GAO and J.R. McCarl. 73rd Congress., 1934. *Congressional Record,* 78, No. 1, 940.

———. Representative Jack Brooks. Speech on "Adolph T. Samuelson, One of the Early Pioneers of Management Audits of Government Programs." 94th Cong., 1st sess., 1975. *Congressional Record*, 121, No. 106.

———. Representative Shirley Chisholm on "Discrimination at the GAO." 92d Cong. 2d sess., 1972. *Congressional Record*, 118, No. 28, 37426-37427.

———. Representative James Good. Speech on the Budget and Accounting Act. 66th Cong., 1st sess., 1919. *Congressional Record*, 66, No. 7, 7085.

———. Representative James Good. Speech on the Budget and Accounting Act. 67th Cong., 1st sess., 1921. *Congressional Record*, 67, No. 2, 1080.

———. Select Committee on Congressional Operations. *General Accounting Office Services to Congress: An Assessment.* H. Rept. 95-1317, 95th Cong., 2d sess., 1978.

———. "Tribute to the Honorable Joseph Campbell." 80th Cong., 1st sess., 1965. *Congressional Record*, 111, No. 14, 18565-18660.

———. Committee on Expenditures in the Executive Departments. *Budget and Accounting Procedures Act of 1950.* S. Rept. 2031, 81st Cong., 2d sess., 1950.

———. Committee on Expenditures in the Executive Departments. *Federal Property and Administrative Services Act of 1949.* S. Rept. 475, 81st Cong., 1st sess., 1949.

———. Committee on Government Operations. *Accounting and Auditing: Practices and Procedures, Hearings.* 95th Cong., 1st sess., 1977.

———. Committee on Government Operations. *The Accounting Establishment, A Staff Study.* 94th Cong., 2d sess., 1976.

———. Committee on Government Operations. *Capability of the GAO to Analyze and Audit Defense Expenditures, Hearings.* 91st Cong., 1st sess., 1969.

U.S. Congress. Senate. Committee on Government Operations. *Congressional Budget and Impoundment Control Act of 1974 (Public Law 93-344): Legislative History.* Committee print. 93rd Cong., 2d sess., 1974.

———. Committee on Government Operations. *GAO Audits of the Internal Revenue Service and the Bureau of Alcohol, Tobacco and Firearms.* S. Rept. 94-752, 94th Cong., 2d sess., 1976.

———. Committee on Government Operations. *Legislative Oversight and Program Evaluation, Hearings.* 94th Cong., 2d sess., 1976.

———. Committee on Government Operations. *Nomination of Joseph Campbell, Hearings* before the Committee on Government Operations. 84th Cong., 1st sess., 1955.

———. Committee on Government Operations. *Nomination of Robert F. Keller, Hearing.* 91st Cong., 1st sess., 1969.

———. Committee on Government Operations. *Nomination of Elmer B. Staats, Hearings.* 89th Cong., 2d sess., 1966.

———. Committee on Government Operations. *Refusals to the General Accounting Office of Access to Records of the Executive Departments and Agencies.* S. Doc. 108, 86th Cong., 2d sess., 1961.

———. Senator John McClellan. Speech on the Fortieth Anniversary of the Budget and Accounting Act of 1921. 87th Cong., 1st sess., June 28, 1961. *Congressional Record,* 10741–10742.

———. Senator Winston Prouty on "The Economic Opportunity Amendment of 1967." 90th Cong., 1st sess., 1967. *Congressional Record,* 113, No. 20, 27378-80.

U.S. Congress. *Review of Economic Opportunity Programs.* Joint Committee Print. 91st Cong., 1st sess., 1969.

OTHER GOVERNMENT PUBLICATIONS

Accounting and Auditing Act of 1950. U.S. Code, Title 31, sec. 66 (1950).

Budget and Accounting Act of 1921. U.S. Code, Title 31, sec. 54 (1921).

The Budget and Accounting Procedures Act. U.S. Code, Title 31, secs. 65–67 (1950).

Federal Property and Administrative Services Act, U.S. Code, Title 40, secs. 486-87 (1949).

Government Corporation Control Act. U.S. Code, Title 31, secs. 850-56 (1945).

Hanes, John, *et al.* "Fiscal, Budgeting, and Accounting Systems of the Federal Government: A Report with Recommendations Prepared for the Commission on Organization of the Executive Branch of Government." Washington, D.C.: U.S. Government Printing Office, 1948.

Legislative Reference Service. "Relations of the General Accounting Office to Congress." Unpublished manuscript, 1944.

Legislative Reorganization Act of 1946. U.S. Code, Title 2, sec. 190d (1977).

Legislative Reorganization Act of 1970. U.S. Code, I (1970).

President's Committee on Administrative Management (Brownlow Committee). *Report of the President's Committee on Administrative Management in the Government of the United States.* Washington, D.C.: U.S. Government Printing Office, 1937.

U.S. Commission on Organization of the Executive Branch of Government (Hoover Commission). *Budgeting and Accounting.* Washington, D.C.: U.S. Government Printing Office, 1949.

Index

Changing Organizational Culture has been composed into type on a Varityper phototypesetter in ten point Times Roman with two points spacing between the lines. Times Roman was also used as display. The book was designed by Jim Billingsley, composed by Universal Publishing Services, printed offset by Thomson-Shore, Inc. and bound by John H. Dekker & Sons. The paper on which the book is printed carries acid-free characteristics and is designed for an effective life of at least three hundred years.

THE UNIVERSITY OF TENNESSEE PRESS : KNOXVILLE